Rethinking English in Schools

Also available from Continuum

Subject Knowledge and Teacher Education – Viv Ellis
Romanticism and Education – David Halpin
Philosophy of Education – Richard Pring

Rethinking English in Schools

Towards a New and Constructive Stage

Edited by
Viv Ellis, Carol Fox and Brian Street

continuum

Continuum International Publishing Group
The Tower Building
11 York Road
London
SE1 7NX

80 Maiden Lane, Suite 704
New York
NY
10038

www.continuumbooks.com

British Library Cataloguing-in-Publication Data
A catalogue record for this book is available from the British Library.

ISBN: 9780826499226 (hardcover)

Library of Congress Cataloging-in-Publication Data
Rethinking English in schools : towards a new and constructive stage / edited by Viv Ellis, Carol Fox, and Brian Street.
        p. cm.
  Includes bibliographical references.
  ISBN-13: 978-0-8264-9922-6 (hardcover)
  ISBN-10: 0-8264-9922-8 (hardcover)
  1. English language—Study and teaching—Social aspects. 2. Literature—Study and teaching—Social aspects. I. Ellis, Viv, 1965- II. Fox, Carol. III. Street, Brian V. IV. Title.

  LB1576.R47 2008
  428'.0071—dc22

                                    2007026644

Typeset by Free Range Book Design & Production Ltd
Printed and bound in Great Britain by Biddles Ltd, Kings Lynn, Norfolk

*For all those drawn to becoming English teachers
in schools – and for those compelled
to be their students*

Contents

Acknowledgements

The editors would like to acknowledge participants in the 'Why English?' Conference held in Oxford in October 2006 all of whom helped to shape the direction of this book: Joy Alexander, Rachel Beaumont, Kate Bell, Jade Broughton, Janina Brutt-Griffler, Tony Burgess, Caroline Dyche, Sue Dymoke, John Edwards, Viv Ellis, Bob Fecho, Carol Fox, Michelle Gemelos, Wendy Glenn, Andy Goodwyn, Joan Goody, Katrina Harrell, Ngaire Hoben, Jenny Hsieh, Melanie Hundley, Tom Hunt, Richard Jacobs, Janet Laugharne, Min-Zhan Lu, Suzanne M. Miller, Ray Misson, Wendy Morgan, Kevin Morris, Naomi Morris, Hal O'Neil, Richard Pring, Ilana Snyder, Brian Street, Patrick Walsh, Lionel Warner and Charlotte Wright.

Thanks to Boda Sedlacek, Erica Oakes, Louise Gully and Dorothy Fitchett (Department of Education, Oxford University) for the administrative and organizational support provided both for the conference and in the preparation of this book. Special thanks are due to Joanne Hazell (Nuffield Review of 14–19 Education) for her invaluable contribution to conference planning.

Viv Ellis would also like to thank Chris Davies (Oxford University), Wendy Glenn (University of Connecticut) and Ilana Snyder (Monash University) for their helpful comments on sections of the manuscript and Richard Pring for his encouragement to pursue these ideas.

As editors, we are grateful to the following authors and publishers for their permission to print the following short extracts: the *Guardian* and Ben Okri for permission to reprint an extract from a poem by Ben Okri printed on 20 January, 1999; 'Epilogue' is extracted from the book *I is a long Married Woman* by Grace Nichols, used with permission of Kernak House © 1983/2007; and Viking Penguin and Gordon Dickinson for permission to reprint an extract from 'Book Ends' by Tony Harrison, published in 2007 in *Collected Poems*.

Finally, the editors would like to thank Alexandra Webster, Publisher, and Kirsty Schaper, Editorial Assistant, at Continuum for their enthusiasm and patience throughout the publishing process.

Viv Ellis, Carol Fox and Brian Street
Oxford, Brighton and London, April 2007

Contributors

Joy Alexander was a secondary school teacher for twenty years before taking up her present position in 1995 as a Lecturer in English Education in the School of Education at Queen's University, Belfast. She has published a number of articles on matters relating to English teaching and children's literature.

Janina Brutt-Griffler is Associate Professor of Foreign and Second Language Acquisition and Director of Polish Studies at the State University of New York, Buffalo. She is the author of *World English: A Study of Its Development*, winner of the Modern Language Association's 2004 Mildenberger Prize, *Bilingualism and Language Pedagogy* and *English and Ethnicity*.

Tony Burgess was formerly Reader in Education at the Institute of Education, University of London. He has been joint author of work on language diversity and on the development of writing abilities, and has research interests in the history of English teaching.

James L. Collins is Professor of English Education at The State University of New York at Buffalo. His primary research interests centre on literacy issues for students in low-performing schools. He currently directs the Writing Intensive Reading Comprehension study of the usefulness of guided writing for improving reading comprehension.

Sue Dymoke is a Senior Lecturer in Education at the University of Leicester where she leads the PGCE English course. Her main research interests are the teaching of poetry and the professional development of beginning teachers. Her previous publications include *Drafting and Assessing Poetry* (Paul Chapman Publishing).

Viv Ellis is Tutor for English and a University Lecturer in the Oxford University Department of Education. He has published widely on teacher education and development, ICT and English teaching, and questions of social justice in education. His research monograph *Subject Knowledge and Teacher Education* is also published by Continuum.

Bob Fecho is an Associate Professor of Language and Literacy education at the University of Georgia. His work focuses on language, identity and critical inquiry pedagogy as they relate to adolescent literacy. His book *'Is This English?' Race, Language, and Culture in the Classroom* received the James Britton Award for Teacher Research.

Carol Fox taught English for many years in London schools and subsequently in teacher education. Her interests are in young children's oral storytelling, multicultural literature and, more recently, comics and graphic novels. She has co-edited three anthologies of children's literature of war arising out of an EU-funded project.

Bruce Horner is the University of Louisville's Endowed Chair in Rhetoric and Composition. His books include *Representing the 'Other': Basic Writers and the Teaching of Basic Writing*, with Min-Zhan Lu, and *Terms of Work for Composition: A Materialist Critique*. His recent work investigates relationships between US monolingualism and composition studies.

Janet Laugharne is Director of Research and Reader in the School of Education, University of Wales Institute Cardiff. Her research interests are in bilingualism, languages in education and critical literacy approaches to UK education policy after devolution. Her current teaching includes MA Education, professional doctorate and PhD students.

Min-Zhan Lu is Professor of English and University Scholar at the University of Louisville. Her books include *Comp Tales* and *Shanghai Quartet: The Crossings of Four Women of China*. Her essays have received the College Composition and Communication Richard Braddock Award and the Journal of Basic Writing Mina Shaughnessy Award.

Suzanne M. Miller is Associate Professor and Director of English Education at the State University of New York at Buffalo, where she teaches and conducts ethnographic research on the sociocultural dynamics of teacher and student learning. She is past-Chair of NCTE's Conference on English Education and co-author of *Why Multimodal Literacy?*

Ray Misson is Director of Learning and Teaching in the Faculty of Education at the University of Melbourne. His work centres on the implications of literary and cultural theory for the English classroom, with particular reference to popular culture, critical literacy, sexuality studies, and the place of creativity and imagination.

Wendy Morgan was, until her retirement in 2007, a Senior Lecturer in Education at Queensland University of Technology. Her books include *Critical Literacy in the Classroom: The art of the possible* (Routledge 1997) and, with Ray Misson, *Critical Literacy and the Aesthetic: Transforming the English classroom* (NCTE 2006).

Brian Street is Professor of Language in Education at King's College, London University and Visiting Professor of Education in the Graduate School of Education, University of Pennsylvania. He has a commitment to linking ethnographic-style research on the cultural dimension of language and literacy with contemporary practice in education and in development.

Patrick Walsh lectures in English Education at the School of Education, Queen's University, Belfast. His research interests include international issues in English Education, the effects of managerialism and the history of education. He is co-editor of *The History of the Book in Ireland: Vol. 5* (forthcoming, Oxford University Press).

Chapter 1

Why English?
Rethinking the school subject

Viv Ellis, with Carol Fox and Brian Street

Our purpose in this book is to raise some questions about English in schools at the present moment and, more urgently, to suggest that it is a subject in need of reconsideration and renewal. We begin our introduction to the book's themes and organization with three provocations which, we believe, are in some ways illustrative of the problem of English.

Provocation 1

A group of US high school students are working with their theatre and language arts teachers to develop a play based on the military experiences of young people from their home town in the Iraq war. They conceptualize the play as a series of intersecting monologues from a range of authentic characters. With their teachers, they begin to research, drawing resources from the published writings of Iraq war veterans, news reports, a documentary film, personal letters and soldiers' blogs. They build characters that are based upon actual soldiers from their town but shaped so as to capture particular perspectives in the highly charged debate about the war and its human cost. They revise the script carefully to strengthen the contrast of perspectives, while also removing some of the more contentious quotations, including a personally critical comment about former US Defence Secretary Donald Rumsfeld.

During rehearsals, news about the play circulates the school and the community. A few students agitate against what they see as anti-war propaganda. One month before opening night, the principal suddenly cancels the performances. The theatre teacher says, 'If I had just done Grease, this would not be happening'

(Cowan 2007: B3). One of the students in the cast says that, in his school, 'people don't talk about the things that matter' (ibid.).[1]

Provocation 2

The boy is 11 years old. He reads every day, has worked his way through the 'Harry Potter' series and has been trying out some science fiction and fantasy novels. He also likes to write fantasy stories as 'they're not just about ordinary things' (Wignall 2004). He would like to be an author; he can see a future in reading and writing. He enters a book review competition run by a BBC TV children's programme and wins. The prize is to join the jury for the Whitbread Awards for best children's book of 2004 and he is actively involved in the short-listing and the selection of the winning title. He attends the awards ceremony and meets the authors.

The boy says his favourite subject at school is English. At the same time as judging the Whitbread Awards, reading widely at home and working out ideas in his fantasy story-writing, in English at school he is 'learning how to use more adjectives' and 'also spotting metaphors in our class book' (ibid.).

Provocation 3

A student teacher is being observed by her university tutor in a comprehensive school in England. She is working with a class of 11 year olds and has been collaborating with the class teacher in lesson planning and teaching for about eight weeks. The class teacher (in his second year of teaching) has been instructed by the head of English to ensure that the class know how to write a 'compare essay', specifically, that they will master the generic linguistic structure for 'argument', as defined in the Secondary National Strategy's approach to teaching English (DfEE 2001). In turn, the head of department feels under personal pressure from her headteacher to demonstrate compliance with this approach to language and literacy teaching.

Just before the observed lesson starts, the student teacher tells her tutor that the poems had not been properly understood by the class the day before but that she had been told to 'press on' with teaching the essay anyway. The student teacher greets the children warmly and manages the usual 'lost pen' routines with patience. She begins the lesson with a recap of the two poems about the sea introduced in the previous lesson. Soon, she is using a laptop computer and data projector to show a PowerPoint slide containing a plan for the 'compare essay'. She explains:

'You will need three paragraphs in the body of your essay. In each paragraph, you must have two PQCs [Point, Quotation, Comment – otherwise known as PEE, Point Evidence Explain]: one PQC about one sea poem and one PQC on the other sea poem. Each paragraph must have a different focus ... so, you compare something different about the two poems in each one. Language is the first one. So that's six PQCs, three on one poem, three on the other, two in each paragraph.'

After a brief silence, many children's hands go up. The student teacher and the class teacher spend the next ten minutes darting around the classroom drawing PQC tables in many children's exercise books. The remaining lesson time is spent talking to individual children who say they are 'stuck' and 'don't know what to say'. A girl sitting next to the university tutor says, 'Can you help me with this?' The tutor isn't sure but has a go, ashamed to be almost defeated by the arithmetic. When the bell rings, the class teacher leaves and the student teacher, visibly defeated, talks to her tutor about the lesson. He has seen many lessons like this over the last few years (Ellis 2003).

The tutor travels to a new school. He observes another student teacher, this time working with a 'bottom set' (or 'track') of 14 year olds. The class is being taught a Shakespeare play for the GCSE exam. The tutor sits next to a boy who is Lithuanian; he has an English/Lithuanian dictionary on the desk in front of him. The boy tells the tutor he knows the play, having read it at school in Lithuania a few months before he and his family came to England. At the same table as the boy, there is a girl with an Autistic Spectrum Disorder, and next to her, another girl with speech and language difficulties. Later, the tutor asks the student teacher why the Lithuanian boy is in the bottom set. The student teacher, coached by her experienced mentor, explains that it is a question of the boy's fluency in English.

The problem of English: unpacking the provocations

These provocations, while not attempting to be comprehensive in their scope, expose some critical aspects of the problem of English in schools, a historical problem partly inherent in its constitution but nevertheless one that has reached an important moment of crisis. First, these examples reveal a hierarchical and objectivist view of what counts as knowledge in English. 'What counts' is determined elsewhere by other people and then 'delivered'. The point of origin for English in schools – and its ownership – is at some distance from those who are meant to be engaged in its practices, denying its participants (both students and teachers) the possibilities of developing new knowledge. Second, the examples expose the disjuncture between the cultural, meaning-making practices of children and young people in their lives outside school and subject English as it is currently enacted in these classrooms. This disjuncture, however, is not simply a function of the emergence of new technologies, or the explosion of new media channels and modes of signification, but is far more fundamentally concerned with the curricularization of language (monolingualistically, English), literacy and culture, and the 'governmental' (Hunter 1988) purposes for which English as a subject was invented. Third, in the provocations we see the marginalization of the aesthetic as a uniquely important way of knowing that draws its power from the integration of the cognitive and the affective. Consequently, feelings and relationships are erased from the analysis of language in a way that renders a text as an occasion primarily for teaching the tools of a bowdlerized form of structuralist linguistics. This is language (English only) separated from literacy. Finally, and arising from such a decontextualized view of language and linguistic structures and the marginalization of the aesthetic, the provocations illustrate the way in which the ideological content of subject English – that which has the potential to engage students and give it a socially critical purpose – has become so easy, and in some cases necessary, to avoid. The 'intellectual project of English', as Tony Burgess puts it (this volume) has been evacuated.

These aspects of the problem of English are not new, of course, and in many ways 'Why English?' is a very old question.[2] In our view, however, these core dimensions of the problem of English in schools have reached a critical point in many countries where English is both a subject and held as a 'national' language. A key factor in the critical point the profession has now reached, we believe, is that all too often English is taken as a given and is *not* regarded as a problem. It can seem an unnecessary distraction to question current practices and attempt to reconceptualize them when teachers are expected to deliver rather than teach. But there are other factors framing the way we understand the current situation of English in schools too. From the perspective of children and young people, recognition of a wider crisis in their social and educational experiences has been provided by the 2007 UNICEF report, *The State of the World's Children* (UNICEF 2006).[3] In addition, large-scale, directive interventions by the state have not proved to be as successful as policy-makers intended, either in raising standards of attainment in literacy and English (e.g. Earl et al. 2003; Ofsted 2006) or, apparently, in improving students' engagement and well-being. The contextual details across settings are not identical and neither are the chronologies, nor what it means in terms of lived experiences. But we believe that current circumstances require a fundamental reconsideration of the purposes of English in schools. Moreover, even though the conditions for such a reconsideration might not seem propitious everywhere at all times, particularly in terms of the political will of national governments, we believe that it is also a question of the political will of the education community – the profession (broadly understood) – and its capacity for action as well as criticism. English Education, in England, especially, has garnered a reputation for witty, sometimes radical, scepticism but we suggest that the kind of rethinking required will not come from dissent alone. Rather, what is needed is what Raymond Williams called a 'new and constructive stage' (Williams 1965: 382) with a 'necessary sense of direction' focused on 'open discussion, extending relationships, the practical shaping of institutions' (ibid.: 383). And while we offered three critical provocations as our starting point in this introduction, we also believe that the 'effects' of policy and the enactment of pedagogies are much more complex than they may at first appear. Opportunities do exist for the practical shaping of the institution of school English (should we wish to take them), as many of our contributors demonstrate.

We hope that this book can play a small part in setting a direction for such a new, constructive stage in the development of English in schools. By bringing together the diverse perspectives of literary studies, sociocultural psychology, ethnography, literacy studies, applied linguistics, post-colonial histories and composition – with an important focus on the generation of questions – our hope is that those who work in English in schools can once again come to regard the subject as an intellectual problem that can be actively worked on rather than as a set of routines that just painfully work on them.

Working towards a new and constructive stage in the development of English in schools

Early versions of chapters in this book were discussed at a conference at the University of Oxford in October 2006. In so many ways, Oxford could have been seen as an uncomfortable place to sit for a discussion that sought to rethink the rationales and purposes for English. In Thomas Hardy's *Jude the Obscure*, Sue captures this possibility of unease in her outsider's gaze at Christminster (Oxford) University:

> At some distance opposite, the outer walls of Sarcophagus College – silent, black and windowless – threw their four centuries of gloom, bigotry, and decay into the little room she occupied, shutting out the moonlight by night and the sun by day. (Hardy 1896/1978: 406)

Working from the 'inside' out, however, the conference built an understanding of the conditions for rethinking and renewing school English that acknowledged the social realities of living in a small city in England's Thames valley where the life expectancy in the university-dominated north of the city is nine years ahead of that in its eastern estates (DH/NHS 2006). Oxford the city is where the student teachers present at the conference learn to teach English in schools where the educational attainment of 15 year olds is significantly below the England and regional averages (DfES 2006). Jude's scrawl on the college wall in Hardy's Christminster in the late nineteenth century is today's street artist's tag that exposes social and territorial divisions arising out of institutionalizing a particularly valued form of elite education with its attendant hierarchies of taste alongside a derided form of popular education deemed suitable for the 'masses'.

The particular setting of Oxford thus exposed for examination an important, historical dimension of the problem of English – the relationship between social and cultural practices, technologies, and political and demographic change that some have referred to as 'new times'. The question of how English should change in response to distinctively (and often distinctively ahistorical) new times has been frequently addressed and, we believe, often leads in unpromising directions that, for example, fetishize new technologies and lead to a decontextualized and deterministic futurism. Rather, we believe it is the historical dynamic of continuity and change that characterizes the nature of the problem of English, a dynamic that Williams described as 'the long revolution':

Our whole way of life, from the shape of our communities to the organization and content of education, and from the status of the family to the status of art and entertainment, is being profoundly affected by the progress and interaction of democracy and industry and the extension of communications. (Williams 1965: 12)

We believe that a challenging, fundamental and potentially productive set of questions can be generated if we situate the problem of English in the context of what Williams meant by the long revolution rather than in some deterministic view of the 'effects' of new technologies. Understanding English as an educational practice within such a long revolution – focused on shifting and competing understandings of language, culture and education (painfully felt by Jude in Hardy's novel) – allowed us at the Oxford conference to begin the formulation of a set of principles that would acknowledge the political necessity of state regulation in a modern democracy but also would allow us to point towards a new and constructive stage in the development of the field.

Given what we have said about English and its production historically, it is worth stating briefly and explicitly why we are retaining the word to refer to a school subject. At the Oxford conference, participants came from England, Wales, Scotland, Northern Ireland, the Republic of Ireland, the United States, Jamaica, Australia, New Zealand and Canada. In their professional settings, what we understood broadly as 'English' was named variously language arts, language and literature, English, composition, and communication on school timetables and syllabuses. In response, we felt that it was important for us to interrogate 'English' itself rather than propose the substitution of another term intended to be somehow more neutral or more representative and leading to the reification of a whole new set of categories. But we pose this as a question and it may be that the principles we are suggesting will lead participants to develop a new formulation for describing their educational practice that varies according to cultural context.

Core principles for English's new and constructive stage
The principles listed overleaf were common themes and directions in discussion at the Oxford conference. Subsequently, they were elaborated by the editors of this volume in response to the chapters that follow. As such, their status here is as a statement of principles around which these chapters cohere. They are also offered as a starting point for further discussion and debate by the wider

community concerned with what we are referring to as English and are focused on the *potential* of English as it might be enacted in schools.

1. English (like the performing arts) acknowledges the importance of the aesthetic as a set of meaning-making practices and as a way of knowing.
2. English fosters active participation in the culture and promotes pleasure – and the theorization of pleasure – as an important educational outcome.
3. English promotes a critical perspective on text and the capacity for a critical rather than a merely operational or cultural literacy.
4. English offers a curriculum space for foregrounding the mutuality of the cognitive and affective in learning and development.
5. English has a central focus on the importance of language as a tool in the social and historical development of mind (specifically, the social practices of talk, reading and writing).
6. English embraces a cultural-historical understanding of the subject as multilingual and as world languages.
7. English is premised on a view of language as a relational, social practice that embraces multiple modes of signification and representation.
8. English, as an educational practice, involves the development of social relationships, collaborative work, and is transformative at the level of the individual and the community.

How this book is organized

Arising out of these principles, the key argument of this book is that English in schools – as an intellectual project – needs to be rethought and renewed. The authors propose that there should be a renewed emphasis on the challenge of the questions at the heart of English and the fundamental nature of the enquiries that these provoke. The diversity of English, involving differences of national perspective as well as different disciplinary enterprises requires a continuing dialogue across apparent boundaries. It follows that there is also a need to situate the teacher and teachers' development, as well as the development of students, in the collaborative activity of English. However, this cannot be an exercise in nostalgia or individualism.

An important aspect of our argument is that account needs to be taken of the politics of language and of a literary education. This move necessarily involves engagement with New Literacy Studies and multimodal perspectives that challenge the dominance of 'schooled' linguistic text and notions of 'Standard' and monolingual approaches to language. It involves instead engagement with multiple literacies, with multilingualism and with plural Englishes. Drawing upon critical traditions in English studies, it also embraces reinterpretations of the aesthetic and acknowledges pleasure and sensory responses. A further direction of the book is to place questions about English arising in the setting of England within wider UK and international contexts, relating these to questions of imperialism and post-colonial histories. The process of questioning is advanced as a necessary contribution towards a new and constructive stage in the development of English in schools rather than the presentation of a generalizable answer. An important dimension of our argument is concerned with how questions from Australia, New Zealand, Jamaica, the United States of America, Canada, Ireland, etc. – as well as broader questions about language and language teaching worldwide – intersect with questions from the UK.

The book is organized in three, thematic sections that reflect important aspects of the problem of English:

1. How history and politics have shaped English teaching
2. Culture as a verb: teaching literatures
3. Language(s), multiple literacies and the question of English.

At the end of each section, there is a response to its chapters by another author that to some extent summarizes the section's argument and also draws out key questions for the English Education community.

Section 1 – How history and politics have shaped English teaching
In the first section, the authors focus on the ways in which English as a school subject has developed, the potential of the subject in young people's social and cognitive development, and the relationship between literacy practices and the realization of a self, a sense of identity. In Chapter 2, Tony Burgess revisits a particular moment in the history of English teaching, especially for the UK, and the work of James Britton and others (including Tony himself) at the London University Institute of Education. Tony shows how the work of the Russian psychologist (and literary scholar) Lev

Vygotsky informed this highly influential view of English teaching as an 'intellectual project' with a close focus on learning. More importantly, he shows how it is both possible and necessary to combine this focus on learning and development with more recent functional linguistic and anthropological perspectives in order to improve pedagogy. At risk, otherwise, is the integrity of English's intellectual project with the possibility of a disconnection from – or 'evacuation' of – the subject's core purposes. Tony shows us how 'Vygotskyan theory helps to keep the person in the picture' and how it positions 'curriculum as a means and not an end'. With particular reference to written composition, the strengths of a Vygotskyan perspective are that purposes in writing are conceptualized as 'more than the mastery of specific text types' and that 'a wider framework' is set 'for considering the place of literacy in development'.

In Chapter 3, Bob Fecho (with Kristi Amatucci and Sarah Skinner) draws on Rosenblatt's transactional theory, Bakhtin's dialogic theory and Gordon's theory of existential meaning-making in a discussion of two adolescent male readers and writers who are in some ways positioned as marginal to a 'mainstream'. Fecho shows how 'Isaac' and 'Andy' use the cultural resources and practices of reading and writing to construct a sense of identity and to enhance their sense of well-being. Fecho's chapter, characteristically, pushes the words of these young people to the fore while also strongly questioning the status quo in English/language arts classrooms. He ends by posing a set of challenging questions: 'Will we, as English educators, enable pedagogies that urge adolescents … to dialogue with and through text with the intention of expanding understandings of self and society or will we as teachers make the divorce between literacy practices and the lives of learners permanent and final?' For Fecho, 'no' is not an option in answer to these questions.

Patrick Walsh, in Chapter 4, explores the role of English (as a subject and a language) in the history of British imperialism, focusing particularly on the textbook industry associated with the Irish National School System (a British colonial invention) in the early nineteenth century. Walsh argues that it is necessary to engage with historical and post-colonial perspectives on the development of English in schools if we are to intervene effectively in debates about the school subject and the language. His chapter offers us a subtle analysis of the 'effects' of imperialism in action that rejects historical determinism. So it is that Walsh suggests that 'in "English" class-rooms the effects of complex, subtle, literary artefacts, and, indeed, even more prosaic functional texts, are determined by interactions between teacher and learner, and in such a context the outcomes of centrally driven administrative initiatives can be wildly unpredictable and may frequently run counter to those intended by administrators'. It is through such an historical awareness and an awareness of the complexity of social interaction that Walsh sees the constitution of English as intrinsically culturally diverse.

Section 2 – Culture as a verb: teaching literatures
The chapters of Section 2 have at their heart the kind of reading that gets done in English. Each chapter in its own way   reasserts the place of literature (with a small l) in the English curriculum. In Chapter 6, Misson and Morgan present a carefully staged argument for returning to the values of the aesthetic in reading. While they unpack the baggage that has come with the term aesthetic in the past, they mount a detailed proposal for reclaiming it and redefining it for the subject English. In doing so, they pinpoint what is special about the kind of reading English demands by taking us through the qualities that characterize aesthetic reading; they then branch out from these into considerations of form, language and content in relation to the kinds of engagement with texts that English teachers hope their students will experience. They propose that aesthetic reading is a process of active meaning-making by which we discover multiple subjectivities in ourselves as we experience texts, a post-structuralist reinterpretation of reader response. They remind us that the aesthetic is also bodily and sensate.

In Chapter 7, Fox also focuses on the aesthetics of literature but this time through the medium of comic books or graphic texts. Drawing on her teaching of *Maus* and other comics to teacher education students, she recommends such texts as rich media for teaching about the formal properties of texts since their authors show the processes of text construction from inside the text. She questions the separability of the aesthetic and the efferent in literature which has a strong historical/political content, and argues that the aesthetic carries much efferent reading along with it because of the high level of engagement that aesthetic texts demand of their readers. Her chapter also discusses the benefits of teaching specific graphic texts and their potential for using the well-developed visual competencies of students today to acquire both the informational knowledge that comes from efferent reading and the literary knowledge that comes from aesthetic reading.

In Chapter 8, Alexander gives a critical account of some currently prescriptive models of teaching English, taking as her starting point the literate person who has not been taught to attend to language in use. She argues that the way to avoid unthinking, jargon-laden language is to improve the pedagogy of English. Like Misson and Morgan she stresses the values of aesthetic reading (citing Rosenblatt's distinction between efferent and aesthetic reading) and advocates metaphor as a way of thinking and feeling. She also proposes that language in English needs to be voiced and heard and that listening needs greater centrality in the English curriculum. Throughout her argument Alexander draws on a broad range of literary texts to illustrate her advocacy of new pedagogies for English.

Section 3 – Language(s), multiple literacies and the question of English

The authors in this section locate English – as both a subject in the curriculum and as a language – in the wider context of contemporary developments in language and communication, taking account in particular of new literacies, Multimodality and multilingualism and the theories that have emerged to make sense of them. They describe the conditions of communicative life that teachers and students can now expect to engage with – the forms of reading and writing and their connection with non-linguistic 'modes' and also the world of linguistic diversity and pluralities of 'English' that most children are reared in. They ask, in a relatively open and enquiring way, how, then, might English address these issues and how can it build upon its traditional strengths in doing so?

Street, in Chapter 10, addresses both practice and theory in these areas. He suggests that changes are indeed taking place in communicative practices – literacy for instance is taking on new dimensions and at the same time multimodal forms of communication begin to dominate the lives of children before they even reach the classroom. But more importantly perhaps for this volume and for the concerns of English teachers, new theoretical perspectives have emerged that address all the variety of 'practices'. He summarizes briefly two such approaches, New Literacy Studies and Multimodality and asks what are their implications for English? Resisting mode or technological determinism he calls for English teachers, then, to worry less about the new technologies themselves than about the theoretical perspectives that have emerged to take account of them. English, certainly, will have to change or at least adapt, as it did when cultural studies likewise proposed new more contextual and social perspectives on 'texts'.

Two other chapters in this section address the significance of English as a language in an increasingly multilingual world. Bruce Horner and Min-Zhan Lu and Janina Brutt-Griffler and James

Collins point out that, contrary to what is sometimes assumed in English-speaking countries, the world is not necessarily moving in the direction of an English-dominated monolingualism, but rather more and more situations are to be found of diversity in language practices. This new multilingualism coincides with large population migrations, with increased urbanization as people from many different regions and language groups come to live in close proximity and as the digital communication systems signalled in Street's chapter facilitate the preservation and dissemination of local languages. Horner and Lu, in Chapter 11, question the persistence of monolingualism in the 'English' curriculum and argue that it often derives from ideological and nationalist leanings or from narrow, economistic interpretations of 'globalization' rather than any under-standing of the nature of the actual communicative worlds children are entering.

In Chapter 12, Brutt-Griffler and Collins likewise call upon work in sociolinguistics and research in classrooms to address the question of 'English as a multilingual subject'. They too see part of the task of rethinking English in schools as involving 'managing the linguistic diversity that manifests itself as English as a multilingual subject'. In response to the question 'Why English?', especially at a time when scholarship is showing linguistic diversity to be the norm, they see justifications for English as a subject as precisely lying in the 'increas-ingly multilingual nature it has assumed in the classroom'. Their chapter argues that we need to transcend the binary of English *versus* other languages in the classroom and recognize the growing reality of English as bilingualism. Like Horner and Lu, they use sociolinguistic literature to 'debunk the myth that English spread was endangering local languages', instead indicating the signifi-cance of social variables such as class and gender in nuanced accounts of language diversity.

The English/language arts classroom, with which both the writers and many readers of this volume are crucially concerned, presents, Brutt-Griffler and Collins believe, 'a vastly under-utilized educational space for encouraging greater societal bilingualism'. The chapters in this section have indicated ways in which that space can indeed be utilized while remaining loyal to the critical and reflexive stance and the intellectual tradition in which English/language arts have developed.

In the final chapter, Viv Ellis suggests how teacher education might contribute to the rethinking of English in schools through collaborative work (between students, pre-service and experienced teachers, and teacher educators) on expanding understandings of learning and literacy and on developing knowledge in the key settings for teacher development – schools. A vital aspect of this form of teacher education work is a close focus both on young people's own meaning-making practices and cultural worlds outside the classroom *and* on the dynamic subject concepts of school English as a field.

Finally, in an Afterword, Shirley Brice Heath reflects on the themes of the book as a whole and suggests ways in which English might be rethought and renewed, ways that take account of several decades of educational research and curriculum development.

Together, and in many different ways, the contributors to this book offer both challenging and productive questions for the English Education community. *Rethinking English in Schools* is therefore offered as our contribution to the kinds of discussion and action that might lead to a renewed sense of direction, one that keeps, as Burgess puts it, 'the person in the picture'.

Section 1

How history and politics have shaped English teaching

The souls of nations do not change;
  they merely stretch their hidden range
Just as rivers do not sleep
the spirit of empire still runs deep.

Ben Okri, the *Guardian*,
20 January 1999

The relation between thought and word is a living process; thought is born through words. A word devoid of thought is a dead thing:

… and like bees in the deserted hive
The dead words have a rotten smell. (N. Gumilev)

Lev Vygotsky,
Thought and Language

Chapter 2

The picture of development in Vygotskyan theory: renewing the intellectual project of English

Tony Burgess

Through the work of James Britton, in the 1960s and the 1970s, English teaching began a long engagement with Vygotskyan theory. Britton's book on *Language and Learning* (1970) and the central theoretical chapter 4 of the Bullock Report (DES 1975), the major post-war report on English teaching in UK, in which Britton played a substantial part, are both Vygotskyan in their orientation. The perspectives were widely influential. What was decisive was the orientation Britton gave Vygotskyan thought for teachers, at a time of wider attention to public education and to curriculum. He invited collaboration in an enquiry. The focus was on how the immediacy of learning contributed to the sociocultural development of mind. Here was first of all a call to teachers to look at children with fresh eyes and to listen to the processes that are set in motion in classrooms. But it was the combination of the significance attached to classroom learning within a wider intellectual project, together with the role this gave in forming pedagogy, which caught the imagination of teachers.

In thinking about English at the present time, I set out from the point of view that there has been a partial break, though not by any means a total one, with this Vygotskyan turn in English teaching, in ways that I shall seek to capture. Teachers inhabit now a different professional culture and new perspectives have contributed to a different intellectual climate. I recognize that hopes attached to language used in learning and to a theory of development may carry too much of the flavour of a certain era. Alternatively, perhaps one direction for the future may be to continue in a search to realize the start that Britton gave us, with a much developed version of Vygotskyan thought available to us than was to him, and to seek to make connections with new emphases within the subject. I want to make this argument here. But I believe this case depends on clarifying the strategic and the intellectual potential of Vygotskyan thought, and I shall cast the argument along these lines.

I need to comment at the outset on the gap between the expectations presently placed on schools and teachers and the earlier turn
towards Vygotskyan thought that I have briefly sketched. Britton's
project arose in part from the efforts of a generation of educators to
use the base of universities to put the cutting edge of work in social
sciences and in educational research at the disposal of teachers. Their
aim was to develop the intellectual base of teaching. The calls made
in the Bullock Report for attention to language in education address
a system prior to government's forging of new structures of direction
and system management, which marked the later 1980s and 1990s.
Thus, the Committee's recommendations are not couched in terms of
targets and objectives, but look instead to the development of teachers'
understandings and to the influence of innovation at school and
local authority level. Seen from a later vantage, there were limitations
in this strategy, in effecting system level change. It may be though that
there were also strengths in an approach that concentrated on
teachers' agency, and on enlisting professional energies, which still
have relevance, even in today's more driven system.

The contrast is apparent in the reports on English, commissioned
following the Education Reform Act (1988), the centrepiece for the
reforms that lie behind the present educational dispensations in the
UK. These reports, the one the work of a Commission of Inquiry into
the teaching of the English Language, chaired by Sir John Kingman
(DES 1988), the other that of a working party advising on the content
of English in the National Curriculum, chaired by Brian Cox (DES
1989), each carried forward much from Bullock. It is forgotten
sometimes how much the making of the National Curriculum owes
to earlier work, in its emphases on processes of speaking and listening,
reading and writing, and in its detail. Equally, the model of language
proposed within the Kingman Report, while this has waited for full
implementation, at the time held few surprises, offering no support
for a return to traditionalist teaching of grammar, which had been
canvassed in some quarters. The brief for both reports, however,
was to offer National Curriculum level descriptors and targets, in
preparation for the approaching system of national assessment and
reporting, and, in this, both reflect, and help to shape, a different
educational culture.

Strategically, it is the shift in teachers' professional culture towards
a system managed through its targets and objectives that represents
a major change from earlier work on language, learning and development. At the risk of oversimplifying, what has been achieved,
through the action of successive governments in the 1990s, contrasts
with that supposed by Bullock: a system anchored in the National

Curriculum as a base and open to fine tuning through the implementation of more specific strategies; one driven and directed from the centre, and managed through targets and objectives, together with requirements at school and local authority level for reporting and inspection. In such a system, there have been gains in managing performance, but hopes for a continuing intellectual progress of the subject, linking classroom learning to a wider theoretical enquiry into development, now sit very differently in the expectations held of teachers. It follows that to make the case for the continuing relevance of English teaching guided by Vygotskyan perspectives must presuppose in part attention to generic issues. I have in mind renewal of attention to the professional space for teachers in the UK setting, and a wider sense of opportunity for teachers to contribute to the development of the teaching subject.

Meanwhile, in the thirty years since Bullock, much has happened in the academic and theoretical worlds that bear on English teaching, which provide a different intellectual context, in which to argue for the relevance of Vygotskyan theory. In higher education, the subject, fortified by an enhanced and diversified literary theory and by a vastly stronger contribution from linguistics, looks very different from the predominantly historical and literary critical inheritance of the immediate post-war years. A sociolinguistic revolution in linguistics has come to approach language as a social phenomenon, best conceptualized through registers and genres, events and practices and texts, together with awareness of cultural difference, both in language and in literacy. A stronger anthropological contribution has built on earlier concentrations on speech events and speech communities, and has heightened critical awareness of different literacies, relating difference to the analysis of social power. I should add to this the challenges and development of theoretical concepts that have derived from concentrations on gender, race and class. The object before English teaching is surely now an expanded and developed sense of literacy in a multimodal culture and a multicultural world.

I shall argue in what follows that Vygotskyan thought, drawing on a central intellectual tradition in English teaching, can play a part alongside other perspectives in building a renewed professional culture with its emphasis on learning in the sociocultural development of mind. It is a case that will reflect my reading of Vygotskyan thought, which is necessarily selective. I interweave three emphases in my discussion: one is on the centrality of a picture of the learner and another on attention to the development of concepts within English teaching, the practices of teaching subjects, more widely. Connecting both these emphases, I argue for attention to the interplay of instruction, learning and development, referring to the account of pedagogy given by Vygotsky, in the last years of his life.

Developmental theory and the pre-school child

I want to start out on my undertaking, not through formal exposition of Vygotsky's psychology, but through pausing on the kind of thinking about children that seems to be most central in Vygotskyan thought. Exposition is better done in many very extensive works (Van der Veer and Valsiner 1991; Kozulin et al. 2003; Wertsch 1985; Daniels 2001). I shall start from emphases, related to the sort of thinking English teachers do and in the spirit of making connections to those changes in the worlds that bear on English teaching that I have already briefly noticed; and I shall pause to work on these, offering my grandson, Orlando, as an example. I begin by listing some key emphases within Vygotskyan thought that might inform an answer to the question concerning the continuing relevance to English teachers of a focus on development.

1. Development is seen as arising historically in the course of interaction with the culture, mediated by tools and signs, by relations with adults and with peers and by both informal and more formal learning experiences.
2. The explanatory concern is with the emergence of higher mental functions and with seeking to explain the genesis of these and their development. A central contribution to the emergence of higher mental functions is made by concepts, mediated by signs.
3. The explanation for development is transformation of existing mental functions as new skills are internalized, in the critical periods of early and middle childhood and adolescence. The world is not the same for the toddler or the school-aged child or the adolescent. They are positioned within it differently and they bring to it new needs and motives. Vygotsky refers to this as the changing 'social situation of development'.
4. Given the historical and cultural nature of development, children are both active and interactive in their learning. To learn is to appropriate resources from the culture. At the same time, such appropriation requires the agency of children and young people, participating in the intellectual and other work of growing up, whether as toddler, school-aged child or adolescent.

I pause on an example, in order to explore these emphases in greater detail. With Orlando, we confront the world of the pre-schooler, and I shall tell a little story, and try to illustrate in comments that I make on this the gains that may accrue from thinking about his behaviour developmentally and seeking to interpret this within a Vygotskyan, explanatory framework. My central aim in this is to present an image, and there are themes and implications, which I will come back to.

With the coming of the status of a grandparent, I get more time with toddlers than I have for quite a while, since we get a loan of them at times at weekends, my wife and I, when one or other comes to stay. Orlando is now four years old, and when he comes the day is marked into a number of rituals, which are by now familiar. There will be visits to the toy shop and the book shop, there will be time spent in the park, on the various activities of the children's playground, or playing football, or walking through the woods. There will be meals of various kinds and baths and bedtime. In between, there will be stories read and long passages of time spent on the sitting room floor, engaged in play. So, here is Orlando playing, and this is where my story tends – to the kind of interaction between thinking, language, action and activity that Vygotsky shows us, and to the kind of intellectual and other work engaged in by the age group.

Much of Orlando's time is spent with objects, and here the central object in his play is a relatively small and pushable tractor, bought on the previous day's expedition and assembled the previous evening, which is another story. But while the play is certainly continuous with the curious exploration of objects characteristic of earlier years, here the object has become what Vygotsky would call symbolic. It is representative of tractors and of forms of human activity that tractors can be involved in. The tractor includes a number of bales of hay, square yellow rectangles that can be loaded, piled and emptied. It tows a trailer. Crucially it contains two plastic men who drive the tractor and who can be inserted and removed and made to do things. It also includes a tiny silver object interpreted by Orlando as a telephone, allowing for messages and phone calls and instructions to be conveyed. Additionally, as the game proceeds, a boat becomes involved, a favourite object from bath time, also kitted out with a captain and a diver, which I, as an attendant adult, have to fetch; and boat and tractor proceed together, in various combinations. The play then is symbolic and it is also partly socio-dramatic, with actions being taken appropriate to captains and to tractor drivers. It is minded and intentional, partly arising through responses to the possibilities immediately presented by the objects at the centre but manipulating these as well to make a narrative account. Lastly, it is collaborative, and requires the presence of a collaborating adult as a fellow participant but also as security and respondent and in some sense mentor.

You will notice in the transcript how we move off from the kitchen to the sitting room and settle down to play at the base camp that has been constructed on the floor, an enclosure framed by various objects and the bales of hay. Meanwhile, Orlando's speech shuttles between the social and the egocentric, between fully articulated utterances, addressed to me, and mutterings and whisperings which guide the actions he is undertaking. This is egocentric speech, on the way inwards, in the analysis that Vygotsky gave us. Through it, Orlando represents the objects at a symbolic level, at the same time as he moves them and enacts an unfolding narrative with them. He also uses language to direct his own behaviour. The speech is partly social – it rises and is more articulated in my presence – but it is also thinking for himself and looking inwards. A further mark of this arises at one point when I leave to fetch the boat from the upstairs bathroom, returning a couple of minutes later. Despite my absence from the scene, Orlando's speech continues unabated in this interval.

Orlando playing

O: *Orlando, aged 4 years, 4 months*
T: *Tony, his grandfather*

T: Have you done it?
O: Yep … we done … I don't want to lift this tyre up
T: Shall I take it … shall I take that one?
O: OK that … I'll take this one
O: Come on …
T: I'm coming

(Sounds of running as we leave the kitchen for the sitting room)

O: I can … you can't run really … you can't run very fast
T: No I can't no
O: This is where our base camp
T: This is base camp is it
O: Up … down … oh … right oh here's the one
T: OK so what do we do?
O: We have to go to the shop

T: All right

O: Here's the shop ... we're here ... oh

T: Here's the man coming

O: Get in

O: We ... it's a long way

T: Yes

O: Prrrrrrrr (engine sounds)

O: I pull ... I'll do that

T: Yes

O: I'll put you in the trailer

O: Ready?

T: Ready ... Oh (registering an accident)

T: Good

(Engine sounds continue)

O: 'Here we go ... bottle' (singing)

O: Oh yeah ... we go this way ... look out Tony

T: OK

O: Now ... now we have to make our own tents

T: OK

O: You get out ... I'm going to get out see

T: Right

O: 'Cos I'm ... and take all the trailer bits out

T: OK

O: What can stay it up ... these bits can't they?

T: Yes

O: OK ... I'll stay it up ... come on get the hay out ... no I'll
   dump it ... see I can do that

T: You can

O: See where they ... shall we built it now? ... yes oh ... we built
   it ... we built it ... this is our little camp ... shall we make
   a little camp?

T: Yes please

O: Here a little camp ... oh yeah that ... oh no ... there that can
   be that bit can it

T: Have we got some more hay or is that all the hay?

O: That all that ... that all the hay ... that can make all the ...
   I'm getting up in a minute ... I'm now ... come on now ...
   where your boat? ... you need to get your boat

T: Right I'll get the boat ... (T leaves to get the boat)

O: (Engine noise continues) ... I'm waiting ... front loader (caddy?) ... OK I'll catch you ... Oh ... you OK ... come ... skip ... he went to there ...There 'Hello' ... he should get up here ... he'll put us up there

(Sound of boat arriving pushed along the floor)

T: Here it is
O: Ready ... we're making a big camp with that ... look ... do it like that ... and do it like that
T: Yes
O: And that how we get through ... and how I get on the machine ... get the machine in ... here get the machine under ... I've got it ... you get in the boat ... we need to buy some food
T: Right
O: OK ... come on ... get in your boat ... have you have you take anybody ... we don't want to be messy ... we don't want it to be messy do we?
T: No we don't
O: You need the ladder ... no I ... we don't need this do we?
T: How do we get on the boat?
O: Um ... oh no ... this ladder
T: OK
O: No look you do it like this
T: Yes
O: Pathway you have to go on the pathway
T: Right
O: What I just did ... you have to do that ... get on the trailer

(Play continues)

The transcript offers just a snapshot. This play in fact proceeded for well over an hour, involving changes to the base camp, endless permutations of the various men, as drivers, loaders and passengers, changes of position, and periodic telephone calls by men at different stations. It seems reasonable to infer from this that Orlando is exploring in his own way the adult world and what men would do in their work and with machines. He is anchored in his own life, imagining the difference. He is also settling and attending and submitting to the constitutive rules of this activity, loose and self-imposed though these may be. The various activities that the men can undertake reflect the limits of the real world he imagines. The geography of the base camp is maintained. In this and other ways,

Orlando demonstrates maturity as a toddler and a pre-school child. His language confidently varies, from social to egocentric to narrative; it is adequate to what he wants to do, conceptually. As I noted earlier, the play is both symbolic and socio-dramatic. Supported by an adult presence, Orlando is self-regulating. His emotions are subordinated to the task in hand; and he is working with emotions cognitively and consciously, not just possessed by different feelings. He attributes feelings to the men who absorb his attention and he relates empathetically to his adult partner.

There are threads of change within this moment, apparent through juxtaposing strengths achieved and challenges not yet confronted, which will lie ahead as schooling enters, as an influence on Orlando's maturing, psychological functions. Thus, the level of Orlando's interaction with the resources of the culture, his use of tools and signs, is still relatively bounded by the immediate. Through play, he is manipulating reality, but his thinking outside play settings is driven principally by perception and by memory and the experience of the moment. He is pre-literate, though exploring several paths to literacy through participating in stories, read and spoken, and engaging with literacy events within his family, such as reading catalogues, translating labels, absorbing written and visual language through the media. He lives within a world of spontaneous concepts, prepared for, but not having reached as yet, the scientific concepts that will come with schooling and instruction. He is self-regulating in his family world, but limited in his relations with the peers and adults, who exist outside it. Cognition and emotion in his play run ahead of what he can do in other contexts, though his capacity to sustain attention and to empathize with others is now considerable.

I have set out in my commentary on this example to do more than just evoke an episode and share some random insights linked to some Vygotskyan ideas. I have hoped to point towards a general relevance. Where Vygotskyan theory focuses attention is on the transformation of existing psychological functions as new resources from the culture are internalized and appropriated. For this there must be both the interaction of the child with culture as well as culture with the child. To work with these perspectives in English teaching is to look towards the place of pedagogy in the lives of children, in their interactions with the culture, and to search beneath immediate transactions for the longer-term development of the mind. I have tried to anchor such considerations through pausing on one example. I want to come now to some aspects of Vygotskyan theory more directly concerned with schooling.

Scientific concepts and schooling

Schooling brings a changed social situation. There will be new relations with peers, which will influence both cognitive and emotional development. With literacy will come a further symbol system to spoken language, permitting greater consciousness in making meaning. Instruction in scientific (academic) concepts[1] will add new levels of thinking and will transform existing spontaneous concepts, achieved within the years of infancy and early childhood. Where the lead activity has been 'play' for infancy and early childhood, Vygotsky argues, we may think of 'learning' as the lead activity for the middle years of childhood and of schooling, and of peer relations as that of adolescence.

Much of Vygotsky's writing about schooling, and especially about scientific concepts and the relevance of instruction in them, was not available to English teachers, in the early stages of working with Vygotsky's thought. Scientific concepts are introduced in Chapter 6 of *Thought and Language* (Vygotsky 1986), but this is not an easy chapter, and draws on, rather than explains, connections between scientific concepts, the role of literacy, the zone of proximal development and a theory of instruction, which are hard to grasp, within a single, unifying perspective. As important, the development of these ideas by Vygotsky's followers, especially Galperin and Davydov, has only recently become available in the West in accessible form. A major contribution here is their dissemination in Kozulin's splendid reader on *Vygotsky's Educational Theory in Cultural Context* (Kozulin et al. 2003), which I shall refer to in what follows.

Partly due to these historical gaps, the scope of the Vygotskyan argument concerning scientific concepts and the influence of schooling has sometimes been foreshortened. At times the focus on instruction has simply been transported into other arguments, where it has really meant no more than a handy justification for explicit teaching. The interplay between spontaneous and scientific concepts has sometimes been forgotten; that to grasp scientific concepts requires a theoretical exploration and not merely learning words and technical vocabulary. For English teachers, it may have seemed that scientific concepts were less central for attention than for teachers of science or the humanities, and therefore greater interpretative weight came to be attached to other aspects of Vygotskyan theory – a point that may be worth rethinking. The focus on the interaction between spontaneous and scientific concepts, together with the part of schooling, informs the major concentration of Vygotsky's later work on the relations between learning, instruction and development.

The relations between learning and instruction, especially effective instruction in scientific concepts, are taken up most fully in the work of Vygotsky's students and successors, most notably Daniil Elkonin and Vassily Davydov. Their work is introduced in accessible form in the Kozulin et al. (2003) collection mentioned earlier. This is not the place for full discussion, but it is worthwhile pausing briefly on these extensions to Vygotsky's thought, and on their development in classroom practice, since they help to indicate the scale and the potential of the Vygotskyan analysis.

Explaining Vygotsky's doctrine of scientific concepts and its implications for school instruction, Yuriy Karpov (in Kozulin et al. 2003), one contributor to the Kozulin volume, distinguishes two sorts of learning: the empirical and the theoretical. Empirical learning is based on children's comparison of several different objects or events, picking out their common salient characteristics and formulating on this basis a 'general concept about this class of objects or events'. Theoretical learning is needed to provide analysis of the essential characteristics of objects and events. Sometimes, this may coincide with understandings arrived at by empirical methods, but often this empirical knowledge, children's spontaneous concepts, may lead to misconceptions.

The example that Karpov gives is that of whales, and fish and mammals. In an investigation he refers to (Davydov 1990), elementary school students when classifying animals, though taught the definitions of fish and mammals, continued to associate the whale with the class of fish. Karpov comments

> It could reasonably be assumed that not being able to use the memorized definitions of these scientific concepts ... (t)hey compared 'typical' fishes among themselves, picked out their common salient features, and formulated on this basis a spontaneous concept of fish, which turned out to be wrong. Probably, this misconception involved the shape of a body, fins and tail, and living in the water as the essential characteristics that are necessary and sufficient for belonging to the class of fish. In the same way, they developed a wrong spontaneous concept of mammals. Then, when asked to classify animals, they analysed them by using the developed misconceptions as the basis for analysis, and that method resulted in associating the whale with the class of fish. (Karpov 2003: 70)

I may add how close this is to my own essentially spontaneous understandings in this area. I can remember having being taught that a whale is a mammal, and have been known to assert this confidently, in visits to aquaria. But I remember this as a piece of random information and cannot even now say why.

Karpov makes a number of points in his discussion. It is not sufficient just to be taught the definitions of scientific concepts; it is necessary to be able to use them and to grasp the principles that underlie them. As well as concepts, it is also necessary to grasp procedures, the 'methods for analysis in the relevant domain'. In the whale example, the procedure is that of identifying necessary and sufficient conditions for classifying instances within a class of objects. He points out that in the absence of instruction in the relevant scientific concepts and procedures, students will attempt to compensate for these deficiencies by 'discovering' for themselves the scientific knowledge that they have not been taught effectively in school but that these attempts will often be mostly unsuccessful and lead to students' development of spontaneous rather than scientific concepts. He notes that '[T]his is why, having elaborated Vygotsky's idea of teaching scientific concepts as the content of school instruction, his Russian followers concluded that scientific knowledge should be directly taught to students rather than being discovered by them' (Karpov 2003: 71).

Put thus baldly, this may sound like no more than an argument for a return to traditional instruction. Set within the larger framework of Vygotskyan emphases – on the trajectory of concepts, on the leading role for instruction in relation to development, and on the zone of proximal development – the implications are for new methods of instruction, formulated on new lines. Those pursued by Elkonin (1972) and Davydov (1990), envisaged methodologies that concentrated on the design of 'learning activities', intended to address the development of theoretical concepts and procedures and comprising practices that treat children not as passive performers and recipients but as agents in their learning, alongside the teacher and their peers.

In a companion piece to Karpov's, in the Kozulin volume, these methods are outlined by Galina Zuckerman (in Kozulin 2003). In essence, they include, in any designed activity, the prior conceptualization of the field of study and the location of the 'big idea' that unifies the material to be grasped. The method of instruction then involves preparing the orientation of the students to this material and the presentation of the main hypothesis, the 'germ cell' of the area of study, which is then explored collaboratively by students through a series of tasks. Echoing Vygotsky's observation that a scientific concept, once internalized, is only at the beginning of its journey,

Davydov talks of the work of exploring the 'germ cell', or 'big idea', as 'ascending to the concrete', the reverse direction from that of empirical learning, as new material is encountered and explored in relation to the informing theory. Galina Zuckerman's account brings out the kind of access to the teacher that is appropriate for pupils in this process and the necessity of joint peer collaboration to reflecting on the learning, within the framework that has been set.

Vygotskyan theory then identifies the central contribution of schooling in the development of scientific concepts, taken on through intellectual work and gradually transforming both the spontaneous concepts of the everyday and young people's capacity for reasoning. The interaction is two way. Scientific concepts are in the culture, in the history of enquiry in various disciplines, but in internalizing concepts and procedures the activity of students, in appropriating these and working with them, is central to the pedagogy. This is the difference Karpov notes between mere 'memorization' and grasping principles.

The development of a pedagogy, in Vygotsky's words, 'addressed not to the ripe but to the ripening functions', is taken up by the post-Vygotskyans, where the 'notion of ascending to the concrete' catches the progress that theory needs to make from instruction to full learning. But the analysis also adds some further questions. On the one hand, more reflection may be needed about the place of scientific, or academic, concepts within a notion of English as a subject and about the conceptual contribution of English within curriculum more widely. On the other, it may be that the holism of Vygotsky's theory, and its reference to areas other than the cognitive, may be something to be reasserted from English teaching.

English teaching and Vygotskyan theory

I return now to the case that I am making: that Vygotskyan theory, allied with linguistics, with critical theory of different kinds and with anthropology, can make a contribution to the formulation of English teaching in the future. I can do no more than notice certain points to bring my argument to a close. Generally, Vygotsky's focus on the 'changing social situation of development' has useful implications for considering the orientation of pedagogy at different phases and at different stages. The ambition of Vygotskyan theory supports a holistic view of students and their learning, which recognizes the interaction between culture and the formation of mind and seeks to keep in play awareness of cognitive and emotional and imaginative dimensions. Where the concentrations of contemporary English teaching prioritize the work of texts and representation, Vygotskyan theory helps to keep the person in the picture, reminding pedagogy of learners' agency, the complexity of learning and patterns of longer-term development.

There is more specific relevance to curriculum issues. Within Vygotskyan theory, there are powerful reminders of the curriculum as a means and not an end. It reminds us, as teachers, that in the moment of instruction, however clearly directed towards outcomes, the concepts and the skills initiated are only at the beginning of their journey. From the interactions of the classroom, it is the travel of instruction – and its intersection with wider patterns of intellectual, emotional and cognitive transformation – that Vygotsky demonstrates to the curriculum planners. His focus is on the work the students do, in order to internalize and to appropriate the skills that planners are seeking to develop.

There are also implications for more specific areas of current educational discussion, where directions are still forming in contemporary English teaching. Vygotskyan theory has particular application to discussions about bilingualism and literacies in different languages in a multilingual society. Its focus can complement that of sociolinguistics or anthropological linguistics, because its emphasis is not so much on learning language, coming to acquire it, as on the inward work of language in the development of mind. Attention to the role of words in developing concepts has important implications for the use of mother tongue in learning. Equally, Vygotskyan emphasis on internalization, and on the long development of words in coming to articulate concepts, has lessons for the learning of a target language and can inform instruction in language teaching. More generally, a theory that addresses the role of language and literacy in the development of mind can deal as easily with bilingualism and different literacies as with monolingual speakers.

In literacy instruction, Vygotskyan theory recalls that purposes in writing run further than the mastery of specific text types and it sets a wider framework for considering the place of literacy in development. The methodologies developed in the various writing programmes of the 1970s and 1980s have seemed to some to be too informal in their underpinning linguistic theory and to pay too little regard to incorporating instruction of certain kinds. But perhaps they also made a contribution by emphasizing learning. The pedagogy offered students a way into writing, with its emphases on writing journeys, drafting and redrafting, and the use of writing journals, learning logs and think-books. The evidence is that students in the middle years of schooling, and also adolescents, at later stages, may value these opportunities for drafting informally, for using written language in the process of thinking and for dialogue with a teacher, as well as writing for more formal occasions. It is clearly possible to think of work directed to mastering genres, and to developing written syntax, as co-existing with the range of writing opportunities that pedagogies for writing in the 1970s and 1980s at their best supplied.

Vygotskyan theory also calls to mind the centrality of concepts to reading and to work with texts. In teaching texts like *Great Expectations* and relating these to their sociocultural background, concepts of the past and poverty and class are central. How children handle such historical and social concepts are fundamental to their reading of the novel. More generally, much of the work we want to do on critical literacy or in comparing texts of different kinds or in addressing media production challenges and develops the conceptual powers of students. Equally, in mastering different writing genres, an argument, or an explanation, depends as much on theory and conceptual confidence in the area concerned as it does on written syntax. Vygotskyan theory reminds us, as teachers, that English, no less than other curriculum areas, works with students' concepts and helps to form them.

But my argument is ultimately two-sided. To realize the potential of Vygotskyan thought, it is necessary to combine intellectual considerations with those that I have called strategic. The power of the ideas requires a corresponding space for the professional work of teachers, to explore the immediacy of classroom learning in relation to a wider picture of development. Both aspects need discussion, if the intellectual project of English is to be renewed.

Chapter 3

Deep winters, invincible summers: teaching English for existential purposes

Bob Fecho, with Kristi Amatucci and Sarah Skinner

The following extracts are taken from a poem written by Isaac, an American adolescent raised in a working-class family who was serving out his high school sentence. Chronologically he was in his final year of compulsory education, but due to complications stemming from his bipolar condition – excessive truancy and time spent at an alternative high school – he would need to complete an extra semester of electives in order to qualify for a diploma. This poem, rendered as he wrote it, showed Isaac coming to some understanding of the impact bipolarity, a disorder marked by gross mood swings between mania and depression, had had on his life. As he wrote:

> … i am alive by desire,/ one ability,/ one need,/ to ignore the,/ demons,/ monsters,/ (or whats most often heard)/ Wolves,/ amongst sheep,/ Samiel appeared,/ to wake, me,/ take me,/ to bleed,/ like a farmer's/ scythe/ harvesting wheat,/ incisions wide which my/ soul leaks, . . .

As the poem continued, Isaac shifted focus away from the effects of his disorder and more towards ways of coping with the complications of the disease

> … This verse my narcotic/ most better than/ 'Cures'/ pills for your 'Sanity'/ A 'Loss of mental Balance,'/ I might be 'insane'/ I might be the ocean/ pushed, / pulled, by tides within'/ I have no control? …

Finally, he wondered about the rationale behind his disorder, but still managed to end on a point of assurance:

> … I laugh at the whores/ of this mediocre appoclypse/ wheres god?/ he chose to abandon,/ when we gave all,/ for thumbs on

our hands,/ silly mammal,/ ego hurt?/ the fall from Eden,/ Hell
on Earth,/ Its a problem Of tempermeant/ Of whoose im unsure./
there's one thing that's certain,/ go read a book.

Two aspects stood out to me upon first reading this poem. To begin,
Isaac wrote with intent; he used his poem to gain some sense of how
bipolarity was and would continue to influence his life. He gave
readers glimpses of his focus ('i am alive by desire,/ one ability,/ one
need,/ to ignore the,/ demons'), his frustrations ('I might be the
ocean/ pushed, / pulled, by tides within'/ I have no control?'), his pain
('to bleed,/ like a farmer's/ scythe/ harvesting wheat,/ incisions wide
which my/ soul leaks'), and his sense of the absurd ('wheres god?/ he
chose to abandon,/ when we gave all,/ for thumbs on our hands').
Isaac composed this collage of images to make meaning of this
seemingly random disorder that had entered his life.

But equally present was Isaac's metacognitive sense that reading
and writing are meaning-making processes and that, in engaging in
such literacy transactions, he expected to gain insight and perhaps
comfort regarding his bipolarity. He acknowledged that the verse he
was writing was 'my narcotic' and that writing it was better than
cures and pill-based therapy. The lines that finish this extract also
finish the poem: 'there's one thing that's certain,/ go read a book.' It's
perhaps the most definitive statement in a verse full of questions. In
terms of thinking through issues, Isaac asserted that engagement in
text is the one surety, the constant upon which he could count.

I feel this poem encapsulates an argument that posits there is a need
within human beings to make meaning of our lives, particularly if
those lives seem too far removed from the norms of dominant
culture. Isaac, caught in the throes of a disorder that caused him to
feel too much or too little, saw himself on the margins of his school
community, looking for a means for self-expression. Through reading
and writing he sought to bring expression to his life so that others,
but primarily he, could make meaning of this seemingly random set
of circumstances that had taken over his daily experiences.

The problem, however, that Isaac and others like him face is that
too many secondary English classrooms are intent on recognizing
only certain cultures and the expectations of only certain students,
primarily those who are white and come from homes where cultural
and financial capital are the norm (Finn 1999; Heath 1983). The
drive for standardization of assessment, curriculums and even dress
are, as Jensen (2004) noted, initiatives 'to make sure students meet
a set of standardized criteria so they will later be able to fit into a
world that is itself increasingly standardized' (p. 5). As a result,

assessment that is mandated with little local input or interpretation (Schultz and Fecho 2005) is driving curriculum and pedagogy, creating a narrow, primarily economic view of literacy (Coles 2003; Darling-Hammond 2004). Already pressed to the wings of the educational stage, students who are marginalized for sociocultural factors such as race, class, gender and sexual identity find it even harder to see themselves in the culture of school (Fecho 2004; Hull and Schultz 2002). Consequently, many throw up their hands. For example, students in the USA living in low-income families were at approximately four times greater risk to drop out than peers from high-income families (Laird et al. 2006).

To reverse these trends, we need to see the teaching of English differently. In the remainder of this chapter, I argue against teaching literature, reading and composition as subjects unto themselves, a practice currently found much too frequently in too many class-rooms. Instead, I argue for teachers in English classrooms to situate the reading and creation of texts as ways of making meaning, as processes through which we develop an existential sense of ourselves as actors in larger social worlds. Through a theoretical framework anchored by the works of Rosenblatt (1994, 1995), Bakhtin (1981) and Gordon (2000), I indicate that, particularly for those learners whose lives are marginalized from the cultural centre, reading, writing and other forms of expression are valuable media through which learners seek understanding of the chaos around them. Using the experiences of Isaac, along with that of Andy, another working-class adolescent, I argue that the teaching of reading and writing needs to be seen as more than the learning of discrete skills to enable future employment. On the contrary, all transactions with texts should be viewed as providing learners with a range of ways to call their lives and the lives of others into scrutiny. Ultimately, I suggest that, by taking a transactional and existential stance on the teaching of English, teachers and learners become inquirers into and ongoing co-constructors of their individual and collective selves.

Theoretical framework

The theoretical framework upon which I drape this chapter is informed by Rosenblatt's (1994, 1995) transactional theory, Bakhtin's (1981) dialogic theory and Gordon's (2000) theory of existential meaning-making. My first intent is to establish dialogue among these theoretical perspectives in ways that are resonant among the perspectives themselves. I also provide a theoretical context for understanding the importance of seeing transactions with texts as attempts to take some control of one's life through the mutual shaping of reader/writer and text.

Rosenblatt and transactional theory

The concept of what I'm calling literacy transactions is in direct reference to Rosenblatt's (1994, 1995) transactional theory of reading and writing. To Rosenblatt, a transaction is more complex than simply giving and receiving. Instead the term describes activity where context, both temporal and spatial, is considered and those persons or objects involved shape each other in ways that create new texts.

What does that mean? When we read, as Rosenblatt (1994, 1995) suggested, for information and for emotional response, we are transacting with the text and new texts are created. Because each of us reads any text by bringing the whole of our experience to that text, all readers bring personal interpretations to all text. These interpretations may intersect with the interpretations of others or they may differ markedly. As Rosenblatt (1995) put it, 'there are no generic readers or generic interpretations but only innumerable relationships between readers and texts' (p. 291). Most importantly, both the printed text and the reader as text – as something to be interpreted and made meaning of – remain in a process of mutual shaping. Readers, through their interpretations, create original texts of the material before them and that material shapes them as they read. A parallel process occurs with writers who, in shaping a text, are being shaped by that text they are creating. I would go a step further and suggest that humans engaging with text are simultaneously but to different degrees always readers and writers of text, that in reading we write the text anew and that in writing we are the first readers of that text.

Although Rosenblatt was primarily interested in transactions between readers and printed text, she conceded that humans are constantly transacting with their environment. Seeing such transactions through the Freirian (Freire 1983) lens of reading the world and the word argues for wider definitions of what counts as text. Consequently, how we read this wider textual range results in a sense that we read everything around us and are in a constant process of transaction. Deciphering the sound of the ocean scattering shells on the shore, enjoying the smell of the first spatters of rain on a beach road, encountering storm flags ripped to attention in heavy gusts, and examining a Doppler radar map streaming repeatedly on a computer screen are, in my parlance, literacy transactions.

Bakhtin and dialogue theory

Akin to meaning in literacy transactions, language in a Bakhtinian (Bakhtin 1981) world remains constantly in flux, tugged between opposing tensions in a process he called heteroglossia, literally different tongues. In this process, centripetal forces pull language towards the centre, seeking stability and unification. Construed benignly, such forces foster communication because they allow large numbers of language users access to a language that remains constant and undergoes little change. However, at their most malevolent, such forces become the tools of oppressive regimes that, through control of the language, seek also to control flexibility of thought. Stripped of personality and fluidity, language becomes, as Bakhtin noted a 'dead, thing-like shell' (p. 355).

Conversely, the opposing force of heteroglossia is centrifugal, urging language away from the centre towards variety and individuality. In a positive light, centrifugal forces allow for language users to find themselves in and have input into the language, creating a personal connection. However, when too much individualism and flexibility occurs, the language loses commonality and the result is diminishing degrees of communication. The language becomes so closely identified with such a small group of speakers that it no longer fulfils the need for wider understanding.

Ultimately, Bakhtin (1981) suggested that a healthy state of language exists at the point where the centrifugal and centripetal forces intersect. As he noted, every speaking turn or writing task 'serves as a point where centrifugal as well as centripetal forces are brought to bear,' where they 'intersect in the utterance' (p. 272). He elaborated: 'Every utterance participates in the "unitary language" (in its centripetal forces and tendencies) and at the same time partakes of social and historical heteroglossia (the centrifugal, stratifying forces)' (p. 272, parentheses in the original). The upshot of this transaction is that language remains in flux and, to an extent, in conflict. What individual words and words in combination mean are entirely dependent upon the context in which they are uttered or written. Understanding comes in response. Utterance, response and meaning – the building stones of dialogue – are merged in a recursive, continual and transactional process.

Gordon and existential theory

Gordon's (2000) discussion of existential thought and the ways such thought historically and currently manifests in black (i.e. African, African American, African Caribbean, Caribbean American) literature expands and particularizes these discussions

initiated by Rosenblatt and Bakhtin. His work has kinship to that
of Fanon (1965) and Sartre (1956), but becomes entirely his own
as he argues that to seek meaning for one's existence is an existential
act. Because so many examples of black literature are meditations
upon the circumstances that have conspired to marginalize the lives
and cultures of blacks globally, Gordon offers that such work –
from Frederick Douglas through W. E. B. DuBois, and up to bell
hooks and Cornell West – is of an existential nature.

Although not necessarily capital E Existentialism – a term that
defines a distinct European philosophical movement – work by
black authors that troubles the absurdity of racism and the consequences such racism inflicts on all our lives takes an existential
stance by trying to bring meaning out of chaos. And, although
European Existentialism is a philosophy frequently regarded as one
from which no hope is derived, I refer to the work of Camus
(1968) who wrote, 'In the depths of winter, I finally learned that
within me there lay an invincible summer' (p. 169), I feel that
Gordon would agree that Africana Existentialism is an attempt to
find hope where it doesn't seem to exist and to do so by calling
upon the inherent strengths of the black community.

Furthermore, Gordon (2000) argued that the more marginalized
one is from the dominant culture, the more one needs to find
meaning for one's existence. To put it in Bakhtinian terms, the more
one sees him- or herself centrifugally in relation to dominant
culture, the greater the need to examine that tension. According to
Gordon, blacks having long been marginalized by dominant
cultures, possess an intense need to write their way out of that
predicament whether through more traditional and formal genres
such as autobiographies and essays or more pop cultural mediums
such as hip hop and the blues. Although not necessarily to the same
degree and certainly not to the same historical intensity of blacks,
I expect that all learners who are marginalized from the mainstream
dominant culture and under the impact of socially constructed and
randomized factors beyond their control have similar needs to
write, read and otherwise express their perspectives and understandings, to bring meaning to the chaos they perceive.

Coalescing the framework
Taken together, the works of Rosenblatt, Bakhtin and Gordon
argue that from dialogue comes meaning – a restless, transient,
ephemeral meaning that is contingent on context and inclined
towards its next iteration. This work also argues that the dialogue
is many voiced, that without a range of voices, meaning often gets

skewed towards the centre and lies in danger of becoming lifeless and inert. In the heteroglossic blur of these literacy transactions where language, response and meaning routinely engage, marginalized learners try to define space for themselves that simultaneously helps them establish a foothold in the dominant culture without subsuming too many of the more individualistic and personal selves within them. In short, they try to retain some recognizable sense of self even as that self is in process. In doing so, they, to varying degrees of intentionality and effect, shape the dialogues they enter.

Sketching the study

To animate this theory, I discuss the literacy transactions of two working-class adolescents. Prior to this discussion, however, I offer a brief description of the foundations of the work.

Isaac and Andy were two of six participants in a study of attitudes of adolescent boys who had embraced literacy and had been raised in working-class families. By 'working class', I meant that the parents held jobs in the service, manufacturing, agriculture or business industries for which they had little say as to their job description, the conditions of their employment and the future direction of that business. Using this definition, an electrician who ran his own business would not consider himself working class, although an electrician who was employed by a manufacturing firm to service their machines would. Although how much money one makes and what one values certainly figure into any discussion of what counts as being of the working class, ultimately for me, a position for which a worker has little power over the circumstances of that position is frequently the deciding factor. Although I suspect there are readers who would contest this definition, I can't imagine any definition of 'working class' that would stand uncontested.

By the phrase 'embracing literacy for their own purposes', I meant that I was looking for young men who routinely read books and/or other print and electronic media and/or routinely wrote via traditional pen and paper media and/or electronic media as a means of making sense of their contexts and their identities and roles within those contexts. More briefly, they read or composed because they had needs to do so. In particular, they engaged in literacy transactions beyond classroom assignments.

Historical context and purpose of the study

This study had its origins in my childhood experience. My father worked in a car-frame factory and my mother in clothing manufacturing mills. The families who populated the rowhouses of my neighbourhood were decidedly working class, by my definition and most likely any definition one could offer. But from the start of my formal education, unlike many of the other boys, I embraced reading and writing. Trips to the library were frequent – I always rented books – and almost always without my neighbourhood pals. Although I never felt fully connected to my boyhood neighbourhood, I also felt separate from the children of professionals who dominated the classes of my junior and senior high schools.

As an educator and researcher, I am acutely aware of what I have gained through my embracing of literacy and formal education, but am equally aware of what I have lost. Furthermore, although I feel that formal education has added to my life, I remain a critic of that very education. In particular, I argue that, too often, I learned in spite of and not because of the way I was taught, which was mostly various iterations of what Freire (1970) has called 'the banking model' – teachers depositing information into my brain for future withdrawal via tests and quizzes. Consequently, as one strand of my research agenda, I have sought to understand what it meant to be a working-class male adolescent who had embraced literacy for his own purposes, using my experience as a springboard into the study that yielded the examples to follow. Through journals written by the participants, vignettes written by teachers, observations, online threaded discussions, interviews and artefact collection, I looked closely at the literacy transactions of six working-class adolescent males who fell within those parameters.

By looking closely at specific literacy transactions of two adolescent males – Isaac and Andy – from working-class backgrounds, I put a face on the theory, to show, in effect, my own praxis. If thought and action mutually inform, then this section vitalizes the substantive, but somewhat abstract discussion to this point, even as it points towards the understandings and challenges to come. Specifically, I use the experiences of these two young men to show the unique and necessary presence of literacy transactions in their lives and the range of possibility and consequence these transactions provoke.

Isaac

I assert that Isaac and Andy were thrice marginalized, although with some variation between them. Regarding Isaac, his growing up in a working-class family in a rural subdivision accounted for two degrees of marginalization. His bipolarity was the third. As discussed above, Isaac transacted with text in order to make sense of and work through his issues with his disorder. For my purposes here, I focus on ways that Isaac used traditional writing as means for gaining insight.

Isaac was a prolific writer and relied heavily on written expression to make meaning of his emotional struggles and develop a sense of identity that simultaneously accepted, but attempted to limit the effects of his bipolarity:

> 'I try to predict my feelings through a lot of things like writing and doing collage work, drawing, things like that. You know, I find my release in those types of things. Made a lot of short stories and things like that, just to try to cope with [my bipolarity] and make things a little better.'

His writings, whether for public sharing or private rumination, tended towards themes many might construe as being ominous and even nihilistic:

> 'It is just some of the things I go for, I don't particularly know why. I guess it's just mind thought, things like that. Like the fact that I'm manic-depressive and things like that maybe influence those areas. I guess I've always kind of been dark about things, usually during points of depression.'

Like much of what Isaac shared, this extract indicated a Bakhtinian centripetal and centrifugal pull occurring within him as he regarded his bipolarity. On one hand, he admitted the disease caused him to write in ways and genres that were disturbing, yet he freely acceded to the idea that these thoughts were ultimately key in shaping his identity.

For Isaac, writing was a way of knowing, and a deeply personal activity. Most of the writing Isaac attempted when he was in a depressive or manic state he hasn't shared – at least not with me – although he discussed the process:

> 'Well they were more like train of thought writings. What it was like, just how the emotion felt, and how I could describe it as best I could through a word and give it a materialistic view. So there were a lot of things that dealt with turning myself to the shadows, picking my pieces from the sand and try to assemble who or what I might have been. That's about how they were, just very

depressed, but at the same time, a cloud to where you couldn't really tell what the meaning was unless I could tell you, you know.'

The language of this extract from an interview is particularly telling. Isaac spoke of picking up pieces of who he was and trying to reassemble the whole. Yet, meaning was clouded. What he had described elsewhere as the 'constant flow of thoughts, just rapid and repeating most of those times' were intelligible mainly and perhaps singularly to him.

In order to release energy that yielded inappropriate social actions and also to 'use my experiences again, just to be stronger', Isaac would let words and thoughts flow onto paper. In terms of making sense,

'Lots of [the writings] do, some of them don't. Some of them were just hateful, at myself and other people. Those I keep just as a reminder that I could go that far – I'm still human – that type of thing. I really wished I had thought better of myself at the time because I felt like I could have done more now than what I had, but I just let it all go. But if I hadn't done [the actions and thoughts produced by my disorder] at the same time, I wouldn't have been able to make those [mania and depression induced writings], and actually see how far I could push myself to any artistic thing.'

The complexity of Isaac's attempts to make meaning is readily apparent in this extract. He simultaneously regretted writing in ways that seemed hurtful to him and others, but also realized how exciting it was to be that artistically aware, caught yet again in that heteroglossic tide between a solidarity with the mainstream and personal expression. He understood that his bipolarity made it difficult for him in social circumstances, but that the heightened awareness could be its own reward. Ultimately this description is similar to ways that Hermans and Kempen (1993) have used Bakhtin's (1981) ideas on heteroglossia to suggest that our identities are always in process, representing ongoing transactions between a unifying identity and various centrifugal identities. We are simultaneously all those identities, with each, to varying degrees contributing to the whole.

In Isaac's story, I perceived that the making of personal meaning was largely processed outside of formal schooling. Although he indicated that certain teachers had opened him to literacy transactions that tugged him in new and interesting directions, for the most part, few took the time to try to understand this complex young man. School had mostly been a place where Isaac worked below capacity and where teachers too often told him he dreamed too much. To an extent, *such indifference* was also the case for Andy. However, a number of life experiences converged late in his high school experience that allowed him to see literacy and, at least his English classroom, as key factors in helping him construct facets of his identity.

Andy

In some respects, Andy was situated in the mainstream culture of the small, but growing city in which he lived. His being white, male and a successful athlete on a school team brought him much social capital. Like Isaac, however, Andy was thrice marginalized. Being raised in a working-class family and attending an urban public high school worked against the accrued social capital described above. Perhaps most significantly, Andy's third degree of marginalization came from his tentative attempts at coming out as gay to his family and peers.

Early in the last semester of his senior year of high school, Andy, through an assignment from his English teacher that asked students to write an autobiography of themselves as readers, confided his sexual identity to her. By discussing young adolescent novels with gay protagonists, he indicated how they had influenced his sense of the lifestyle he was defining for himself. Throughout the ensuing spring, Andy and his teacher, via formal and informal means, kept a running dialogue of how his reading choices influenced how he constructed himself. In the following vignette written by his teacher, she described a literacy transaction between Andy and her that blurred the line between the more formal ways we approach literature discussion in school and the more informal ways we engage those conversations outside school. She picked up this vignette where she was wondering if Andy was still reading *Someone is Watching* (Roeder 2004), a young adolescent gay novel that had proved somewhat worrisome to him.

'Whatcha reading?' I asked, looking at the title, *Prayers for Bobby*, of the book he carried.

'It's this true story, written by someone else. That's a...a...a biography, right?' He looked at me for approval of his use of literary terminology.

So I smiled my approval. 'Yeah. A biography.'

'Yeah. It's this biography about a guy named Bobby. He was

gay, and his parents were really religious – worse than mine – and they wanted him to get healed from being gay. His mama put a lot of pressure on him until he finally killed himself. But they didn't think he had been planning it, 'cause he had just bought a new mattress and a bunch of other things, so it's like a mystery what made him finally decide to do it,' he explained.

'He didn't leave a note?'

'No. He just did a back-flip off this highway overpass and landed on the back of a semi-truck. It killed him instantly.'

'Whoa. That's heavy,' I say.

'But the cool thing is that after he died, his mama decided to change. She goes around the country now speaking out about gay teens and how they need support and all.'

'Oh, so at least something positive came out of his life and death.'

'Yeah. That's what made me like this book so much. And 'cause Bobby seems a lot like me. Not like the suicide part, but just the family issues.'

'So you're finished with this already? You read it quickly.'

'Yeah. I got so into it I couldn't put it down.'

'Does this mean you decided not to finish *Someone is Watching*?' reminding him of the last book we chatted about.

'Yeah. I might start it again later. But not now. It just doesn't feel right.'

Finally the bell chimed. As I straightened up a row of desks, Andy scampered back to his corner to shove his books into his backpack. On the way, he almost bumped into DaQuan, another student in the class who was rushing through the door, back from a trip to the library. He was holding a copy of *Rainbow Boys*, one of the books Andy had asked the librarian to order.

'That's a good book,' Andy said quietly to DaQuan as he headed out the door for another day.

This vignette illustrates several points. First, the dialogue between Andy and his teacher was fairly relaxed and the relative distance between the traditionally defined roles of teacher and student were somewhat bridged. For example, he talked and she responded in casual ways about how the subject of the book committed suicide. Still, we detected the heteroglossic play of language occurring here, the more central tug of the formal classroom jostling with the more centrifugal, individualistic informality. In particular, Andy seemed to be trying on usage, checking with his teacher if his calling the text a biography was correct, before more confidently using it subsequent to her affirmation. Importantly, the two of them used classroom time to act increasingly like two friends having a chat about books at a coffee shop rather than taking the inquisitor/rote responder roles seen all too frequently in too many literature classrooms. The dialogue, especially from Andy's stance, was seen as having immediate purpose, as commenting upon current and shifting conceptions of self rather than some far away and probably not even hoped for identity as literary scholar.

Also in this exchange, Andy, who was a reluctant reader and learner in school, indicated his willingness to use transactions with text as a way of making sense of facets of his in-process identity. He was simultaneously engaged with two novel-length texts and offhandedly recommended a third, all of which he sought on his own. In car trips to area bookstores, Andy consulted reviews in magazines catering to young gay men and would then seek internet sites for suggestions on what to read. Back at school, he contacted the school librarian to order titles of interest. He checked out several books simultaneously and read them whenever time and space permitted him to do so. Though he floundered with indifference through accepted school texts like the plays of Shakespeare and examples of Romantic poetry, he sought and talked about the young adult literature he was reading with confidence and excitement.

Consequently I see it as no fluke that Andy's ongoing construction and awareness of his sexual identity occurred in concurrence with his self-admitted blossoming as a reader, both of which were also concurrent with his acquiring a licence to drive. We don't think the juxtaposition is merely curious. His willingness to engage printed text, particularly lengthy printed text, seemed to correspond to his need to make greater sense of himself as a sexual being and what that might mean for the ways he transacted with peers, teachers, parents and others. Importantly, the freedom that accompanied driving, particularly in a city of growing sprawl, enabled this exploration by providing time, opportunity and privacy. Couple all this to access provided by the internet and the result is a young man with many avenues for pursuing a greater understanding of self within the larger community.

Finally, this vignette showed how Andy's dialogue with the young adult literature he was reading shaped the decisions he was making about how much to expose himself to fellow classmates and, indeed, to the world. The literature he read was transacting with life, helping him to use his experiences with a range of texts to compose an identity and keep that composition a work in progress. And those transactions informed the ways in which Andy was able to discuss a text that was useful to him – *Prayers for Bobby* (Aarons 1996) or *Rainbow Boys* (Sanchez 2003) – as opposed to ones culled from the literary canon that were read but not put to work in his life. Andy was making sense of himself and his experiences through reading. He was rehearsing future performances, reconstructing the cultures he knew. The comment made to DaQuan, an openly gay student, in the moment when the classroom was almost empty, indicated to us Andy's pushing of the boundaries. He used transactions with texts to improvise on the edges of identity by, yet again, trying on newly constructed facets of his identity in ways that felt somewhat secure and in control to him. Unlike Isaac, Andy had more closely meshed his inside and outside school literacy transactions so that both were in service of his ongoing identity construction.

Understandings and challenges

In looking at the lives of Isaac and Andy, I saw two young men who despite or perhaps due to their various marginalizations were actively constructing facets of their identities through literacy transactions. They both felt compelled to read and write with the intent of better understanding themselves in terms of larger social worlds around them. Although Andy may have more frequently and directly used the formal constructs of school as a means for identity exploration, both Isaac and he saw the need to transact with text in multiple ways. They sought to continually engage in ongoing dialogue about how they felt marginalized and what such marginalization meant for their ongoing identity construction. However, as we argued above, Isaac and Andy are more the exception than the norm among working-class families.

   To counter these trends, we urge teachers to see the teaching of English as an opportunity to support adolescent existential explorations. If teachers embrace the idea that the texts we encounter shape us as we shape them, then literacy transactions within their classrooms take on immediate and enduring existential importance. The acts of reading, writing, listening and speaking become ways of making meaning and the intention no longer becomes teaching the literary canon or even young adult novels as texts with discrete knowledge contained within the pages. Instead, the purpose becomes using those and other texts to help teachers and students make sense of the many complex social worlds within which they transact. Importantly, the more someone becomes self- or other marginalized, the more necessary it becomes for him or her to use literacy transactions to make meaning of the marginalization (Gordon 2000). I would add that, in the making of meaning, the need to improvise and act upon the meaning-making becomes critical. Without proactive measures on one's behalf, the reflection remains somewhat distant, sterile and ineffectual.

So the question is formed: for whom will English be taught. Of equal importance, how will it be taught? And to what end?

Will we, as English educators, enable pedagogies that urge adolescents like Isaac to dialogue with and through text with the intention of expanding understandings of self and society or will we as teachers make the divorce between literacy practices and the lives of learners permanent and final? Will we support uses of reading and writing that provide students like Andy with open forums for construction of identity or will we continue to look the other way in some farcical and potentially destructive game of 'Don't Ask, Don't Tell?' Will we encourage complex transactions with a range of texts that allow marginalized learners to realize their dreams and aspirations without sacrificing their cultures and adolescence or will we continue to expect them to merely replicate and reify a culture that will continue to marginalize others? Will we design explorations into a range of media that will make all learners uncomfortable about current social conditions and thus more willing to seek better responses to those conditions or will we continue to teach in ways that only make the marginalized cringe at the ignorance of the mainstream? Ultimately, will we provide opportunities for literacy transactions that will help all students, in the depths of their personal winters, find their invincible summer? If not, why not?

Chapter 4

English in the history of imperialism: teaching the empire how to read

Patrick Walsh

English has a presence as a global language which is related to British history and the history of imperialism over the last 300 years. This kind of geographical perspective and long view of the history and significance of the language in today's world is necessary if we are to have more than a parochial view of what constitutes the school curriculum subject of English. Some of the issues this perspective addresses are represented by such concerns that appear in the present curriculum as 'Literature from other cultures' and 'Varieties of English'. But this is little more than gestural – designed to obfuscate rather than confront unsettling questions that are posed by the history of imperialism and colonialism.

What is also required is a perspective which denaturalizes English in the imperialist context and uncovers ideological configurations that still operate in oppressive ways in many countries with a colonial history. This endeavour should include an analysis of the history of British imperialist education policies and the relationship of these to the use of English in colonial territories, particularly in regard to the heyday of British imperialism in the nineteenth century. Such perspectives relate not only to post-colonial countries but also to the context of the home countries of former imperial powers such as Britain which now contain diverse communities originating from mass emigration from former colonies in the second half of the twentieth century. This chapter argues that if we are to understand the significance of present-day polices in relation to the school subject of 'English' and be equipped to intervene effectively in the debates which shape them then such an historical engagement is essential.

Britain, of course, was not the only European colonial power. France, for example, had Asian and African colonial possessions and linguistic and educational policies that were comparable, if contextually quite different, to those of the British. But the geographical and economic reach of the British Empire was more extensive, and in the

English language it possessed a cultural resource which, in the American twentieth century, went on to dominate international discourse across a whole range of important contexts so that it has far outstripped any of its European, nineteenth-century competitors. The advent of the electronics revolution and the spread of the internet have contributed to the enhancement of the role of English as the dominant lingua franca of educational discourse. In this context the increasing convergence of cultures and political systems in today's globalized world raises theoretical and ethical questions that can be related to the effects of cultural hegemonic practices in colonial contexts. This has become a discourse that is vitally relevant for uncovering practices of domination and control in a world where the unequal and asymmetrical distribution of power and economic resources is becoming ever more entangled with issues relating to the place of culture, history and languages within national curricula in many parts of the world (Green 1990).

Often in colonial situations in the nineteenth century an important part of the administration of the colonial territories included ideological projects linked to establishing English-based systems of education to service native, administrative élites, and many post-colonial writers and scholars have reflected on the complex patterns of influence that these systems have left in the wake of the end of the period of formal colonization (Achebe 1975; Ngũgĩ 1986; Viswanathan 1998). Central to the imperialist initiatives was a commitment, usually expressed in terms of Christian, religious morality and/or the importance of economic and industrial development, to the diffusion of the English language. Learning to read and write, increasingly meant reading and writing in English and thus gaining access to 'civilization' and the 'modern world'.

These perceived benefits were, of course, not seen as applying exclusively to the colonies. Bringing education to the British working classes was part of the same project. It should be noted that the technologies of social control were usually more centralized in colonies than imperial homelands where the relationship between the ruling class and the general population was perceived to be more culturally 'organic', being mediated through a political system more responsive to modern, democratic, political mechanisms. The developing labour movement in Britain proved capable of intervening and setting limits on the dominant social and economic agenda of the ruling classes. In the British colonies of Africa and the East Indies the relationship between 'progress' and education was more explicitly tied in with access to *the language* of English. In Britain the working classes were to be taught to *read and write* while in the colonies they were to be taught to *read and write English*. The distinction is important because it emphasizes that in the colonies there were competing languages, cultures, religions and communal ideologies from which the colonial subjects were to be weaned through the use of the English language. Many of those active in providing education to the 'natives' in the colonies, therefore, conceived of it in terms of access to the English language. In this specifically colonial elaboration of the 'Arnoldian' conception of culture the colonial subject was to become a British subject through the subject of English. Teaching English would assist in the project of civilization and also serve as an ideological bulwark against the emergence of democratic ideas tied to demands for national independence. Eventually this struggle of ideas was played out between the imperialist administrators and the rising nationalist movements that rose to oppose British rule.

Beyond the United Kingdom, where, as we shall see, Ireland's deeply ambiguous status and anomalous religious composition produced state interventions structured along colonialist lines, nineteenth-century India was the colonial site where these policies were most carefully formulated and elaborated, and India provided the model for the introduction of such policies in other parts of the empire. Macaulay, chairman of the Governor-General's Committee on Public Instruction, was the authoritative, administrative ideologue of this principle. He came down decisively on the side of a policy of using English in the education system as against a competing one of education based on 'orientalist traditions, through Sanskrit, Arabic, or Persian' (Phillipson 1992: 110). The outcome was the administrative decree of 1835:

> [T]he great object of the British government ought to be the promotion of European literature and science among the natives of India; and that all the funds appropriated for the purpose of education should be best employed on English education alone. (Phillipson 1992: 110)

Misra (1982: 150), quoted in Phillipson (1992: 111), sums up the consequences of this decision for the Indian subcontinent: 'English, became the sole medium of education, administration, trade, and commerce, in short of all formal domains of a society's functioning.' Such policies were reproduced throughout British Asia and British sub-Saharan Africa. 'In the words of the head of the British Council's teaching operations for many years [writing in 1961], "Macaulay determined what we should do, quite literally, from Hong Kong to the Gambia"' (Phillipson 1992: 111). This, it must be stressed, does not imply that a fully articulated strategy was applied mechanistically across diverse societies and widely dispersed geographical regions. What is being argued is that a discursive and administrative trend evolved into a powerful, hegemonizing paradigm across the British Empire. Such policies, of course, had to confront differing sizes of populations at different levels of technical development situated in very culturally diverse communities. They were applied in differentiated ways that were adaptable over time. This is to emphasize that British colonial policy was historically situated and responded flexibly to changing circumstances. By the end of the nineteenth century the British administration was facilitating primary education for native Indians in vernacular languages, and indeed they were also mindful of the practical need for the provision of some bilingual education even for elites – who also needed to mediate in indigenous languages between ruler and ruled. But for those few who progressed to secondary education, English remained the dominant, prestige medium of instruction. Similar subaltern status was provided to African vernacular languages in African countries under British rule (Phillipson 1992: 111–12).

We should, of course, distinguish between what imperialist policies intended and what they actually accomplished. They were not applied to *tabulae rasae* or to completely compliant populations, but to frequently resistant communities drawing on their own traditional, cultural resources and on adaptive responses which engaged with these policies in combative ways leading to often unforeseen outcomes. The nineteenth century, of course, was also the age of the rise of nationalism in Europe, and in the colonies similar democratic struggles rose to oppose imperialism. In the British Empire, English frequently became the principal means by which diverse language groups propagandized and solidarized for common, revolutionary purposes. In a theoretical engagement with Phillipson's concept of 'linguistic imperialism' (Phillipson 1992) Pennycook has insisted that it needs further nuancing, particularly in regard to the policies of 'Orientalism' and 'Anglicism' employed at various times by imperialist educational administrators. In regard to the former it was argued that British interests would best be disseminated through indigenous languages and this dovetailed with a long tradition of empathetic, British and European scholarship in this area. In regard to the latter, education for elites was to be promoted through English and this was, of course, the policy that was adopted after Macaulay's decisive intervention in 1835. Pennycook (1994: 75) asserts, however, that the former was not politically innocent and that earlier 'policies of the British in India encouraged colonial officers and administrators to develop a better understanding of Indian political structure, language and culture in order to establish a sound basis for British rule and administration'. He therefore argues for a more complex reading of the relationships between languages and imperialist policy:

> It seems that rather than Anglicism replacing Orientalism, the two ideologies in fact operated alongside each other. This observation goes beyond a redressing of an understanding of colonial education policies because it suggests, first, that promotion of education in local languages was as much part of colonialism as was promotion of English and, second, that the denial of access to English may have been as important for colonialism as the insistence on English. (Pennycook 1994: 74)

The point to be emphasized here is that neither imperialist policy nor native responses to it were static, but adaptable, and that if this is to be understood then any analysis needs to be diachronic as well as synchronic. It also allows for a conception of language as dynamic and flexible, and of human beings as actors and agents, rather than passive recipients, of language policies in education.

Brutt-Griffler (2002) has attempted to refute Phillipson's (1992) theory of 'linguistic imperialism'. She argues that because imperialist policy was more concerned with producing educated elites for administrative purposes tied to economic imperatives than with any explicit commitment to cultural proselytization, that it is economic globalization, rather than colonial ideology, that has produced 'World English'. The existence of this world language, she goes on to assert, has provided access to a global 'econocultural system' for a diverse range of national communities. But she exaggerates the significance of the difference between economic and cultural activity which are frequently one and the same thing. Economic activity cannot take place in a social vacuum. She also underplays the asymmetry of power involved in the contact of languages. English is not only overwhelmingly powerful in terms of geographic spread and economic presence but is capable of reconstructing the 'local' in ways that are not as multidirectional as her account of 'language spread' suggests.

One of Brutt-Griffler's concerns has been to problematize the representation of residents of the colonial 'periphery' as passive recipients of language and educational policies. In a comparable, though ideologically very different, engagement with Pennycook's analysis Canagarajah has also attempted to nuance such representations by insisting on the 'need to go further and see how the dialectic between the discourses (Orientalism and Anglicism) also spawned native resistance against the colonial project' (Canagarajah 1999: 58). He successfully shows how in the example of Ceylon (now Sri Lanka) there was a multiplicity of competing and sometimes contradictory agendas among both colonized and colonizer and that positions shifted over time. For example, religious and caste differences among the indigenous population worked in favour of the advance of English so that 'its social and cultural conditions influenced the community to participate in its domination' (Canagarajah 1999: 62). Paradoxically, among the colonizers religious and economic agendas sometimes diverged to the benefit of the vernacular language. Tamils educated through English used their education to get government jobs and spurned the role of 'native preachers' for which the Christian missionaries had been supposedly preparing them. Thus, frequently the churches favoured education in the vernacular languages, much to the chagrin of the colonial administration which wanted a 'cadre of functionaries who could help economize their rule' (Canagarajah 1999: 64). And, of course, doctrinal and national divisions in the churches led to subtly differing attitudes to English and the vernacular. Many of the missionaries in Jaffna were from the United States and did not owe much allegiance to Britain, and Portuguese Catholic missionaries favoured the vernacular as a bulwark against 'social evil' and the political disunity along linguistic lines among the Tamils that education in English was perceived to be faciltitating. Most importantly, Canagarajah convincingly establishes that the native population were not wholly prostrate before the economic and cultural hegemony that imperialism strove to impose, but succeeded in a whole variety of ways of appropriating English to their own agendas:

> Paradoxically, within Anglicism itself there were the seeds for its destabilization – planted by English education, which created a breed of natives influenced by enlightened liberal democratic discourses, who demanded such values from colonial rulers. Opposition to colonialism and Anglicism was expressed by natives in subtle and sometimes partially expressed ways. Encouraged by local discourses, cultures, and philosophical traditions, this tradition of resistance later played an important function in the post-colonial context, engendering related forms of linguistic resistance and appropriation. (Canagarajah 1999: 58–9)

It has been convincingly established by recent scholarship that the emergence of the subject of English in schools, and later in universities, was heavily influenced by the educational policies (tied so closely, as these policies were, to the teaching of the English language itself) of imperialist administrators in the colonies (Viswanathan 1998). The ideological link between the subject's civilizing mission in the colonies and its comparable role among the proliferating industrial working classes in Britain's cities has been traced to Mathew Arnold's influential *Culture and Anarchy* (1869) where he agues for a specifically civilizing mission for literary culture. And, of course, Arnold had a long career as an inspector of schools. Claims have also been made for a link between the establishment of the subject in British universities and the tradition of courses in Rhetoric and Belles Lettres in Scottish universities (Crawford 1998). This latter suggests a Celtic connection generally. Both Scotland and Ireland had quite distinct, but nevertheless comparable status as peripheral, subordinate national cultures within the United Kingdom. Both also played an important role in providing personnel to staff the armies of empire, and in the case of Scotland the provision of a disproportionate amount of personnel for the imperial administrative staff. Both also provided large emigrant populations to the 'white settler' colonies of North America, Australia and New Zealand. This link between these populations and the administrative demands of the burgeoning English education systems that were being established throughout the empire is particularly stark in relation to the establishment of the Irish National School system in 1831: '(T)he first state system of popular schools in the English-speaking world' (Akenson 1970: 58). The sets of textbooks that were developed by the British government to serve the needs of these schools played a role in English-language education in diverse imperialist settings. In these books it is possible to discern the outlines of the emerging subject of English and establish a clear line of influence to the pursuit of imperialist, ideological aims throughout the empire.

The Irish National School system was established in 1831 by the British government's Irish administration. Catholic emancipation had been granted in 1829 after a mass campaign orchestrated by Daniel O'Connell and supported by the Catholic hierarchy. In an overwhelmingly Catholic state, at least outside the north-east where the religious composition was more evenly balanced, the British government had long supported Protestant ascendancy in its governance and excluded Catholics from political power. In addition, between a third and a half of the population still used the Irish language in their daily lives. All this made Ireland radically different from the rest of the UK and more prone to political disaffection and outright rebellion. The establishment of the school system represented the latest in a long line of strategic attempts by the British to bring this disaffection under state regulation and render it more amenable to political control. This was of a piece with other administrative technologies of control emanating from the political centre. In the 1830s Ireland got national school and police systems and an ordnance survey, long before any of these were attempted in Britain itself (Akenson 1970; Andrews 1975; O'Sullivan 1999).

Right from the start the state administrators endeavoured to create and control a series of textbooks, or 'readers', that would become the ideological cornerstone of the system. These 'readers' constituted an attempt to construct a prototype of an English curriculum. In fact they subsumed *all* of what we would now call the 'humanities' subjects on the curriculum under the heading of 'reading'. Because this system and its books represented a coherent intervention in the direction of mass education, many of these books proved attractive to administrators in Britain itself where there was a growing movement to develop secular instruction in schools which were still largely under the control of voluntary, religious organizations (Goldstrom 1972a, Chapter 3). In the 1860s one observer judged that the Irish national textbooks were the most popular series of textbooks used in *English* schools. They were also used in many other countries of the empire. 'The commissioners [of Irish National Education] supplied books to schools of more than a dozen countries, in addition to Scotland and England' (Akenson 1970: 229–30). Thus the Irish education project had a resonance congruent with the reach and power of the British Empire. It should be seen, therefore, as one of the first of the bureaucratic initiatives of empire that was 'universalist' in ambition and scope. It is not being suggested here that the conditions of the nineteenth century allowed for a fully articulated bureaucratic unfolding of such a scheme. Uneven levels of development, difficulties with communication and travel and, of course, the often chaotic economic and social conditions of colonial underdevelopment made such a fully coordinated bureaucratic project virtually impossible. Nevertheless, the logic of imperialism called forth from imperialist administrators and bureaucrats initiatives that were transnational and global and that followed the economic, political and ideological logic of empire.

We can illustrate the reach and ambition of imperialist administrators in regard to what we might term 'education for empire' by looking at the convergence between the Irish National School system and that of another British colonial possession, 'British Canada', that is, the area covered roughly by the modern province of Ontario. Typicality for either of these countries is not being claimed; in many ways both were very untypical of the experience of British colonialism.

For example, Ireland was a white, European country and its ancient domination by Britain was, historically, articulated in very complex ways. And Ontario was part of the mass 'white settler' component of the empire and thus quite distinct in how it was governed as compared to India and the East Indies, or sub-Saharan Africa, which were generally controlled by relatively small, white, administrative elites. Nevertheless, in Ireland and Ontario the books and the school systems in which they were embedded are best understood as components of the colonial administrative apparatuses. The basic administrative principle of the Irish National School system was that it would be overseen by a Board of Commissioners composed of appointed representatives of the government and the three main Christian churches in Ireland, which would disburse grants and centrally oversee the schools that would be set up and managed by local, voluntary trustees, in effect clergymen. While formally preferring applications by groups of joint religious trustees this was not compulsory (Akenson 1970). In Ontario the 1846 Common Schools Act established a Board of Education (the name was changed in 1850 to the Council of Public Instruction). Like the Irish National Schools Board it dealt with local 'trustees' (elected local boards, unlike Ireland where the schools were set up and effectively controlled directly by clergy) who were to establish schools which had to conform to the Board's regulations if they were to be officially recognized and to be awarded grants (Curtis 1988).

The chief centralizing mechanism by which the curriculum was to be standardized in both countries was through control of textbooks. The letter from the Chief Secretary, Lord Stanley, to the Irish Lord Lieutenant in 1831 became in effect the constitution of the Commissioners of National Education in Ireland who were appointed to oversee the system. Control of books was dealt with explicitly:

> They [the commissioners] will exercise the most entire control over all books to be used in the schools, whether in the combined literary, or separate religious instruction; none to be employed in the first, except under the sanction of the Board, nor in the latter, but with the approbation of the Members of the Board of the persuasion of those for whom they are intended. (Goldstrom 1972b: 74)

In Ontario the new Board took powers similar to the Irish Board:

> [The Board was] to examine and recommend, or disapprove, of all Books, Plans, or Forms which may be submitted to them, with

a view to their use in Schools: and no portion of the government
Grant shall be given in aid of any School in which any book is
used and which has been disapproved by the Board, and of
which disapproval public notice shall have been given. (Parvin
1965: 21)

The Irish Commissioners set about producing their own series of
books and granting free stocks of these to the schools every three
years. They were closely scrutinized and jointly agreed on by representatives of the three main Christian denominations on the
National Board of Education. Although never compulsory, by
1863 they were so securely established that the commissioners
were able to charge for them, though at a rate much cheaper than
the going commercial one. After a preparatory tour of various
countries, including Ireland where he met with the Irish system's
administrative founder, Lord Stanley, who was by then working at
the heart of government in London, the Chief Superintendent of the
Ontarian system decided he had no need to commission a set of
books (Akenson 1985: 146–7). One that answered his purposes
was already to hand. He immediately commissioned 31 of the 50
publications of the Irish National Commissioners then in existence.
'During the next twenty years, the Irish series remained almost the
only authorized textbooks in the Province' (Parvin 1965: 26). In
1866, out of over 4,000 common schools in the province, only
around 150 failed to report that they were using the Irish National
Readers (ibid.: 29). This congruence of the two systems offers
convincing evidence of the international coherence of the efforts by
imperialist educational administrators in widely flung territories of
the empire.

The Irish National School Board's books were all-purpose reading
primers and were graded according to age and developing ability.[1]
Texts for the older pupils contained reading extracts chosen from
the 'great' writers of English literature. One of their peculiarities,
given that they were specifically developed for Irish schools, was
that they contained practically no material on Ireland and, while
they were suffused with religious matter, they nevertheless avoided
anything that was specifically doctrinal. The former was in
deference to the politically sectarian conditions of Irish society –
conditions, of course, for which the British government, through
its enforcement of the Union and its support for Protestant ascendancy, bore primary responsibility. The latter was part of the
arrangement by which the three religious denominations agreed to
support the government's 'non-sectarian' school system. Many of

those who have written about these texts have been impressed by them from a purely educational perspective. This is understandable, because from a pedagogical viewpoint they were clearly in advance of most of the books then in existence in Britain and its territories. As well as being used extensively in Britain they had a big influence on subsequent school books series published in Britain: 'The popularity of the books invited imitation. In 1840 the British and Foreign Schools Society published its first school books with secular material. They were closely modelled on the Irish books ...' (Goldstrom 1966: 137). Those who devised them had a comprehensive design brief that was unimaginable at that time in any other part of the UK: to design from scratch a rational, graded curriculum – because that was what the content of the books amounted to – to be taught in elementary schools that were aimed at the whole available population irrespective of social circumstances. The close pedagogical engagement involved, and the articulation of design within and between each book were unheard of in Britain. They were also in the English language and, given the imperial spread of the British Empire, they were available to educators working in that language in very diverse circumstances. Although understandably unremarked on by their enthusiasts in places like Ontario, it was their detachment from the specifics of locale that made them so peculiarly adaptable. They also encouraged a view of the world that placed Britain, Christianity and the English language at the normative centre from which social and moral value and effective political power derived supreme authority.

We can illustrate this further if we look at the strategy adopted in the books for describing the world. The series was envisaged as a coherent, sequential course so, while the following extracts from one do not purport to be a detailed survey of their content, they should be seen nevertheless as representative of an important approach in the series as a whole. Very similar extracts, for example, could be taken from the *Third Book of Lessons* which preceded this one. In the *Fourth Book of Lessons for the Use of Schools*,[2] published in 1859, under a section titled 'Descriptive Geography' we see a systematic attempt to describe the various parts of the world for school pupils. The author adopts a 'pedagogic voice' suitable for his young readers – one is tempted to say 'listeners' because it is very much in the teacher's classroom mode of address. Knowledge is situated in Britain at the seat of empire and the world is understood in these terms. At times rapt and interested in the peculiarities of the habits, customs and physical descriptions of the various countries he describes he (for it certainly is a 'he') is always conscious of a norm, a stable point of view to which he returns. For example, the section begins with 'The British Islands':

> The British Islands are, to English and Irish people, of course, the most interesting portion of the globe; and a tour through the countries of Europe, such as we propose to make, must naturally begin from home. The Island of Great Britain, which is composed of England, Scotland and Wales, and the Island of Ireland, form together with the little Isle of Man, in the Irish Sea, and the numerous islands about the northern coasts – the British Empire in Europe. The people of these islands have one and the same language (all at least who are educated), one and the same Queen – the same laws; and though they differ in their religious worship, they all serve the same God, and call themselves by the name of Christ. (p. 52)

Having established this normative view he then proceeds to mould his descriptions to conform to it. For example, Gaelic Ireland is marked out as 'different' and marginalized:

> On the west coast is the province of Connaught. It is a wild district, where Irish is a good deal spoken, especially in one beautiful but barren tract, called Connemara. The people here dress differently from those of the other provinces. (p. 55)

Other parts of the empire and its inhabitants are described in terms of their progress (or lack of progress) towards British civility and away from 'wildness'. For example, Australia's Penal Colony past is noted and the role of education is explicitly promoted in a framework that makes clear the ambitions of the authors of the Irish National School Books:

> Their [the convicts] sufferings are great during this period (of imprisonment), but very often, after a certain time, they are set free, and then, if they are well conducted, industrious, and persevering, they sometimes grow rich, and live just like other settlers. It is certainly not an agreeable thing to live in a Penal Colony, but convicts are no longer sent to New South Wales; nor indeed were they ever sent to the more recently formed colonies of *Victoria* or *Southern Australia*. To these promising, and already flourishing colonies, great numbers of enterprising and respectable emigrants have been attracted from all parts of Europe; particularly from

Great Britain and Ireland. And if you were to emigrate with your parents to any of these settlements, you would find schools there quite as good as your own; and, in fact, the very same books are used in them that you are now reading, for large supplies of the Irish National School Books are constantly sent for by the colonial authorities, and by clergy of all denominations who are cooperating with them, in promoting popular education ... We may therefore hope, that at no very distant day, civilization and Christianity will be extended, not only round the coast, but also into the very heart of this immense country. (pp. 153–4)

Native barbarism, which is the main target of this civilizing mission, is described in terms which make clear the role of education:

They are among the lowest and most ignorant savages in the world ... They are divided into tribes, and these tribes are continually at war together ... Now what makes the difference between one of us Europeans and these poor savages? Evidently it is *education*. If one of you had been left alone on the coast of New Holland while an infant, and had been brought up among those savage tribes, you would have grown up like one of them. How thankful, then, ought you to be, that God has placed you in a Christian country, and granted you the benefits of a good education, and the light of the Gospel, of which so many nations are still ignorant. (pp. 154–5)

The section ends with a poem entitled 'A Voyage Round the World', 24 verses long, where the speaker recapitulates his journey in poetic form. Each verse glances at the inadequacies of various countries – 'Jealous China', 'Strange Japan' – all haunts of 'slavery', 'ignorance' and 'despotism', until at last:

I have seen them, one by one,
Every shore beneath the sun,
And my voyage now is done,
While I bid them all be blest;
Britain thou art my home, my rest,
My own land, I love thee best. (pp. 157–61)

Thus the normative framework, both explicitly racist and imperialist, is established and the 'universalist' ambition of the strategy which is made explicit in the books of the Irish school system becomes clearly visible.

Both in regard to the example of the Irish National School books and to the other crucially important example of British educational policy on the Indian sub-continent we can see the emergent dominant paradigm of education in the empire. In Ireland, the idea of total systemization was first translated into policy. Concomitant to this we see in the Irish books an attempt to reify British civilization into a coherent series of textbooks, carefully articulated with one another, where information was imparted in a manner that ordered the world in terms of the priorities of that system, and, as we have noted, it was only one of a number of technologies of control which began to emerge from the British state administrators around this time. The use of 'great writers' in school books was, of course, not new; this had been common to many textbooks before this time, but their deployment in a total administrative system, recognizably modern in its bureaucratization, was. It was only another step from this to the conception of an idea of the values of English civilization being transmitted to a mass, non-elite population through regulated, annotated and selective encounters with these authors. In Ireland, where the English language had become, by the second half of the nineteenth century, the dominant mother tongue of the great majority of the population, the relationship between this new school subject of 'English' for English subjects and the language itself was not fully transparent. It was only in a non-English speaking context where it could fully become so. As Robert Eaglestone puts it:

So it was in India then that the British formed the idea of a school and academic discipline called English, which involved reading and writing about novels, plays and poems written in English. This helps to explain why the subject is called 'English' and not, as in many other countries, 'Literature'. (Eaglestone 2000: 11)

The subject therefore emerged from imperialist, administrative policies, and was deeply implicated in the project of empire.

It has been emphasized throughout this chapter that policies, no matter how powerful their agents, do not fully determine outcomes. The target populations frequently managed to insert their own agendas to ameliorate their effects, or even to redirect them towards ends determined principally by the colonized. That the subject of English, and indeed mass schooling itself, emerged from imperialist education policies does not imply that this precisely determined uniform experiences for millions of pupils over vast geographical areas and widely differing cultures. In 'English' classrooms the effects of complex, subtle, literary artefacts and, indeed, even more prosaic functional texts, are determined by interactions between teacher and learner, and in such a context the outcomes of centrally driven administrative initiatives can be wildly unpredictable and may frequently run counter to those intended by administrators. The development of mass literacy, which was one of the inescapable effects of compulsory school systems, facilitated the emergence of mass democracy, and one of the outcomes of this was the end of formal colonialism. Schooling in English also opened up the diverse riches of the language to many who might never have availed of them. A love of English writers allied with equally strong attachments to local, cultural traditions produced unexpected, fruitful interactions between colonizer and colonized. Nearly all of the sites of empire produced immigrant populations and writing that returned to trouble and challenge the political and cultural complacencies at the centre of empire. And it is this complex heritage that should constitute the 'English' subject that we teach in our schools. This would mean that rather than constructing notions of 'varieties of English' or 'literature from other cultures' at the periphery of the subject, makers of curriculum policy would recognize that such 'cultural variety' is inscribed within the development of the language itself. In the same way that British imperialism has left a continuing political, economic and social legacy for the post-colonial world this colonial heritage has reconstituted the language as a global phenomenon which goes far beyond its national origins, and this should be reflected in the way the subject is taught. Practically, this would mean not only acknowledging the 'variousness' of the language but also embracing opportunities to acknowledge that its colonial heritage has inscribed trauma into its historical development.

Chapter 5

The personal, the community and the society: a response to Section 1

Janet Laugharne

My response to the previous three chapters is framed at the levels of the personal, the community and the society, examining the history and politics of English as a school subject and as a language. As Luke and Kapitzke noted in 1999, 'change in literacy education is no matter of personal genius or scientific truth. It is a historical process, located within shifts in local political economies of languages, textual practices and text-based social relationships' (Luke and Kapitzke 1999: 467).

Being a Welsh speaker from a small country, Wales, tucked in between the Irish Sea on one side and England on the other, this 'historical process' is of particular interest to me, when rethinking the subject English. For example, how does English work in a country, where there is a bilingual language policy? I am partisan, of course, but one can contrast the terms National Literacy Strategy in England with *Iaith Pawb (Everyone's Language)* in Wales. These were policies produced within five years of each other; 1998 for the National Literacy Strategy and 2003 for *Iaith Pawb*. One is a policy intended to drive up 'deficient' standards and refers to a rather narrow range of activity in language, 'national' meaning England and 'literacy' meaning in 'Standard English' only. The other, *Iaith Pawb*, asks 'everyone' to take responsibility in attending to the *languages* of Wales. Language is seen in the plural, rather than the singular, English. There is, too, a potentially more egalitarian concept in the phrase 'everyone's language', in contrast to the more abstract sense of 'national' and 'strategy'. 'Everyone's language' suggests, I think, the inevitability of literacy as plural and diverse social practices.

This is one example of rethinking English in practice. Fecho, Burgess and Walsh in the previous chapters point us to other ways. Fecho argues that there is not enough attention given to the varying needs of individuals and too much to assessment. Walsh shows that, if the context of study is ignored and the focus is on a text and a particular policy initiative, the effect is autocratic and limiting. Burgess stresses the need to link the subject English to the work of universities, to learning theory and teachers' development, while at the same time keeping the individual firmly in mind.

From this position we can see that we don't want teachers of English to leave their learning from university at the classroom door, to pick up a prescribed text, in a modern-day version of what is discussed in Walsh's chapter, and pass on its thin gruel. Such an approach smacks of scripting the subject; and stagnation. We want English teachers and their students to be fed on the pleasures of English, its languages and literatures, and to be strong in their knowledge and understanding. After all, this is the main aspiration of new teachers (Marshall et al. 2001; Ellis 2003). And they are right to have this aspiration for themselves and for their students!

The personal in English

Fecho and Burgess focus particularly on this aspect. They speak of different ages, different countries, different lives, but, for both, the individual self is at the centre of their discussion. We see that learning about English occurs at home, as well as at school, and that English is a means of bringing meaning and understanding to one's life, rather than content to be received. A further point is that learning to use language is subsumed into the purpose of the activity and not a test of discrete skills.

Walsh, then, draws our attention to the displacement between the lives of people and the language of the textbooks of empire they studied. He makes the point that, although the textbooks he discusses were ahead of their time in pedagogic design, being a set of graded readers, the ideology they conveyed was a narrow one, of a ruling British Empire. This left little room for the person receiving them to do more than feel how different their lives were from the 'norm' being portrayed in the textbooks.

It can be noted, also, that Burgess, Fecho and Walsh all dwell on matters of identity in their writing. This is no accident and lends additional emphasis to their chapters. Fecho talks of his experience in school as somewhat an 'outsider', by virtue of his working-class childhood. Burgess speaks personally, both as a grandfather and of his professional experience of the cycles of English teaching. Walsh writes of English and imperialism from the perspective of a university lecturer in Northern Ireland; and, with the ironic distance of history, considers the paradox of a local outpost to empire being the flagship for doctrine carrying imperialism to its other parts, while, ultimately, being the agent of change which shakes its certainties.

What does a focus on the personal show us, then, when we rethink the subject English? We might, for example, consider where is its centre and where its margin. Burgess has shown that the centre is where the individual child is at that moment in time. Fecho, too, argues that this is where the centre should be, while demonstrating that in many cases the centre is somewhere else. Walsh shows that when the centre is the textbook, the personal is displaced.

Fecho, further, raises important issues about language and power, class and privilege. The individuals he describes are not comfortably accommodated in society, or school. A focus on the personal, then, raises questions about English in school as prescription, and how an assessment-driven curriculum marginalizes many young people.

Community in English

Here I define community as, mainly, the community of teachers. I don't wish to relegate the importance of students and their diverse communities but I want to emphasize the importance *for students* of teachers' professional communities. It is important for teachers, especially new teachers, to understand the history and politics of English, in order to develop a sense of professional identity and to argue for more collective autonomy focused on the education and well-being of young people. Politics and history, then, help explain the present in the subject English.

The direct questions raised by Fecho at the end of his chapter are vital, when he asks how English should be taught. Of course, in one sense, it is the most common question asked about the subject. Moss (2004), Goodwyn and Findlay (2003), Ellis (2003), Marshall (2000), Marshall et al. (2001) and others have written about this topic and, often, they show that English teachers are struggling with precisely the questions Fecho raises, frequently in a context of prescriptive policy and an assessment-driven curriculum. As one of the students, Sue (in Marshall et al. 2001), said, 'Some of the things I thought I could just ignore – well you can't. All those systems – they don't leave you space to think, to say stuff like ... but what about the kids, what about their learning?'(p. 200).

Indeed, for the community of English teachers, in many countries, the experience of teaching their subject is of its delivery through thickets of continual policy change. In 1999, Luke and Kapitzke talked of 'seemingly endless government searches for final solutions to the literacy problem' (p. 468); and there is little sign of this search diminishing. Much media discussion continues on standards in English and the place of countries in the global economic market in relation to their literacy standards.

Is English a divided subject?

English has a history of dynamic oppositions in its development: language and literature; aesthetic (literature) and functional (skills); grammar and creativity; 'robust' standards and dynamic innovation. The complexity of English is underlined by variations in what to call it. Is it language arts, literature, communication, cultural studies, knowledge about language, literacy, or 'English'? We note this is very different from the certainties of the textbooks of empire in Walsh's discussion, where 'English' was, essentially, 'reading'.

In the UK, there have been broad oppositional shifts since the beginning of the twentieth century from reading (literature); to speaking and listening, language across the curriculum and the use of English in the 1970s and 1980s; to a focus on writing in the National Writing Project (NWP) (1985–1989) and grammar in the Kingman report (1988). The strong legacy of the last two can still be seen in the National Curriculum English documents (DES and WO 1990; PfEE and WO 1995; DfEE 1999) and, more recently, in England, in the National Literacy Strategy (NLS) (1998) and Literacy Framework (2001).

Some of the movements in English described above have been 'top down' (for example, the NLS) and others 'bottom up' (for example, the NWP). Significantly, the latter operated at regional level and took place across the UK, while the NLS is resourced by, and focused on, England. The NLS in England, as Lewis (2004) noted, was the most heavily resourced and prescribed pedagogy ever in the UK. It also had the least theoretical basis in research and wider reading at its inception, although it was evaluated post hoc (Ofsted 2003; Earl et al. 2003; Beard 2001). The 'top down' approach offers less professional autonomy for teachers. Post-UK devolution, there has been a general narrowing of exchanges between practitioners across the countries of the UK. This is illustrated in the research on teacher education by McKie and Jackson (2006: 37) who said: 'one of the most significant matters raised by this report is the fact that each nation's representatives had only a vague and, perhaps one could say sometimes opinionated, view of their neighbours' experiences'.

Related to this, it is noticeable that Burgess, Fecho and Walsh argue for the need for teachers to continue to develop their knowledge and understanding. Fecho links meaning-making in texts to the existential state of being. Burgess reminds us of the value of a collaborative approach in English teaching and the potential of Vygotskyan theory. Walsh says a critical approach is needed, 'a geographical perspective and historical long view'. All these points relate to surface and deep understanding in the community of English teachers. The soundbites of policy directives are often perfectly acceptable as statements, but lack depth, and, as Alexander shows in her chapter later in this volume, they are curiously unsatisfying when not firmly anchored in a meaningful context. This is where teaching can become prescription and teachers find themselves in danger of delivering a script. The imbuing of meaning to policy comes from the skill of teachers as they interpret, extend and adapt it. This requires knowledge and understanding of a high order, an ability to be reflective and to apply professional judgement.

In contrast Marshall (2006: 106) refers to comments from an Ofsted report for 2000–2005, which says that 'for too many primary and secondary teachers objectives become a tick list to be checked off because they follow the literacy frameworks for teaching too slavishly'. They also note that there is a sharp decline in student enjoyment of, and interest in, reading. Here is a question for us in rethinking the subject English.

Further, observing a lesson taught as part of the *Framework for Teaching English*, Marshall commented, 'at no point were students encouraged to think beyond the given remit' (2003: 88). Would this be true of their teachers as well? Burgess, Fecho and Walsh very clearly demonstrate in their chapters that there is a problem with not thinking 'beyond the given remit'.

Continuity in the community of English teachers
Reading Burgess' piece, I am reminded of the continuities in the community of English teachers, which should not be forgotten. As Fisher (2004) said, the philosophy and related identity of a teacher is far less subject to rapid change than changes in classroom practice, such as the adoption of a particular government policy. Harmonization of identity, as an English teacher, with the pedagogy of the subject is essential if we are to avoid scripts and prescription.

The short transcript of conversation with his grandson in Burgess's chapter took me back to my PGCE English year in the 1970s in the London Institute, where he had just started, and to other focused extracts of student talk that so influenced me in his work and that of Britton (1970), Rosen et al. (1973), Martin (1976) and others who showed us how language and context help learning. I wonder where this approach and the accompanying idea of talking to support learning reside now in the communities of English teachers? The language across the curriculum approach, which was evident at that time, was not at the expense of literature, unlike current debates which seem to place language in opposition to literature. Clearly this is a flawed argument.

It is important to use knowledge from the history of the subject to inform practice. As teachers and researchers into English in education the idea of being part of a community is extremely useful. It helps to create a sense of the intellectual project of English, as Burgess says, and links English teachers in schools with English researchers/teachers in other contexts. Then, some of the outcomes of literacy/English research can inform teaching in a natural and helpful way, such as, for example, the work on literacies in the community (Barton and Hamilton 1998; Barton et al. 2000). Much of this work is very harmonious with the ideas expressed in Burgess's and Fecho's pieces and acts as an antidote to prescription in English. Equally, the work on critical literacy in many English university departments and the way this approach engages with texts is invaluable to English teaching in schools. It seems, here, that the false dichotomy that was created between language and literature by the overemphasis on language, arising from government policy in the 1990s, is a legacy that critical literacy can help overcome, especially since many of its techniques come from literary study as well as literacy education (Williams 1983).

The earlier work in English of Burgess, Britton and others, then, created conditions in which English teachers could be critical literacy researchers, although the term wasn't used at the time. To recognize this is to be able as a teacher and/or researcher to develop a sense of the continuities and turns in the history of English.

Such knowledge is all the more important in order for English teachers to work out just what they are doing, and why, in their teaching; and to relate this to the history of their subject, realizing its continuities as well as fractures. This shared knowledge is mutually beneficial in creating a community of scholarship in English. It represents a knowledge-building which allows the subject to be properly considered and delivered and which, in turn, has a strong and positive impact on students' learning.

The English curriculum

Sometimes it seems that the most interesting, innovative work in English is happening outside the school setting, in home and community literacy. There is, for example, the work in the UK Economic and Social Research Council's Teaching and Learning

Research Programme (Smith 2005) and the ethnographic work of Martin-Jones and colleagues (2007) in North Wales, working with young people in the 16–19 age range. The striking aspect of this work is the way it reflects the day-to-day literacy practices of young people. The teaching opportunities of this approach are rich and seem to connect closely to the real lives of young people. This has the potential to create learning situations of purpose and currency, for example, work on hypertext novels, internet blogs, email and text messaging, as well as text blends of the visual, auditory and verbal in response to literature texts.

It seems that these approaches are less welcome in the 5 to 16-year-old stages of statutory education. Of course, such learning is more difficult to measure and assess, mixing as it often does the visual and auditory, the transient and non-standard. Fecho's point about assessment driving the curriculum has resonance here.

Finally, English teachers are committed to helping students gain the best uses of English possible, especially if these same students have poverty, family and health problems to contend with. How English teachers do this is still a challenge, as it was in past decades, which is another continuity in the history of the subject. English teaching is always, too, related to the context in which it occurs. Thus, the community of English teachers, wherever they are working, needs to be able to rethink English for themselves; and the school and society in which they live.

Society

A question one might ask is who owns English and so can regard it as 'their' subject? Given the position of English in online communication and the usefulness of the language to multilingual speakers, it is foolish to ignore global and international dimensions. It may be that the real owners of English are non-native speakers, with respect to their numbers around the world and their use of the language, not speakers in, for example, England, America or Australia. It is likely that there will be a re-evaluation of this aspect of English in the future, which will affect how it is taught in schools. It is to this aspect of society, in the global as well as local sense that I will turn finally.

There are debates about the spread of English as an international language and its effect on local languages and cultures (see, for example, Marti et al. 2005). The point is made also, as Brutt-Griffler does, later in this volume, that it is monolingual English speakers who ultimately lose out, culturally and economically, when English is so widely used. Thus English teaching must, surely, consider English as one language of many, while also discussing the implications of it being an international lingua franca.

Xianqiong (2005), writing about global English in a very interesting way, uses the analogy of a river to describe the rise and fall of languages over time and says, 'The coexistence of two or more cultures and languages is probably the best recipe in today's world to arrive at some degree of the tolerance and understanding that are so desperately needed' (p. 341). This is particularly pertinent to Walsh's chapter and his comments about English and empire. Equally, Burgess, in his discussion, writing from a future rather than past perspective, encompasses multiliteracy and bilingualism as a natural part of his interpretation of English.

Street (2003: 77) observed, there is 'a new tradition in considering the nature of literacy, focusing not so much on acquisition of skills, as in dominant approaches, but rather on what it means to think of literacy as a social practice'. This is an essential premise for the future of English in schools. From my own experience as a teacher and researcher in Wales, I know there are opportunities for good work to be done within this paradigm. From such a starting point in English there are numerous places of departure: into other languages, into literature, into grammar and into multimodal approaches to text. The key thing is that these are all anchored in an understanding of English as a set of social and cultural practices rather than as a once imperial object that must be transmitted and received.

Conclusion

Burgess, Fecho and Walsh give us an insight into how history and politics have shaped, and continue to shape, English in schools. In doing so, none of them, interestingly, focuses explicitly on many current debates in the subject: the role of literature, of technology and Multimodality, of 'key skills' and creativity. They offer new insights into more fundamental questions, which we must not lose sight of. They speak of emotion *and* intellect, of language *and* power, of learning *and* development.

I have tried, in my response to Section 1, to reflect back some of these themes. Several issues stand out clearly. One is of the need to consider the personal in context in the practices of English in schools. Another is the inherent danger of stagnation of a prescriptive approach to pedagogy and an objectivist approach to text. Finally, all three authors show that English cannot be taken as 'given': it is simply too complex. They tell us that teachers must have opportunities to develop understanding of the history and politics of English as an integral part of their own *and their students'* development. They invite us in their chapters into this knowledge-building process. And they pose some important questions:

- How can teachers reconstruct professional communities that allow them to work actively with their students on the problem of English in schools?
- How do we find ways to help participants in English (meaning students *and* their teachers) actively engage with their own and others' cultures and languages?
- How can we reposition English, so that learners and their development are established as more important than their assessment data?

Section 2

Culture as a verb:
teaching literatures

Back in our silences and sullen looks,
For all the Scotch we drink, what's still between 's
Not the thirty or so years, but books, books, books.

Tony Harrison, 'Book Ends',

Every great book we read became a challenge to the
ruling ideology. It became a potential threat and menace
not so much because of what it said but how it said it,
the attitude it took towards life and fiction. Nowhere
was this challenge more apparent than in the case of
Jane Austen.

Azar Nafisi,
Reading Lolita in Tehran

Chapter 6

How critical is the aesthetic?
The role of literature in English

Ray Misson and Wendy Morgan

The word 'Literature' exerts a great deal of power – it has connotations of solidity and stability and old-fashioned values – and if one wants to think about it in fresh ways, the power of the word needs to be undermined. This was done in the 1980s and 1990s by using the word 'text'. The most influential voice here was probably that of Roland Barthes and his little essay 'From work to text' (Barthes 1977). English teaching came to be about texts, all kinds of texts, films, TV shows, comics, advertisements, etc. This was a quite exhilarating liberation, but, perhaps against expectation, it did not effect a redefinition of the word 'literature'. Instead, battle lines were drawn up between those revelling in the world of textuality, and those solidly committed to the study of 'literature'.

Our move to talking about 'the aesthetic' is for the same reason that people started talking about 'texts': we see it as a useful way of getting rid of a lot of baggage that the word 'literature' has accrued and so of reshaping the debate around the value of literature. (We do, incidentally, also accept the expanded definition of 'literature' as 'text' and so will readily talk about films, TV programs, hypertexts, etc., as literature, as well as classic novels, poems and plays.)

Some might feel that the word 'aesthetic' comes with even more baggage than the term 'literature', since, for literary students anyway, it is often related to an extreme and effete sentimentality and preciousness, most notably evident in the extravagant other-worldliness of pre-Raphaelite poetry. (Bunthorne in Gilbert and Sullivan's *Patience* is the caricatured epitome of the connotations the term often brings with it.) However, in philosophy and in the (non-literary) arts generally, the term is used in a much more interesting and robust way to denote the distinctive ways in which the arts (including literature) work, although beyond that there is little agreement on how one should precisely define it.

How are we using the term 'aesthetic'? There is only space for a few pointers here (see Misson and Morgan, 2006, for an expansion of these):

The aesthetic is a way of knowing

The aesthetic represents the world to us in certain ways or gives us a particular set of lenses through which to see the world. The crucial feature of this way of knowing is that the rational is not contrasted with or privileged above the emotional, but the intellectual domain is held in tension with the affective.

The aesthetic generalizes through representing particulars

In aesthetic texts we will usually see a representation of particular experience that somehow seems generally important to us. We see the represented experience as indicative of more general patterns in human existence, and the more precise and complex the representation becomes, the more deeply we contemplate the wider implications. This dynamic means that the aesthetic is often both profoundly embodied in that it draws our attention to precise physical and emotional detail, creating embodied reactions in us, and at the same time it seems to open up perspectives on the immaterial and even spiritual world.

The aesthetic is marked by intensity and engagement

Intensity and engagement are the words we have used to gloss 'beauty' and 'pleasure' respectively, two words often associated with the aesthetic. The aesthetic has a strong power to draw us in and engage us with the experience it is creating. It does this by investing the experience with a kind of intensity beyond the ordinary, which can be an intensity of beauty, but equally well can be an intensity of emotional distress or horror, as in tragedy.

The aesthetic is both personal and social

While we experience the aesthetic individually, it is nevertheless a product of social conventions and inscribes social values, since all language and texts are inherently social phenomena. The aesthetic thus, far from being abstractly pure, is a very powerful carrier of ideology, not least because we experience the social values so immediately and personally.

We are talking here of literary texts, and literary texts are the most obvious kinds of aesthetic texts (although the aesthetic is by no means limited to literature: it is potentially an element in all texts).

However, our immediate aim is to reassess and reassert what is valuable in the study of literature in English classes, by looking at the textual workings and benefits of the aesthetic, and how we as readers and teachers engage with it.

Engaging with the aesthetic

In most English classes students will encounter texts that invite an aesthetic response. These kinds of texts offer them ways of sensing, knowing and being that are different from what is available elsewhere in the curriculum, including English in its more functional or analytical-critical aspects. If for no other reason, this is justification for the subject. But it will not do, as teachers or students, merely to gesture to the presence of the aesthetic in texts; we need to understand how we become engaged aesthetically. Thus the first part of this chapter considers three interlinked aspects of those engagements: first, the texturing of texts, as readers experience them; next, the social, ethical and ideological stances texts offer; and finally the selves or subjectivities that are developed through readers' negotiations with texts. The second part of the chapter considers how these aspects might figure in English classrooms.

Textuality and experience
Under this heading we consider aspects of form, language, and content.

The form of a text is as we experience it in the reading.[1] In a typical narrative, for instance, we are presented with a selection of events in sequence, characters gradually revealed through those events, the point of view that offers an angle on those events and characters, the pace of narration that propels us through the story, and the like. If we have read other texts from the same family or genre we will be able to anticipate something about this text's purposes, its organization and range of content. The genre conditions us to expect that our desires, experiences and satisfactions in reading will be structured in certain ways to certain ends. In an aesthetic text, the features of the genre are shaped to produce a particular affect/effect through the structuring of our experience.

In a narrative, for instance, depending on whether it is a murder mystery, or a sitcom, or a coming-of-age young adult novel, we know what kind of meaning we will be asked to make of the plot as it moves towards its denouement, and we know what range of feeling and thinking responses will be called up in us. If the text is a tragedy, we expect that the structuring will build a chain of events that will intensify our sense of their fearfulness and pathos. In *Macbeth*, motive finds opportunity, causes breed consequences and atrocities are reduplicated, as the Macbeths collaborate with the witches' prophecies. But at the point of the characters' and our exhaustion and despair, Macbeth is finally destroyed, and we sense with the victors the glimmerings of a new order. The more we have felt the horrors, the greater is our relief. This of course opens us to the play's ideology of social and political stability – which we have invested in, as we have worked imaginatively to make the characters' experiences real for ourselves and to make meaning of them.

Talk of form brings us to the matter of language, since the range of diction a text draws on is also part of the genre 'package', whether it is a lyric poem resonant with metaphor and its hovering meanings, or a war movie whose characters speak in a restricted range of monosyllables, or an advertisement for perfume, with pastel colours and sensuously soft-focus textures.

For our purposes here, in talking about language, it is useful to consider discourse in aesthetic texts. The term 'discourse' refers to a particular way of using language that is shared by members of a social group. They use the discourse in talking and writing about a common area of knowledge and interest, in accordance with certain shared attitudes, beliefs and values. Any text is a tissue woven of such discourses. Some texts mobilize one particular discourse,[2] others present the clash of opposed discourses as these are voiced and acted out by characters. Jane Austen's *Pride and Prejudice*, for instance, can be seen in just such terms, as older and newer discourses about marriage, status and property are played out by the characters, in their words, actions and attitudes. These discourses are woven into the very form of the text, as its particular problematics are worked through and resolved.

Thus discourses work on us aesthetically, by contributing to our sense of how a text's form and language have been crafted. Any discourse is designed to engage us emotionally as well as intellectually and ethically – and by these means it invites us to align ourselves with its ideology. That is, the texturing of language implicates us in a text by giving its concerns an aesthetic and affective dimension, and not just an intellectual or ideological one.

So to content. Some English teachers focus almost exclusively on the particulars of experience as represented in the text their class is studying. If it is a narrative, they ask why characters speak and act as they do and how students respond to those characters in action. But teachers sometimes neglect the ways those particulars are selected and shaped in order to engage our feelings and thoughts. Now of course we do rehearse in our imaginations the passions the characters know and show. But emphasizing the 'reality' of characters can hide their textuality – and deny students the chance to understand how their responses have been shaped.

Shaping of response derives in large measure from the distinctive framing of the content in an aesthetic text. The everyday may be intensified – perhaps comically, as in a sitcom, or ironically, as in *The Simpsons*, or tragically, in a tear-jerker. Or, in a poem, aspects of situations can be presented in ways we have not perceived before, and this expands our sense of the possibilities of human interaction and understanding. Through the particulars we are given in a text we infer a more general significance. Often we sense or intuit this rather than simply deliberate on it. That is, aesthetic texts are generally more open in their interpretative possibilities than other kinds of text, and the affective and aesthetic components are central to our response.

This does not mean teachers and students cannot or should not investigate the text's content, construction and uses of language strategies. It is crucial if we are to develop a better understanding of the ways that aesthetic texts offer us a 'value-added' product. They frame and interpret aspects of the world for us in particular ways – in ways we could not otherwise experience. This distinctiveness is why we value them. But it also makes them partial – incomplete, and interested. This brings us to the social, ethical and ideological.

The social/ideological/ethical

It is impossible to talk about texts and our experience of them without also touching on how they engage us with a world of human, social experiences, and how they invite us to respond in ways that are both personal and positioned. As we have seen, the aesthetic shaping of form, language and content in a text engages our desires and satisfactions – both thinking and feeling ones. It thereby invites us to take a stance towards what it shows us and the ideology that infuses it. This is why teachers and students need to attend to that shaping, and why, if the aesthetic is dismissed as merely decorative and all the focus is on the represented content, we will come nowhere near understanding the nature of our engagements with the text.

For instance, when dealing with digital role-playing games (RPG) some teachers may ask their students to take a politically critical stance by critiquing the stereotypic gender-role representations or the ethic that says individual strong-arm tactics are the only path to success. These teachers want students to take a distanced stance and make a reasoned critique based on their own ethical principles. Of course it is important to trace how players are enrolled within the discourses on offer. This involves understanding how players project into their avatar's identity, and exercise agency as simultaneously player and character; how immersed participants become in the text when their decisions shape the narrative direction and its outcome; how these engagements not only transform the text but also the capacities and subjectivity of the player. That is, in evaluating an RPG, one needs to give due weight to the aesthetic elements of its form (such as the novelty, elegance or cleverness of the game structuring), its visual language (such as first-person shooter perspective) and not just its content.

Ultimately our affective and ideological engagements with texts contribute to our becoming ethical beings. Aesthetic texts offer a range of human experiences for us to imagine ourselves into and thereby feel and understand on that basis. It's not that we have unmediated access to those represented experiences, nor is our experience a merely individual matter: we are always subject to cultural, social and material forces, many of them conveyed through texts.

This (post-structuralist) argument is rather different from that older humanistic defence of the role literature plays in our growth to moral maturity. It is based on a different understanding of 'identity'. Through our encounters with aesthetic texts we can come to know ourselves as selves who are capable of participating imaginatively in the range of thoughts and feelings, actions and experiences they offer – those manifold ways of being in the world. These make us as we make sense of them, imaginatively and aesthetically. But also ethically. We can also know ourselves as selves who are capable of assessing those texts, not in some cold-blooded abstracted way but on the basis of what we have experienced. Because when we know the aesthetic satisfactions of a text, we do not give up our capacity to evaluate them. In fact, there is no way to assess what attitudes, values and beliefs a text is offering us except through knowing the meanings and pleasures it offers and weighing these up with the values we espouse. That is, the aesthetic aspects of the text are crucial in evoking in us those imagined experiences, which can and should feed into our ethical understanding and any social critique we may make of the text.

Subjectivities
This discussion highlights a vital point: aesthetic texts help develop our subjective repertoires. As we engage with a text, we experience the attitudes, beliefs and values it offers. Across the range of texts we

read, we take up a number of stances towards the particulars of those texts and their associated discourses and ideologies. We are offered reading positions and therefore subject positions – those ways of knowing and being that fit within a particular discourse and practice. These positions on offer are diverse, perhaps even contradictory. And so, over time, as we take them up we come to know ourselves as multifarious beings with a broader repertoire of ways of being and knowing than we might otherwise have.

This is more than a matter of simply being subjected passively to all the texts we encounter. As readers we work actively – intellectually and imaginatively – to create the 'value-added' experience we want the text to give us. We participate in reconstructing the form and giving it significance. We engage with the play of language and meaning. We invest our interest in it. We negotiate with its meanings and our values; and even when we have reservations about its form and content, this is also a source of our involvement. And so we collaborate in producing ourselves as subjects who take and make our aesthetic satisfactions – and our aesthetic and ethical judgements.

In these ways, then, aesthetic texts are crucial in making us who we become. This is not to smuggle back in that older way of thinking about the self as a single, coherent, unfolding human being. (That leads to the argument that studying Shakespeare makes the reader a more mature, morally sensitive self.) 'Who we become' is more fluid, more diverse and more multiple than that. Each of us as readers is many in our capacities for thinking and feeling; we may be many contradictory selves, and that multiplicity is itself part of our plasticity as human beings. And insofar as aesthetic texts contribute significantly to that capaciousness, they are valuable.

One final point needs to be made in this discussion. As neuroscientists are increasingly demonstrating, our mental operations and emotional states are bodied – dependent on hormonal chemicals and neural pathways. Much recent theorizing by post-structuralists, feminist and post-colonial theorists, among others (e.g. Bourdieu 1977; Butler 1990; Foucault 1990), has helped us see how central the body is to our social dealings, no less than to our intimate and emotional lives.

It follows that the aesthetic is no disembodied, ethereal phenomenon, but fundamentally a sensate one. Our aesthetic responses may not manifest themselves in palpably physical ways (tears, groans, hair standing on end, and so forth); they may be subtle, all but imperceptible, even to ourselves – but they are of the body nonetheless.

Take those matters of textuality mentioned above. When it comes to form, for instance, the way a narrative is focalized provides us readers with particular sight-lines and a visual perspective on the events. This locates us bodily, in relation to the action. When we read a poem, its pattern of rhythm is registered in our ears; and the line and stanza breaks cue our breathing pauses and thus the pacing of the poem and its dimensions in time and space, with its layout.

Discourses too have their bodily dimension. This concerns all that our ear is keyed to register and interpret: whether we hear the sounds of words as harsh, mellifluous, rapid or ponderous; and whether the patterns of intonation, pronunciation or syntax say 'us' or 'them'. The very ways words are produced by the face and throat and projected via lungs and stomach – these derive from the speaker's *habitus* (Bourdieu 1977), those learned bodily habits and dispositions that locate him or her within particular communities, modulated by ethnicity, gender, class and the like.

The way particular characters are represented as moving or holding themselves involves bodily *habitus* too: the proud 'carriage' or comportment of a Darcy or a Lady Bracknell is a world away from the cool 'attitude' of an urban adolescent. As we (almost literally) take a stance towards those characters, in imagination practising their bodily *hexis*, the ethical aspects of our aesthetic responses are engaged.

When we feel empathy for this or that character in action, we rehearse often intense emotional states, and these are manifested physically in an increased heart rate, for instance, an indrawn breath, the slackening of tense muscles – or a grunt of exasperation (for our emotional responses are not always aligned with those the text seeks to produce in us). In such ways, we perform with the characters – or the speakers of poems – diverse ways of being in and responding to the world, socially and ethically. These are all inscribed on the body, in their (and our) emotional and attitudinal styles of address to the world.

Thus engaging with aesthetic texts enables us to extend our repertoire of bodily dispositions and therefore emotional and mental ones – and therefore contributes to our producing our subjectivities.

And this brings us to schooling in English.

The aesthetic in the curriculum

Whatever irrationalities may surround it, or whatever irrationalities may be found within it, schooling is nonetheless a rationalist institution. Similarly, whatever its role in developing private subjectivities, and whatever kind of liberation learning might bring, schooling is a public, social institution and regimented to a high degree. There is an issue then, given the aesthetic's intuitive, emotional and personal dimensions, of how we develop the capacity in our students to see and create aesthetically. It takes a clear sense of purpose, an openness to a broad range of texts, and the utilization of a whole battery of classroom strategies.

Part of the difficulty is that the aesthetic is not just an aspect of texts, nor is it just a way of perceiving; it is a complex interaction between the text and the person reading it. One does not simply 'appreciate' the aesthetic within a text, since that assumes the aesthetic is something objective to observe and admire. If the aesthetic is a way of knowing and potentially constitutive of the students themselves, then we are after much bigger game: students need to be led into operating within the aesthetic mode as readers and writers.

In some ways, this is comparatively easy with writing, and we would not want to underplay the importance of aesthetic writing in the classroom, including attention being paid to the aesthetic and imaginative elements in the kinds of texts students write that are not normally considered 'creative', such as reports and arguments. Nor should we underplay the significance of the link between reading and writing: we can learn to read well through writing and vice versa. But aesthetic reading of texts in itself is a more difficult case.

There is the fundamental problem when we are dealing with reading, that the only way of accessing how the student is understanding a text is through another 'text' that the student produces. Very often this will be an oral text – the teacher asks a question and the student responds – but it can be a written text (and these are often most valued): the teacher sets a question or a task and the student produces their text in response, whether it be an exam answer, an essay, or a creative response of some kind (stylistic imitation, changing the point of view, etc.). As teachers we develop our students' understanding of the aesthetic through initiating these texts and responding to them in turn, and so it is vital that our initiation of them and our response to them is guided by a strong sense of what we want our students to learn.

Hence the importance of purpose. The kind of classroom that we are advocating will not look as if it is employing a lot of new strategies. Many of the same things will be being done. But they will be framed by a particular sense of purpose, and so will be set up in particular ways, and, most significantly, will be reflected on in particular ways at the end of the lesson or the cycle. In fact, one of the problems with a lot of teaching is that the strategy can so easily lose its purpose and become an end in itself. It may entertain the students (or even us as the teacher), but it isn't necessarily teaching anything significant.

As we have suggested, there are three fronts to be worked on: the textual, the ethical and the experiential/personal. These three can be (and indeed are) combined in our aesthetic dealings with any text, but, as so often with education, we may need to separate them out, and we are not likely to be working on all fronts at the same time with the same text (although we can). Indeed, we will often make strategic decisions to focus on one or two of them with a particular text, because we can see that that is the best way to approach it. Similarly we will often choose texts to work on that highlight one or other of the aspects, so as to develop students' understanding of that aspect without muddying the waters by complicating things up.

So, let us take those three areas – the textual, the ethical and the experiential – and think about our purpose in developing students' understanding in each of them and why it is important that we do so.

Textual

The main purpose with the textual area is to develop in students an understanding of the ways in which the shaping of the text is meaningful in itself. The textual strategies used are carrying meaning and making us see the experience (and making us experience the world) in particular ways. Analysis of textual strategies can be arid if it is done in the abstract, but it is not necessarily so.

The range of teaching practices that can be most useful here are ones where the text is played with and varied, and the effect of the variation is discussed. Take something like metaphor. Students can be asked to suggest other metaphors than the one used in the text, and then talk about the way the effect and meaning differs with the various metaphors. This can focus attention on the implications of the particular metaphor that is being used. Alternatively, one can set students the task of rewriting a passage substituting negative metaphors for positive ones, and see the effect of this.

Metaphors are local, as are things like stylistic quirks of a particular author (e.g. the use of parataxis, the use of passives). We can see what happens when these are changed, again defining more clearly the effect and meaning of the original text. One can also work at a more macro level with such things as changing the narrative from first person to third person, or changing the genre.

Genre-shifting is particularly popular, especially below the senior years – taking *Romeo and Juliet* and writing it up as a news story, or having Juliet write a letter to a lonely hearts column, and so on. It has almost become a default activity in some classrooms (in Australia, at least) and it often is one of those activities mentioned above that are more entertaining (or time-filling) than meaningful. Not that there is anything wrong with entertainment, and it can make the students aware of the features of the target genre (the newspaper or the lonely hearts letter), but it often does not help a great deal in developing understanding of the original text. The importance of careful debriefing and comparative discussion cannot be stressed too strongly if the purpose is to get further into, rather than further away from the text being studied.

Why would one do this kind of thing? There are practical reasons and there are more theoretical ones.

Practically, students need to know something of the mechanics of textuality because it gives them greater power in their own writing if they understand that meaning is not only carried in the denotative content of the language, but in the way the language is shaped and the way in which it is used. It extends their capacity to create the meaning they want, but also to explore meaning, since language is constitutive of 'reality', and so we explore what we mean by rearticulating it in various ways, using different textual resources. A knowledge of textuality also gives them greater power as readers, since if they are aware of how the text is functioning and how it is communicating its meaning they will be more fully able to activate that meaning for themselves.

Theoretically, highlighting textuality is important because it relativizes the 'truth' of the text showing its constructedness. Representations have power, and the texts we call literature present some of the most powerful representations around. To see how they are constructed out of the available discourses, using common textual strategies, within particular genres does not make them less truthful, but it can relativize their truthfulness, make us see that this is just one version of the truth. It can help in defining what the value of this particular truth is, and also in reminding us that there are other ways of seeing available.

This leads us on to the second of our three areas: the ethical.

Ethical
The main purpose in this area is to develop in students an understanding of what values the text is promoting and to get them to engage with these values critically. This, if you like, is the critical

literacy agenda. Students need to understand that every text comes with social values implicit simply because it is representing the world in a particular way, as argued above. It is asking us to subscribe to its view of the world and take on those values. We, as readers, can do so or not. This is clear to students in argumentative texts, but less clear in aesthetic texts where the ideology is more naturalized and, to that extent, more powerful.

When it comes to classroom work, therefore, what is fundamental is not taking the textual representation as natural, but engaging with it as a particular view of the world. Many of the strategies we were looking at in the textual area can actually serve this purpose well too, since they intervene to show the constructedness of the text, and this can be turned to the purpose of defining through contrast the particular belief systems implied by a particular metaphor or a particular genre. Writing tasks that shift the point of view from one character to another, allowing the 'untold' stories to be told, are a common but potentially powerful strategy for delineating the ideological slanting of the text. For example, some students were asked to take Miss Bingley seriously in *Pride and Prejudice* and to write something from her point of view. It produced some excellent work, with the students thinking through what it might mean to be a woman in that society who didn't have many options except to get married and who didn't have the natural charm of an Elizabeth Bennet who could just be fallen in love with.

Developing an understanding of the ethical implications can, of course, be achieved through discussion, a very powerful strategy, often overlooked (or rather not talked about much) because of its simplicity. In discussion, students can engage with what the text is showing about its world and what matters implicitly and explicitly within it. A valuable entry point to such discussions can be political/theoretical frameworks. The most obvious is the feminist one: feminist readings of texts have become mainstream, and it is more or less standard practice these days to ask how the text is constructing gender and gender relations, but often questions drawing on theoretical framings of social class, sexuality, ethnicity and so on can open up how the textual representations are ideologically implicated.

The importance of all this kind of work is obvious if we want to develop a critical awareness in students that will allow them to make informed ethical judgements. It is also important in developing their understanding of how human action is always ethically implicated, and may be judged from different positions. It gives them some control over the kinds of representations they are allowing to become part of their own way of interacting with the world, become part of themselves.

Which leads us on to our final area: the experiential, or the creation of individual subjectivities.

Experiential

This is the most significant element of all in many ways. Probably the main purpose for working with aesthetic texts is that they allow us to experience a whole range of events, ideas, emotions that we would not normally have the chance to engage with, whether that be through the stark tragedy of *King Lear*, the excruciating comedy of *Little Britain* or *The Office*, or the terror of *The Shining*. They allow us to feel things and develop our emotional imagination and so our emotional repertoire. They allow us to react to things and so develop in us different possibilities of interacting with the world. There is nothing sinfully vicarious about this; we all rehearse emotions and reactions through the texts we read and view.

However, we should not stress the narrowly emotional at the expense of intellectual engagement: texts also, by engaging us with shaped experience, give us a spectrum of ways to understand our lives as human beings and understand the many worlds we live in. They can open up to us perspectives on how we relate to other people, both in a psychological and a sociological perspective.

In the classroom, discussion is again fundamental here, talking about what is happening in the text, motivations, reactions, why we laugh at something that would objectively not seem particularly funny (as in *The Office*), or our almost visceral involvement in the moral dilemmas of Clint Eastwood's *Mystic River* or *Million Dollar Baby*.

Indeed, as suggested before, much of our involvement with texts has a bodily (if not always visceral) element. This can be very difficult to deal with in the classroom, since classroom management often requires bodies to be disciplined and still. However, there are many drama techniques that can be used, since a lot of the work in developing our students' perception of the experience texts offer is about understanding what is going on for characters within particular situations. Getting students to embody the characters or situations through performance, improvization, or other strategies involving physical expression externalizes and extends the internal understanding.

We also often forget that voice is a bodily phenomenon: reading out loud can be a significant part of the textual experience. This is obvious with highly rhythmic texts, since the rhythmic drive will normally be fundamental to the experience the text is offering and to the pleasure that it gives. It is perhaps even more significant in texts with more varied and subtle rhythms. Shifts in stress can carry feeling and change meaning. Indeed, reading literature cognitively is an interpretative act, and the interpretation can be sharpened, developed and expressed by reading literature vocally, since interpretation depends on how one 'hears' the text, and even something as simple as how one is forced to breathe when articulating it.

Writing is also a physical act, and when combined with role play can produce in the performance of the act of writing, a sympathetic sense of character. Having students write emails, diaries, accounts of scenes not actually shown in the text are all possibilities. Not just writing, but also other graphic representations. The body exists in space, and texts have spatial dimensions too that the body can position itself within. While conceptual mapping can seem to be a purely intellectual exercise, it can also give a material sense of the text, of the tensions and harmonies within the disposition of the materials, and the way that the text has written itself on the reader.

The importance of all of this is because texts do constitute our subjectivity. The richer the range of texts we bring into our classrooms, the more deeply we engage with them, and the more fully we understand what they are asking of us and doing to us, then the more capacious our subjectivities are and the better we are able to comprehend human variety and the various worlds we live in.

Why literature?

While for convenience and clarity here, we have separated out the textual, the ethical and the experiential elements, it is important finally to stress their fundamental inseparability for us as English teachers. The textual is what we have to work with: we are the people who develop in students the capacity to produce and respond to texts that represent their world in various ways, whether it be a job application, the news, or obviously aesthetic texts like *The Bill* or *King Lear*. We develop in students the capacity to critique the experiences texts offer and to understand their right and responsibility to make ethical judgements about the texts they write and read. We also develop in them the capacity to understand themselves better through textual experience, giving them the material to create for themselves richer subjectivities. That, however, in itself stresses the importance of not divorcing the ethical from the subjective textual experience. Students need to develop the capacity to make ethical as well as emotional decisions about what they want to be. The study of literature, broadly defined, gives them the capacity to develop their emotional and ethical imaginations and so imagine themselves more powerfully as human beings.

Chapter 7

History, war and politics:
taking 'comix' seriously

Carol Fox

In this chapter I discuss comic books, or graphic literature, as a medium which offers very rich reading material to students and young adults. I begin by sketching in the international background through which I first became aware of comics as a resource for literature teaching and learning. I then focus on some comics that have war and politics as their major focus, particularly discussing the work of Raymond Briggs, Art Spiegelman and Ho Che Anderson. I argue that comics bring adult and children's literature into a close relation to one another since the authors of many graphic texts write for both readerships and, indeed, muddy the traditional distinction between them. While I have no problem in acknowledging and celebrating that aesthetic reading has always found its natural home in the subject English, and that the aesthetic aspects of literature need to be valued and maintained (as English is the one subject domain that gives them a central focus), I argue that the efferent reading demanded by these texts is equally important and is carried by the aesthetic and affective involvement readers have in encounters with such works. As I write I notice that the *Guardian* newspaper is producing little booklets of some of the great speeches of the twentieth century. While it cannot be denied that such speeches were made in order to persuade opinion of this or that ethical, political or social point of view, and that their uses of rhetoric undoubtedly lend themselves to aesthetic reading, yet it seems obvious, at least to me, that they need to be read efferently at the same time. I cite this example because one of the texts I recommend here is Ho Che Anderson's *King* (2005), a very detailed comic-book biography of Martin Luther King which includes all his major speeches. This is a work of history and politics produced within an aesthetic medium, but the history and politics remain as kinds of knowledge which are accessed through the text, although in a form which is very much more powerful and engaging than most textbooks or information books. Indeed, I would propose that the distinction aesthetic/efferent does not really stand up when the works I am discussing here are considered, since the two kinds of reading that those terms represent become so very closely intertwined that it is extremely difficult to pull them apart as we read.

The aims of this chapter, building on the chapters by Misson and Morgan and Alexander in this section, are to reassert the place of literature in the English curriculum, to persuade readers that comic/graphic texts have a place within what we call literature and need to be read in secondary schools and beyond, to recommend specific texts that have been powerful for my own students, to question whether the efferent and aesthetic can always be distinguished in the historical/political texts that I discuss, to propose that the efferent reading these texts demand is as important as the aesthetic readings that they also demand, to argue further that comic books are particularly effective in drawing readers' attention to their formal constructedness and to their processes of production, and finally to suggest that visual media as part of literature, exemplified by these comic books, are particularly accommodating to students today

I arrived at my interest in comics from several different directions. I very much enjoyed comics as a child although soon gave them up for 'proper books'. Later I became interested in newspaper cartoons and even thought of becoming a cartoonist myself. In the mid-1990s I visited South Africa several times and it was there that I encountered the most significant uses of comics I had ever seen. Peter Esterhuysen and his collective of artists and writers, the Storyteller Group, had created comics for the new democracy (Esterhuysen 1996). The comic about how to vote, *Our Time to Choose*, was published in a print-run of millions and distributed everywhere; it overcame language and literacy barriers and helped people to participate in the election (Esterhuysen 1994a). Other comics covered AIDS education, environmental issues (*The River of Our Dreams*, 1991), science education for teacher training (*Spider's Place*, four volumes, 1994b), English literature for Matriculation examinations, and even romantic fiction with a post-modern spin (*Heart to Heart*, Watson and Esterhuysen 1994). In a country where books were scarce and very expensive, where bookshops and libraries tended to be rare in the townships, and where there were huge literacy and schooling problems for the majority, the comics served an urgent social and political need. Peter attended a symposium held at the University of Brighton in 1995 and in my introduction to his piece in the ensuing book I wrote:

So skilfully wrought are the comics that the practices of reading and writing are woven into the stories they tell in ways that help readers to reflect on what their literacy practices are and might be. Books and stories, reading and writing, play a critical role in the narratives so that those who read them learn how specific literacy activities can be materially, psychologically, and socially transformative. In this respect Esterhuysen's comics are examples of Barthes' (1970) 'writerly texts', that is texts that foreground the processes of their own construction rather than concealing them. (Fox 1996: 146)

In other words, some of the comics were showing readers how texts work, making them good candidates for study with my teacher education students.

Towards the end of the 1990s I joined a European Socrates project about the children's literature of war in three countries, Belgium, Portugal and the UK;[1] in preparing three anthologies of European literature for this project I and my partners encountered some comic-book texts that were among the most distinguished examples of literature about war that we found, among them several books by Raymond Briggs (Briggs 1982, 1984, 1998), Spiegelman's *Maus* (1987 onwards), and Tardi's (1993) *C'était la Guerre Des Tranchées* (*Trench Warfare*), though none of these were written for children. I began to see comics as adult works which were capable of covering the most serious aspects of life in the past and the present, and as the years went on I encountered several other superb comic-book makers – among them Joe Sacco, Marjane Satrapi, Ted Rall, Robert Crumb, Ho Che Anderson and many others. I need to add that although I describe these comics as serious, they do, rather miraculously and in different ways, retain their comic character, the irreverence, subversion, irony and wit that we associate with the form.

I discovered that Dr Seuss had been a cartoonist for US newspapers during the Second World War and that his post-war children's books emerged from the weird and wonderful creatures he had drawn and the wacky rhymes he had invented in his antifascist cartoons in America (Minear 2001). For example, *The Sneetches* (1961), a very funny morality tale, in which the Sneetches, the usual absurd Dr Seuss creatures, are either plain-bellied or star-bellied, an obvious reference to the star which Jews were forced to wear under the Nazis. I was impressed by how seamlessly these techniques translated from the hard bad world of Second World War political comment to the gentler world of children's literature (though we have to ask if the world of children's literature actually is a gentle one). Children's literature is not very gentle in Raymond Briggs' political works – *When the Wind Blows* (1982) and *The Tin-Pot Foreign General and the Old Iron Woman* (1984), though the readership for these works is ambiguous. *When the Wind Blows* is clearly for older students and adults, but Briggs' savage satire on the Falklands campaign of 1982 is told verbally as a traditional children's fairy tale with anonymous characters, while the pictures, in contrast to the words, show cartoons of Mrs Thatcher and General Galtieri as crazed and grossly sexualized warmongers made of iron and tin. Over the years when reading this work with my education students I have always experienced the deep silence which descends on the class when Briggs disrupts the lurid cartoon style of the first half of the book to show, in smudgy charcoal drawings, the dead and dying soldiers. The emotional impact of the change of tone on the reader is very powerful. I also became aware with time of the visual competencies of my students and began to use those competencies in assessment tasks and in free and open reading journals that they were encouraged to keep. It seemed logical and natural to move on to comic books with them, particularly since they were well educated in the ways in which children's picture storybooks work, including those by Briggs and Seuss.

How do we think of comics? Art Spiegelman (*Maus* in two volumes 1987 onwards) prefers to call them '*comix*' in order to distance them from ephemera for children while keeping their comic association and history. Chris Ware's publisher calls his book (*Jimmy Corrigan: The Smartest Kid on Earth*, 2000) a 'graphic novel' in order that it should be taken seriously as an adult work of literature. My students are often surprised to find that I'm recommending a comic-book text as part of an English literature course, and while there is usually at least one female student whose initial encounter with *Maus* is tinged with a certain amount of disdain, there is equally often a male student who has immersed himself in comic books for years and who suddenly finds himself the expert in the class (new for him), as he explains to us the mysteries of Manga[2] and the like. Comics do seem to be gendered still, as they were when I was a child, with most comics very male-centred. However, writers like Marjane Satrapi and many of the female writers of Japanese Manga are opening up comic-book art by and for women. Put briefly, comics are commonly regarded as: for children; as ephemeral, funny, irreverent, subversive or downright crude (*Viz*);[3] as nothing serious in either their artwork or their written text; as certainly not the stuff of literature courses at university except in those places which have *dumbed down*; and as cheap in both literal and metaphorical senses.

Though there are several serious critical works on comics these days, newspapers and websites remain the best sources of information and comment on this genre. In any case comic strips have a close association with newspapers and magazines, which is where many of the major comic-book writers started. I think this is one reason why many modern comics authors write so well about politics and war. Politics and war comics on the one hand, and children and children's literature on the other, seem to be poles apart, yet they share common traditions while their authors often express themselves in both media.

Comics straddle at least three disciplinary areas in my university. The same sorts of text are used by me as part of English in Education, by a colleague in another School as part of Cultural and Media Studies and in the Faculty of Art and Design as part of the study of graphic art. They may also have a role in areas like film-making, printing and ICT and you could make a good case for including quite a few texts in the study of politics, peace studies and history. Today's comics are multimedia texts. It is interesting to watch the university library's collection of comics expand while the section given over to graphic novels in the local branch of Borders bookshop has doubled, giving competition to our local comic-book emporium which used to have a monopoly. All of this suggests that comics have grown up and come into the mainstream, though, sadly, in my view, school English departments, in England at least, mostly still have to catch up.

I realize now, looking back to when I was growing up in the 1940s and 1950s, that even at that time children saw comics as both funny *and* serious – they were amusing and ephemeral but also inspired great passion to get hold of and devour them. Needless to say many adults did not favour comics, even our parents who supplied them to us. Schools looked down on them and left them to be an out-of-school pleasure, all the more precious for that. Most writers of comic books have been influenced by the comics they read as children, so even in the most adult works, such as Joe Sacco's books about the Balkan and Gulf wars and the Palestine/Israeli conflict (Sacco 2003a, 2003b, 2003c), a sense of childness remains, a certain larger-than-life-ness that is also found in texts about super-heroes and in myths, legends and fairy tales. Spiegelman's comic book about 9/11 – *In The Shadow Of No Towers* (2005) – pays homage to the comics of the past in America and those that impressed him as a child, one of which, strangely, seemed to prefigure the attack on the twin towers.

At this point I need to mention my concern that many young people, at post-16, and university/college levels, do not have much political or historical education; the kind of modern comics that interest me tend to have war and politics as their subject matter, and many are very current in their content (though there are also excellent comics about the past and even about literature of the past). The fact that literature, among other things, can extend our knowledge (by this I mean the kind of informational knowledge implied by the efferent kind of reading that Joy Alexander refers to in this volume), should not be ignored, and while this is not the prime criterion for choosing texts to study in English, nevertheless literary texts can transform what students know about the world, thereby stimulating their interest and giving them a pathway to other texts. Literature often lays before us great events seen through a specific individual's eyes, and the comic books I'm discussing here usually have first-person narrators, like Art in *Maus* or Sacco himself in all his books or Satrapi in hers, whose intimate up-closeness to their subjects makes them essentially personal. In an interview Spiegelman comments:

I'd say that autobiography has become the primary mode of underground comics – like what superheroes are for the other branch of the comic family tree. (Spiegelman, in Juno 1997: 10)

And later in another interview he adds:

comics have that quality of personal storytelling. In a sense it's like an overly developed handwriting. So it seems natural to start using *the word 'I' and continue from there.* (Campbell 2004, *Guardian*: Review, pp. 12–14)

I shall return later to the matter of 'content', that is, the efferent element, in these works.

The comics I want to teach are profoundly multicultural in the sense of bringing readers into new worlds where they see things through others' eyes. Marjane Satrapi's autobiographical works about her early life in Iran (*Persepolis: The Story of a Childhood* 2003), her adolescent years in Europe before her return to her homeland (*Persepolis 2: The Story of a Return* 2004) and her adult life in Iran (*Embroideries* 2005) are exemplary of the way in which well-written and well-drawn comic texts can be transformative for readers in the West, used as they are to having Iran and Iranians depicted as belonging to the 'axis of evil', to rogue states swamped by alien and fanatical beliefs, to the ranks of an 'othered' people who are at best to be feared. Satrapi's comics have a certain Persian style about them too, expressed in the kinds of repeating patterns that form the motifs of much Islamic art. Repeated images are powerful rhetorical devices, not available to prose novelists, in graphic texts. Tardi uses repeated images to great filmic effect in *Trench Warfare* (1993) a masterpiece about the First World War. In his pictures the repetitions are particularly effective in bringing the reader closer and closer to a character or an event, as a camera would, so that we enter into an emotion such as fear or horror. Incidentally *Trench Warfare* was one of the very few texts we came across in our European project of war in children's literature that paid homage to the enormous number of combatants from the European colonies world-wide who were drawn into the conflict.

I'm aware of the irony that the literature I prefer to teach as part of English is usually not from England or the UK. In this sense, though I think I know what I mean by the educational discipline 'English', I'm ambivalent about the fitness of that title. I prefer to give myself the scope to think of literature *in* English rather than English literature, and I include translations. It's the quality of texts that's more important though it is difficult these days to use the term quality with any confidence, since it is so often identified with the traditional English canon, with texts which are force-fed to examination candidates and with an authoritarian elitism that is best consigned to the past. I mean by it texts that are complex, multi-layered, subtle and rich, whether they are children's books, modern novels, canonical works or, indeed, comics; for my students, reading texts that will not only satisfy their intellectual curiosity, give them pleasure and nurture their imaginations, but also extend their capacity to read other texts, should be what they are aiming for in teaching their future pupils. I do not see how they can do this for their pupils unless they have experienced such reading for themselves at their own level. By becoming aware of how such readings are enabling and transformative for themselves they ought to gain insights into the development of reading processes in children – Meek's proposal in *How Texts Teach What Readers Learn* (Meek 1988). The comics I refer to here are capable of doing that since their authors often expose visually the processes of meaning-making from inside the text. Esterhuysen points out that because his comics reveal their own workings and composing they are essentially subversive of dominant literacy practices

> our comics have begun increasingly to focus their own frames both in a literal and metaphorical sense; to talk about their own production and the limits of what they can say as popular educa-

tional media. They also paint pictures of contexts in which they and other texts interact in meaningful and critical ways. (Esterhuysen 1996: 148)

'Focusing the frames' to me means showing what the set-up of a work is, where it's coming from, how it achieves its effects and why those effects are there – as Briggs does by his abrupt change of style in *The Tin-Pot Foreign General* ... Painting 'the picture of the context' implies that however 'involved' readers feel they are in a work they are simultaneously given distance from it by the author's inclusion of his/her composing processes or the conditions of the production of the work that make this reading rather than that reading possible; such distancing helps readers to have a critical view of what is going on when they read. The pictured narrator in Spiegelman's *Maus* and in Sacco's and Satrapi's books narrates the story of which he/she is a central part while at the same time narrating the story of *how I come to be doing this* and *why I'm doing it like this*. Thus in *Maus* there are several scenes where we see Spiegelman at his drawing board wondering, for example, why he should be penning yet another work about the Holocaust, and why he is using the comic medium to do it.[4]

Literary theory is useful because it helps students to see how texts get read in different ways, and, importantly for them, how there are no exclusively 'correct' readings. It should help them to understand how texts work and make hitherto 'unreadable' texts more accessible to them. If they are going to learn about semiotics, or psychoanalytic readings, or the layers of complex chronology in narrative discourse, all of which are useful in reading *Maus*, I think it makes sense for students to study those aspects of literature in the context of their current reading of specific works – which is usually what the literary theorists did in the first place. I am not talking here about privileging form over meaning, or separating form from meaning, but helping students to understand the very indivisible relationship between the two. Comic-book texts have the marvellous ability to *show* rather than *tell* students how narratives work, how literary texts achieve their effects. This makes ideas which may seem forbiddingly abstract if encountered out of any reading context[5] very accessible and useful for students' reading of other non-comic book texts. With its dual narration, multiple chronologies, large framing metaphors, variations in duration, point of view and narrating voice *Maus* becomes the ideal text for showing, visually on the page, how literary devices work, not only in this text but in other prose texts. But, of course, to discuss *Maus* merely as a convenient vehicle for taking students on to a reading of, for example, Sebald's *Austerlitz* (2001) or other complex prose works is to miss the point. When students read *Maus* they become deeply involved in the story it tells as well as distanced from that story by its own storytelling techniques. Although it is a work of non-fiction it reads like a work of fiction because it demands the kind of aesthetic reading referred to by Alexander and Misson and Morgan in this volume. However *Maus* also demands an efferent reading, since it deals with the very real events of the Holocaust. This must be true of all literature based on history.

If efferent reading is reading to find out, to take away information, then I would propose that works like *Maus* or Anderson's *King* or Sacco's *Palestine* offer as much efferent reading as aesthetic. Indeed in all these works the efferent reading is extremely important. Spiegelman takes account of potential Holocaust denial in *Maus*, which is after all a very personal recalling, by including such details as the layout of Auschwitz as a camp plan and other drawings of the documentary evidence; although there are implications that Vladek, the Holocaust survivor, might be an unreliable narrator in certain respects, nevertheless the facts of the Holocaust as essentially real have to be present in the text. My students bring various amounts of factual knowledge of these events to their reading of Holocaust literature, but it would be true to say that texts like *Maus*, and non-graphic works like *Austerlitz* and Levi's *If This Is A Man* (1966) teach them much more than they can bring to their reading – and we need to bear in mind that *Austerlitz*, unlike the other two, is a work of fiction. Interestingly in *Austerlitz* and, indeed, in all his other books, Sebald places photographs on the pages, partly to give some documentary support to the facts of what really happened (the little fortress of Terezin, the new Bibliothéque Nationale in Paris, the old fortifications outside Antwerp, are real and can be seen in grainy black and white photographs in the book) and partly as an integral part of the text – the photographs are not add-ons but form part of the whole aesthetic text, much as Spiegelman's graphics do in *Maus*. The eyes of the nocturnal animals which stare at us out of the photographs in the early pages of *Austerlitz* may demonstrate that such creatures are real and are to be found at the zoo in Antwerp, but their function is also metaphorical and aesthetic. Uncovering the suppressed memory of Austerlitz, the book's eponymous central character, is the driving force of the narrative, but readers do not know this at the beginning. My students are always puzzled and sometimes irritated by the narrator's leisurely and lengthy ramblings around Antwerp station, clocks, architectural features, historical fortifications and nocturnal creatures in the zoo in the early part of the story. The grand metaphorical structure of the novel into which all these themes, and others, are woven, only becomes clear as they read on. Their experience of *Maus* helps them in the enterprise of reading the prose novel because the metaphors of the comic text can be *seen*. In the meantime plenty of efferent reading gets done as they are busy finding out the facts of the cultural world of Europe that Sebald presents to them. We have some interesting discussions about how the cultural codes (Barthes 1970) of the text have impact in works of fiction, and students come to understand that such works may offer to, and draw out from, their readers a wide and, in the case of *Austerlitz*, demanding range of cultural references. But it's not a matter of knowing or learning this or that piece of information to add to the cultural store. This efferent reading also, and particularly in relation to Holocaust literature, makes conceptual demands.

In relation to *Maus* and *Austerlitz* some of the conceptual demands are to do with reaching an understanding of what there is to know about the Holocaust. For example, the concentration camp in *Maus*, Auschwitz, is a different kind of camp from Terezin, the little fortress outside Prague which is at the centre of *Austerlitz*, and both are different from Chelmo, Treblinka and Sobibor, which were exclusively devoted to mass murder; Drancy, the transit camp outside Paris which also plays a part in *Austerlitz*, is again different from any of these. Understanding such differences is not a trivial matter if readers are to appreciate how complex, organized and extensive the Nazi Holocaust was. The students begin with the idea of Auschwitz which they see as the one camp signifying the whole Nazi project, but gradually refine their concepts of the camps to understand the different functions and different constitution of each. This broadening and refinement of knowledge happens as they extend their reading. The racism of the Nazi Holocaust takes longer to understand because for many students it means changing or adapting from previously formed concepts. Some students can think that Jewish people had something about *them* – their religion, customs, rites, clothes, etc. – which projected them to the ranks of otherness. It takes many a long time to understand that Jews could be Christians, atheists, fully assimilated into the non-Jewish cultures they were part of, indeed that they could be and were as diverse as any other communities in Europe, and that Nazi racism was about *race*. We are never told in *Austerlitz* that Austerlitz himself is Jewish until, about two-thirds of the way through the text, he comes to know his own identity; up to then, he is just another European (albeit a rather extraordinary and solitary example). The concept of the Other is a further development which takes students into other works of literature, ad infinitum really. In their encounters with these texts students want to explore such knowledge and concepts because their aesthetic reading, framed for them by the hugely metaphorical structures of these works, involves them at both intellectual and affective levels (indeed the two cannot really be divided), and makes them want to learn more.

We need to expand the range of the non-fiction that we include in English. In spite of the recognition by the authors of the National Curriculum for England and Wales in recent years that non-fiction may be the preferred reading of many boys, and the recent attempts to make such texts available to young readers in secondary school English, I feel we have made only modest progress so far. Texts chosen for their generic features, to illustrate particular purposes for reading and writing – to inform, to persuade, to argue – often demonstrate those generic features in very dull and mundane ways. Instead we need more texts like Anderson's *King* whose language is carefully crafted by the author and by the protagonist himself, Martin Luther King, but whose whole text is mediated through the aesthetic qualities of words and images working together. The subject English may not usually be regarded as a site for efferent reading, in the face of so many other subjects in the school and university curriculum which are dedicated to it. It can be argued that topics like the Holocaust or the Civil Rights movement in America are best handled by subjects like history or politics, though I believe that such important and humane topics are more often to be encountered in English than in other subjects. But I would argue that getting at knowledge, ideas and concepts through literature is often more powerful, engaging and stimulating for students like mine precisely because English is the subject where their aesthetic senses and affective sensibilities are employed in both learning texts and learning from texts.

If English is about language we might ask what the role of language is in the comic texts I have been referring to here, and why I think the study of such texts belongs to English rather than to other subjects like art (aesthetic) or history (efferent). In *King* (pp. 142–50) Anderson gives readers Martin Luther King's great speech at the march on Washington in August 1963. The oration is presented over eight pages in a series of speech bubbles set against a graphically turbulent background. This background is not there simply to give the speech a visual context, to illustrate the words as it were, though it is very useful for students to have a visual representation of the physical context; it does much more. By mixing semi-toned old photographs, full-page drawings, black/white/grey/and full colour in a collage behind the words that span the eight pages, Anderson communicates the *impact* of the speech, the power of the words, not only in real time *then*, but down the decades to readers *now*. Each graphic image on top of which the verbal text is imposed speaks to us from behind the words about what the words mean, what they imply, for now as well as for then; in other words the combination of words and pictures, working together, speaks of a revolution, with the figure of King dominating the pages as, indeed, he dominated the march. Large sections of Anderson's text are about dialogue, talking heads arguing and counter-arguing the politics of the Civil Rights movement, like characters in a play. Few concessions are made to the verbal compression of classic graphic texts but so much of the real speech of real characters recorded at the time is offered to readers that one feels this text has a soundtrack as well as pictures. *King* is an excellent example of a text which insists that efferent and aesthetic reading work together.

The verbal text in *Maus* is a different matter. The words are just as complex and significant as the pictures and work in synchronicity with them. Indeed Spiegelman claims to be a writer first:

It's easier for me to write than to draw, I suppose. Comics are an art of compression. You allow your thoughts to decant, until they achieve their maximum density. (Campbell 2004, *Guardian*: Review, pp. 12–14)

The verbal text is extremely rich which partly arises from this compression:

Comics are very condensed thought-structures. It has maybe more to do with poetry than it has to do with narrative prose. (ibid.)

The need for compression arises from the necessary economy of space within speech bubbles and picture frames and, more, from the way the words work *with* the pictures. In discussing the relationship between pictures and words in comics, David Carrier makes the point that speech bubbles externalize thought:

The word balloons, by externalizing thoughts, makes visible the (fictional) inner world of represented figures, externalizing their inner lives, making them transparent to readers. (Carrier 2000: 73)

Even the hand-written orthography in *Maus* carries layers of meaning. The layout and framing of the pages mean that one does not necessarily read the words from left to right and of course one reads the pictures simultaneously with the words. There is also the matter of the words which are in speech bubbles and the words outside them, often representing the difference between the time of the story and the time of telling the story (though this is not consistent it is helpful in sorting out what is going on in terms of the complex time-scales of the text). The language of *Maus* is rich in the voices given to the main characters. First we have the dialects of the two main narrators – Vladek's East European word order and grammar (with some Yiddish vocabulary) and Art's more conventional New York English. Vladek's immigrant dialect is rendered with great humour (and often pathos) placing him both spatially in Europe and temporally in the past The text is full of jokes and ironies, not often to be found in Holocaust literature. Just as in children's picture books the language can subvert the pictures and vice versa. Indeed there is so much to be gained from close reading of words and pictures in *Maus* that our reading has to be slowed down if we are not to miss the many subtleties of the text. Joe Sacco, in contrast to Spiegelman, presents his readers with very long prose passages, often occupying most of the page, while in Anderson's *King*, as I have shown above, most of the major speeches are given verbatim across several pages (Anderson 2005). The point I am making here is that the comic-book texts I have been discussing are verbally as well as visually challenging for their readers. Reading comics is not a case of abandoning words for pictures, nor of reducing the verbal emphasis that belongs to English.

I am aware that many of the graphic texts I have referred to in this chapter are the 'classics' of the medium. I have been discussing them in the context of teaching literature to future teachers in Higher Education, but I would like to see comics, both those for children and those for older readers, popular and ephemeral as well as serious works of art, given a place in the secondary school curriculum in England (they have a well-established place in the Scottish school curriculum). There has in the past in Britain been considerable prejudice against comics but with the current flowering of the medium and the developed visual literacies of young people now such prejudice appears to be increasingly wrong-headed and irrelevant. The following anecdote may illustrate this point.

Sitting on the train a few years ago in a crowded carriage on my way home from the university I was peacefully reading my *Guardian* newspaper. Opposite me was a group of sixth form girls who began giggling and pointing at the back of my paper. They asked me to hold the paper still and one of them photographed on her mobile phone whatever it was that had amused them so much. I turned the paper around and saw it was a stunning cartoon about the Iraq war by the distinguished British cartoonist Steve Bell in which George Bush appeared starkly pink and naked. Having photographed the cartoon the girls forwarded it as a text to their friends.

Chapter 8

'The uncreating word':
some ways *not* to teach English

Joy Alexander

I am at an educational conference listening to a speech by a high authority in the field. I know him to be a good scholar, a dedicated servant of society, and an admirable person. Yet his speech is a muddy river of clichés, flowing stickily into a delta of banalities at the peroration. The content of the speech does not do justice to his mind: what it does reflect is the state of his literary education. It is not that he has never read good literature, for he has the literary tastes that one would expect a cultivated man to have. But he has never been trained to think rhetorically, to visualize his abstractions, to subordinate logic and sequence to the insights of metaphor and simile, to realize that figures of speech are not the ornaments of language, but the elements of both language and thought ... The result is that he is fluent without being articulate, and cannot break out of an armour of ready-made phrases when he tries to express his real convictions ... [N]othing can now be done for him: there are no courses in remedial metaphor.

(Frye 1970: 93–4)

Ouch! Forty years on, Northrop Frye's challenging observation is, if anything, more apposite than ever. We have all listened to an educated person such as this. What they got from their English education is that it enabled them to speak and write lifeless prose. In the final sentence Frye infers that this is a failing that cannot be repaired. It's a salutary reminder of the power and the responsibility of English teaching. That being so, I want to address a simple question: how should English be taught so as to avoid producing people who use language as Frye's educationalist does? In seeking an answer to this question I intend to review the contours of the intellectual project of English which Tony Burgess has examined in Chapter 2, as evidenced in publications over the past four decades or so, a period of time which coincides with my own experience of English classrooms as pupil and teacher.

'The uncreating word'

The urgency of my question is attested by the current glut of clunky, inert, managerialist prose spawned by the so-called information society. At work, my 'strategic aims' are 'to develop and further a dynamic, world-class education portfolio'. Meaning is made fuzzy by cliché and bombast. Meanwhile my eyes glaze over trying to discern the meaning in official documents advocating literacy in schools.[1] When Roger Knight was editor of *The Use of English* he used regularly to apply his literary critical skills to the opaque, sloppy language of government reports on English. One example will serve, on the use of language in the NLS *Framework for Teaching English, Years 7–9*:

> This is not the writing of someone whose thought has been conspicuously empowered by language …
>
> Typically, in the *Framework*, the jargon closes off thought. The writer is not writing 'effectively' because he is not writing imaginatively.
>
> These generalizing phrases avoid the issue; they provide a refuge from the need to think concretely. (Knight 2001: 194–6)

However, jargonized officialese[2] is an easy target and any professional will be readily able to supply multiple examples. More to the purpose is to consider how these chickens come home to roost in the English classroom.

The current literacy drive in England and elsewhere is not motivated by an altruistic concern for young people to attain high literacy levels so that their lives may thereby be enriched:

> Whereas literacy was in the past taught to give access to the truths of the church or the strength of the nation, the literacy of greatest concern to the modern industrial economy is that of 'functional literacy', the competence to deal with modern bureaucratic institutions. (Olson 2003: 202)[3]

The privileging of Standard English and the reification of literacy stem from their promotion by a government supposedly anticipating modern society's needs. Compared with the literacy mandate, debates about the place in the English curriculum of literature and the canon, of creativity, of popular culture, or of multicultural and multiliteracies perspectives seem peripheral. In fact, these elements of English become absorbed as means by which the literacy agenda can be pursued; for example, extracts from literature are used to 'deliver' literacy goals. The literacy juggernaut appropriates and shapes teaching schemes, learning goals and assessment. Pedagogy also is twisted into a kind of 'service'. The pressure to raise standards can lead to transmission-type teaching, to atomized skills which are amenable to measurement and to the proliferation of learning outcomes which can be enumerated and audited. An example would be an English lesson I watched on ballads, where the first thing that happened was that the pupils were asked to copy down a definition of a ballad.[4] I find it hard to believe that before the literacy era any English teacher in their right mind would have introduced such a lesson in such a way. Compare this with the approach suggested in a book on English teaching compiled in 1952 for the Incorporated Association of Assistant Masters in Secondary School. The pupils imagine they are retainers in their lord's hall, the teacher says – 'I am the bard, with a good ghost story for you. I tell you the story as it was passed on to me, by one from further North, where an old woman is called "a carline wife"' (IAAMSS 1952: 108) – and 'The Wife of Usher's Well' is read. But literacy now dominates the English curriculum, with a consequent loss of equilibrium between the whole (English) and its constituent parts (one of which is literacy), between the bigger picture and the details which it frames but which give it definition. It is reminiscent of Henry Reed's poem 'Naming of Parts' in which the mechanical rifle lesson in the classroom is a sterile parody of the fecundity and beauty of the garden outside: 'the point of balance,/Which in our case we have not got.'

My argument at this point runs parallel to that advanced by Robin Alexander with reference to the government's Primary Strategy (Alexander 2004). He relates the following anecdote:

In 1997, as a founding board member of QCA, I asked the then Minister of State Estelle Morris why the Literacy and Numeracy Strategies were run by the Department and the rest of the curriculum by QCA, when the new body had been set up expressly to bring coherence to the hitherto fragmented worlds of curriculum, assessment and qualifications. 'Ah but Minister' one of her aides smoothly interjected, 'literacy and numeracy aren't curriculum, they're *standards*, and standards are the

Department's responsibility, not QCA's.' Literacy is standards, not curriculum: ponder, for a moment, this brutal dismissal of the civilizing ideals of universal literacy and of the efforts of the many who have fought for them. (Alexander 2004: 24)

Similarly, educational *realpolitik* has advanced literacy ahead of English to an extent that it is a 'given' of the situation, leaving English teachers to find ways to operate within this context. The government has answered the big question of 'what is English?' The title of Alexander's essay – 'Still no pedagogy? Principle, pragmatism and compliance in primary education' – outlines his argument that teachers have settled for a pedagogy either of pragmatism or of compliance and that they should instead develop a principled pedagogy, one which has 'educational meaning'. Similarly, it seems to me that English teachers, while they may have limited room for manoeuvre as regards the content of English, may be able to make elbow-room for their professional endeavours by re-engaging with and proposing a worthy pedagogy for their subject.

In some respects also, my argument shadows at a distance that of Ken Jones in an article which explores how 'the principles of a new project for English can be developed' (Jones 2006: 80). Jones acknowledges that 'the opportunities for local experiment and alternative "envisioning" have been lessened by powerful and strongly enforced orthodoxies' (ibid.: 81) and that contemporary education is characterized by 'highly specified programmes of study, emphasizing the acquisition of official knowledge, and implemented in top-down fashion' (ibid.: 89). Nevertheless he sees hope in the possibility that policy which is eager to appear neo-liberal may stimulate – in a delightfully astute phrase – an 'excess of practice over stipulation' (ibid.: 89), whereby classroom practice subverts official prescription. While declining to offer 'a discussion of strategy' (ibid.: 89), Jones suggests that English teachers can find the space to practise purposefully and with integrity despite all-too-real constraints.

It might be helpful to summarize here the main lineaments of the argument I am putting forward. Literacy is the main show in town and dominates the current agenda for English. Not to come to terms with this reality would be Canute-like folly. Though the literacy *de nos jours* is a matter of curriculum content, it has exerted huge pressure on pedagogy, which has responded to the demand for an instrumental approach, skills, systematization and prescription. To return to my original 'problem', Frye's sub-literate scholar: he is a victim of the wrong pedagogy. His teachers may have smiled at their success in achieving their 'learning outcome', a literate student, but they have utterly failed him by the means they employed to attain that end. It is in the area of pedagogy that there is room for English teachers to negotiate their practice, thus applying their profession-alism and salvaging their integrity. In the remainder of this chapter I will develop this proposal in relation to: (i) handling metaphor; (ii) critical literacy; (iii) listening in English. In doing so, I am advocating particular pedagogical orientations which would still require to be worked out in practice.

To illustrate how the broader educational climate has moulded the way English is taught in the classroom, I would draw attention again to a tendency I have already mentioned. A scheme of work on KS3 poetry, in my recent experience, will more often than not be approached through form or through figures of speech, that is by progressing through the limerick, acrostic poem, cinquain and so on, or through simile, metaphor, personification et al. Undoubtedly these are topics which belong to the English curriculum, but two things surprise me about this painting-by-numbers approach. One is the seeming belief that this is *the* way to 'do' poetry with junior classes. It is as though the information society has combined with control-freakery to delude people into thinking that the whole of reality can somehow be captured on a page, preferably in a grid or in bullet points. Thus English is commodified and classified so that it is amenable to tick-boxes. What surprises me even more about this approach is its oddity; it seems strange to read poems principally as exemplars of a form or figure of speech. It is not the best method to read, understand and appreciate poetry. It is stimulating to explore form with pupils as long as it is seen, not in isolation, but as an aspect of meaning. It is to this very conclusion that W. B. Yeats comes in his meditative poem 'Among Schoolchildren': 'How can we tell the dancer from the dance?' Seamus Heaney finds in these words 'a mode of thinking which we should cultivate in ourselves and try to awaken in our pupils: munificent, non-sectarian, energetic and delightful' (Heaney 1983: 16). The subject English offers a way of thinking and feeling about life. A more rewarding pedagogy could be derived by reflecting on values with regard to handling literature or to young people's classroom experience, or on why we read poems in English and on what are the best ways to do so.

Characteristic of the curriculum as it is presently devised is a reliance on what Peter Abbs calls

> ... a crass model of economic learning entirely antithetical to aesthetic education. Here the transmission of skills – all of which are seen as measurable, all of which are deemed to be transferable

to other tasks – is conceived, without reference to any other philosophy, as the centre of the educational task. (Abbs 2003: 60)

The 'skills' outlook arises from a 'purely mechanistic view of human action and human relationships', where 'the dominant perception of human nature is one which construes our interaction as a matter of techniques' (Palmer 1988: 55). From this perspective, mastery of English consists in the accretion of discrete skills which can be improved by exercises and tasks, the outcomes of which can be measured and evaluated. A more constructive approach has been proposed by Costa and Kallick, who have developed a curriculum built around 'Habits of Mind'. A habit of mind is a 'disposition toward behaving intelligently when confronted with problems, the answers to which are not immediately known' (Costa and Kallick 2000: 1), it is directed towards 'authentic, congruent, ethical behaviour' (ibid.: 13) and it 'requires a composite of many skills, attitudes, cues, past experiences and proclivities' (ibid.: 1). That composite, as they describe it, includes a number of qualities such as persistence, metacognition, imagination, responding with wonderment and thinking interdependently. English is more about habits of mind than skills; it is more concerned with the whole than with the parts of which it is composed. A fundamental value which still applies is David Holbrook's assertion that teacher and pupil 'meet in *the word*. The essential process of teaching English is that of a concern with whole meaning' (Holbrook 1967: 145).[5]

To return to my original question: how should English be taught so as to avoid producing people who use language as Frye's educationalist does? How can English teachers cast their bread upon the waters so as *not* to encourage half-baked language use? Flannery O'Connor once expressed the view that universities don't stifle enough writers, opining that 'there's many a best-seller that could have been prevented by a good teacher'. How can an English teacher actively hinder the germination of a rain forest's worth of turgid prose? I have been arguing that Frye's conference speaker has been taught skills separated from meaning and settles for cliché because of deficiencies in the way he has been taught to handle language. I argue that this is a tendency likely to be produced in a regime where there is a functional or instrumental approach to language and where it is taught as though it is a science rather than a craft. Such a literacy regime offers little space to effect changes in curriculum content; instead more meaningful pedagogies for the English classroom could be explored.

From genre to metaphor

Although I am proposing negative outcomes, I actually want to consider positive ways in which certain outcomes may be avoided. However, I will begin by suggesting one way not to teach, or at least, one method which is over-prevalent. The genre approach is widespread but there is a real danger that it could exacerbate the incidence of formulaic writing. Of course there is a necessary place for encountering genre in English learning but it can encourage a clinical division of writing into compartments with their own rules and amenable to methodical teaching and assessment. It is not really so different as a methodology from the clause analysis and parsing which was a significant part of the English diet when I was a pupil. Where it results in the application of a formula in order to structure language, it can lead to language use which, in Frye's words, is 'fluent without being articulate'. The focus is on the formal features of a text so that the attention to what is being said is consequently more superficial. Form prevails over meaning rather than being an expression of the meaning.

Urszula Clark summarizes the limitations of the genre approach:

> Critics of genre theory argue that texts rarely fit one generic type, being in fact multi-generic, and therefore to teach that one particular textual 'model' can be taught to accommodate specific social functions is linguistically unsound. A further criticism is that imposing generic models on children will suppress individual creativity and even the ability to learn through linguistic expression and exploration. Such an approach also comes under attack from critical pedagogy, in that it fails to engage with the ideological aspects of texts, other than as a means of teaching powerful genres to the powerless, with scant consideration as to why they have such power and the source of that power. Finally, the theory of instruction associated with genre theory could be construed as a revival of transmission pedagogy with its teaching of formal language 'facts' isolated from social contexts. (Clark 2001: 216–17)

If genres are treated in a rigid rather than a flexible manner, they may become a straitjacket inclining teachers to deliver a regulated curriculum. Bethan Marshall has shown that 'rather than being an aid to effective writing, the knowledge of the conventions becomes an end in itself and so limits imaginative engagement' (Marshall 2004: 24). The failing of the genre approach is that it diverts attention from content to form; the antidote therefore is to redress the bias away from content, as Frye indicates in his pithy reference to metaphor. In addition he advocates visualizing abstractions and making figurative language a way of thinking. It is a move from skills to a habit of mind, from metaphor as a singular figure of speech to metaphor as an inherent part of meaning, from knowledge of metaphor as naming of parts to metaphor as a way of knowing and perceiving the world. Frye argues that:

> For a student who is going to engage in any verbal activity, the study of literature, not in itself a practical subject, is a practical necessity. (Frye 1982: 110)

and again that:

> Poetry should be at the centre of all literary training, and literary prose forms the periphery. In a properly constructed curriculum there would be no place for 'effective communication' or for any form of utilitarian English. (Frye 1970: 94)

The underlying justification for both of these propositions is that poetry is a method of thought as well as a means of expression (ibid.: 97). Those familiar with Kieran Egan's work on the imagination and learning will know that he regards metaphor as a crucial element in what he calls the cognitive tool-kit for learning, stating that it 'lies at the heart of human intellectual inventiveness, creativity and imagination' (Egan 2005: 3). He emphasises that:

> If we see the educational task as simply to put literacy in place, we risk undermining the very foundations on which a rich literacy must rest. Stimulating children's imaginations, metaphoric fluency, and narrative sophistication can become a more prominent aim of early education. (Egan 1999: 33)

Wayne Booth provides a memorable example of metaphor informing and impacting on thought:

> a lawyer friend … had been hired to defend a large southern utility against a suit by a small one. [He] had thought at first that he was doing fine … Then the lawyer for the small utility said, speaking to the jury, 'So now we see what it is. They got us where they want us. They're holdin' us up with one hand, their good sharp fishin' knife in the other, and they're sayin', "you jes set still, little catfish,

we're jes gonna gut ya.'" At that moment my friend reports, he predicted, accurately, that he had lost the case – 'I had fallen into the hands of a genius with metaphor.' (Booth 1988: 304)

This is persuasive speech all right, but not according to the conventions of the genre. The lawyer has a crafty (in every sense) understanding of what he wants to say and he has a shrewd awareness of his audience; above all, he thinks rhetorically through metaphor. I believe that a proper pedagogic task for English teachers would be to discover curricular methods for thinking by means of figurative language, not least because it would discourage over-reliance on cliché, jargon and dead language. It would mean, for example, developing in young people a habit of mind that understands, when reading Robert Frost, that when he talks about the road not taken he is not just talking about two diverging paths in a wood, or when he says he has miles to go before he sleeps it means more than literal travel to an actual bed.[6] It would be a worthwhile pedagogical project to investigate ways to induct young people in the English classroom into subject-specific forms of cognition such as metaphorical thinking.

From efferent to aesthetic

A different version of the same idea is to consider the move from genre to metaphor as a shift from the efferent to the aesthetic. The distinction between 'aesthetic' and 'efferent' reading is crucial to Louise Rosenblatt's formulation of reader-response theory. In efferent reading the 'primary concern of the reader is with what he (*sic*) will carry away from the reading' (Rosenblatt 1978: 24), as, for example, when we read to gain information. Aesthetic reading is 'reading for its own sake' – 'the reader's primary concern is with what happens *during* the actual reading event' (ibid.: 24, her italics). It is unfortunate that the word 'aesthetic' has accrued connotations of 'effete' or 'arty' because what it means in reader-response theory is something entirely positive and beneficial. Reading itself – not just what happens beforehand or afterwards – becomes a very active process:

> The reader's main purpose is to participate as fully as possible in the potentialities of the text. (ibid.: 69)

Rosenblatt acknowledged that there were 'powerful educational implications' attendant upon a belief in 'the development of the individual's capacity to adopt and to maintain the aesthetic stance, to live fully and personally in the literary transaction' (ibid.: 161). One great advantage of considering aesthetic reading within the English curriculum is that it provides English with content that belongs distinctively to its preserve. The profile components of English – talking and listening, reading and writing – are a part of most curricular subjects. But whereas the reading that takes place in history, science, music, etc., will almost always be efferent reading, aesthetic reading should be a major concern of the English curriculum. Literary training can therefore be defined as 'the refinement of the student's power to enter into literary experiences and to interpret them' (Rosenblatt 1995: 51) and the teacher's concern is with 'the creation of a situation favourable to a vital experience of literature' (ibid.: 59). Actually reading the text has precedence over knowing about the text, establishing its contexts, applying a theory to it, or whatever other experiences of texts pupils may have in the English classroom.

English teachers need to maintain a balance between efferent and aesthetic reading; however it is arguable that English classrooms at the present time are afflicted by a surfeit of efferent reading. The emphasis on literacy together with the predominant genre approach means that there is a tendency to read poems or extracts from novels not for their own sake but because they are good vehicles for teaching personification, use of adjectives, etc. Denis Donoghue writes of Rosenblatt's formulation of reader-response theory:

Her argument for making aesthetic reading the basic model of reading seems convincing. Such an approach would transform expository writing programs in our schools, colleges, and universities: it would show how reductive and demeaning the current fixation on the literal, cognitive and referential aspects of language really is. (Donoghue 1998: 13)

Donoghue regards this type of reading as a defining characteristic of English: 'a work of literature is a work that calls for an aesthetic reading and gratifies it' (ibid.: 13). English classrooms should therefore be places where young people are frequently gratified as they engage in reading aesthetically. The aesthetic principle can be applied to writing also, as Donoghue does. It is time to discover a pedagogy for English that is the practical outworking of such a principle.

From literacy to critical literacy

I can pass over this point more quickly, not because it is less important, but because it will be more familiar. However, while critical literacy as an approach is readily endorsed, I see less evidence of its being exemplified in the classroom, except in the hoary old topic of advertising. Where there are tendencies to a prescriptive curriculum and to transmission teaching, it is all the more important to stoke criticality and subversion of the normative. Once again, it is a matter of discovering how to permeate English teaching and learning with critical literacy, in deed and not just in word. Stevens and McGuinn trenchantly question genre by coming at it with the help of critical literacy:

> A pupil might ... write an essay (or a publicity brochure for a *Macbeth* video) which achieves top marks in an examination – without ever asking such fundamental, ideologically charged questions as: 'Why is this particular genre privileged in this way?' 'Who does or does not have access to this genre and why?' 'How does this genre construct the world for its proficient user?' 'What alternative forms of communication might serve equally or even more effectively in place of this one?' ...

> A truly empowering literacy curriculum would ... teach its students how to 'construct' the genre rather than be 'constructed' by it (Stevens and McGuinn 2004: 85, 88).

In a classroom where critical literacy is practised, pupils will be alert to the power that inheres in many uses of language and will be helped to use language more powerfully themselves.

From unvoiced text to listening

The chief characteristic of jargon-ridden prose is that it bypasses the ear. The writer did not have the time to listen to what they were writing and, in reaching for the ready-made, paid the heavy price of losing contact with the communicative immediacy of the human voice. Jerome Bruner would have diagnosed Frye's conference speaker as a case of cloth ears:

> why is it that man through his entire life as *Homo scribens* will continue to write with no improvement in his sense of craft and little improvement in his use of mind? It may well be that to

become aware of what one has written requires that one hear it, listen to it, compare the written with the spoken version ... Then let the student write some more and listen, listen, listen. (Bruner 1966: 111–12)

The robotic prose of Frye's lecturer is not the language that would naturally issue from the mouth of a human speaker, whereas a distinctive feature of almost all literature is that voice is intimately part of the construction of meaning. It may be a characteristic of factual or functional writing that it is principally written for the eye and not the ear. A significant part of being 'good' at English is having the ability to 'read with the ear' and to hear what you write. Listening is, of course, along with talking, reading and writing, one of the four profile components of English. It is however the Cinderella of the quartet. For the first half of the twentieth century these elements were represented as follows:

expression   –   talking; writing
understanding   –   listening; reading

As a rationale, this was coherent; in practice, it proved productive. When this was realigned in mid-century to: talking and listening; reading; writing, it diminished to tokenism the contribution of listening to learning in English. It is ironic that the component that is most unique to the subject – listening to language – is the most neglected.

Attentiveness to language, in whatever medium it is expressed, is at the very core of English and is its distinctive concern in comparison to other subjects. To link listening to reading safeguards a particular kind of reading and allows listening to be meaningful. To pass over listening is a deleterious omission because it threatens the loss of an attentive, ruminative, receptive stance towards language. Reading and writing with the ear, listening to language – these are vital facets of learning in English. It is not difficult for teachers to find ways to increase the listening dimension in their English programme. I take for granted the familiar formulations both of listening skills and of listening as a partner of speaking. These are already well understood and their contribution to the curriculum is fairly nominal. I am suggesting enriching the subject of English by linking listening to reading and to writing. This goes beyond a surface change of emphasis to a more radical conception of the substance and purpose of English within the wider curriculum. To highlight listening as reading with the ear is to accentuate an aesthetic response to texts such that English develops an appreciative hearing of language. Other subjects make efferent use of texts; uniquely in English is crafted language heard and enjoyed for itself alone. A potential obstacle is that in an era which places an exaggerated emphasis on pace, 'hearing' reading and writing takes time. The dividends paid by such a strategy in terms of more sensitive reading and shapelier writing would reward a more assertive and rightful role for listening as a profile component of English. In reclaiming listening from neglect, I am not seeking for it an over-prominent place in the English curriculum; it has to be held in balance in a holistic programme. However, a renewed emphasis on a pedagogy and practice for listening in English is overdue.

Great Expectations

The need to find new paths in English is starkly exemplified for me in an English textbook in which pupils are set the task of identifying typical ingredients of a text. The example given is of the first three sentences of *Great Expectations*. The opening words, 'My father's family name being Pirrip' are labelled 'subordinate clause', 'I called myself Pip' is labelled 'first person', and 'Mrs. Joe Gargery, who married the blacksmith' is labelled 'retells events'. (It is ironic that this process is applied to a book which has profound concerns with literacy and to a passage where Pip is 'reading' the history of his own life – a Freirean reading of the world – by interpreting a grave-plot and deciphering a tombstone.) It might seem incredible that what is deemed worthy of remark about the first words of this great novel is that it begins with a subordinate clause, but this is the modern way to 'do' Dickens at Key Stage 3: literature is categorized into genres (in this case, narrative); the genre's characteristic features are discovered (first person, retells events, etc.); to be literate is to be able to 'deploy' these genres 'appropriately'; pupils have to show that they can identify the features of the different genres correctly. Literature is mined for excerpts that facilitate this mechanical procedure. At every stage there is a gradual moving away from the living voice of the writer speaking to, and communicating with, the reader.

How very different are the examples of literacy in Dickens' actual novel! We are given an example of Pip's writing:

MI DEER JO i OPE U R KRWITE wELL i OPE i sHAL soN B HABELL 4 2 TEEDGE U JO AN THEN wE sHORL B sO GLODD AN wEN i M PRENGTD 2 U JO woT LARX AN BLEVE ME INF XN PIP.

It is a letter[7] to Joe, which it takes him a couple of hours to print on his slate. Joe, who only knows two letters of the alphabet, J and O, reveals one of his own oral compositions, an epitaph for his father:

> '... And it were my intentions to have had put upon his tombstone that Whatsume'er the failings on his part, Remember reader he were that good in his hart.'

> Joe recited this couplet with such manifest pride and careful perspicuity, that I asked him if he had made it himself.

> 'I made it,' said Joe, 'my own self. I made it in a moment. It was like striking out a horseshoe complete, in a single blow.'

Both Pip and Joe have been assisted, but not ruled, by genre. A human voice speaks powerfully through their words. Each has been helped most in their literacy by having something that they very much wanted to articulate. For both of them, their writing is a source of immense personal satisfaction. In an article on *Great Expectations*, Tom Paulin speaks of 'literary texts which surprise their readers by voicing a living language' and contrasts this with Dickens' love of parodying 'the junk language of bureaucrats, lawyers and hack journalists' (Paulin 1992: 112). For Paulin, the confrontation between 'living language' (especially oral) and 'junk language' (what James Joyce in *Finnegan's Wake* called the 'jinglish janglage') underlies *Great Expectations*:

> Before print was the human voice – the unofficial voice of poetry powerless against the state and the status quo. (ibid.: 114)

Joe Gargery writing his couplet is the perfect oppositional figure to Frye's conference speaker. Joe has no need of 'remedial metaphor'; metaphor springs naturally to his lips. He 'strikes out' the words as though shaping a horseshoe on the anvil. He communicates with the reader in his own voice and expresses what he genuinely feels. An English teacher with Joe in the class would want to foster these qualities and not smother them with system and regulated instruction. How can the teacher ensure that 'teacher-bird' lessons do not send Joe along the cul-de-sac at the end of which is Frye's speaker?

I am not hopeful of influencing definitions of *what* English is as a subject, but I believe that there is room 'between the lines' of exter-nally mandated agendas for fresh thought and creativity about *how* the subject is done. I have tried by indirection to find direction out and considered first some less desirable ways to 'do' English, when judged by their consequences. New directions I have proposed are: a greater emphasis on 'aesthetic' than 'efferent' approaches; linking figures of speech to meaning by nurturing metaphorical thinking; infiltrating critical literacy into all aspects of the English curriculum; giving due recognition to the place of listening and also of voiced text in classroom practice. This is a challenge for English pedagogy, but the guiding aim and foundational principle are surely that 'the way to develop one's mastery over English is to live within a rich context of its lively use' (Holbrook 1961: 23).

Chapter 9

Refreshing the aesthetic:
a response to Section 2

Sue Dymoke

The three chapters in this section all concern themselves with the
aesthetic nature of texts. In their different ways, the authors
challenge current literary teaching practices and question precon-
ceived or official notions of what constitutes 'literature'. They
highlight the need for English teachers, and those researching
English teaching, to release literature from the stagnant curriculum
backwater in which it appears to have been forcibly moored and
seek out the aesthetic within twenty-first-century classroom textual
practices. The writers argue that this act will foreground
engagement with literary texts for meaningful purposes and reshape
the values associated with literature. Foregrounding will enable
young readers, listeners, writers, producers and performers to
actively enjoy their textual encounters in ways which have a long-
lasting and enriching impact that is currently lacking in their
assessment-driven, extract-based textual work. In determining to
locate the aesthetic, the readers and writers of the good ship
Literature should set sail across high curriculum seas, risking
stormy conditions and oppositional readings, encountering unspecified whole texts, wide screens and complex inter-textual kingdoms,
and experiencing ways of thinking which will shape their understandings and future creative practices. The journeys of *Endeavour*
or even the *Starship Enterprise* are not what is being proposed here.
Neither, on the other hand, is literary study to be perceived as a
Sunday afternoon boat trip or a package tour. (It may in fact be
more like a journey in Dr Who's *Tardis* – an unassuming police box
on the outside but inside, a vast and complex hub offering galaxies
of unexpected new experiences and revisitings.) My response in this
chapter represents one such journey in that it explores key questions
raised in this section. It draws out threads, makes connections
between discourses, puts forward suggestions and asks questions
of English teachers and researchers about the refreshment and

renewal of current pedagogy, as well as exploring potential new directions within the field of literary study.

Current contexts

We have been offered timely reminders that English can be taught in a soulless, impersonal way to suit 'stand and deliver' (Harrison 1994: 104) modes of assessment. The authors ask us why this should be so and what alternative approaches might be preferable. Alexander points to the increasing managerialism of schools which is, in part, responsible for this state of affairs. Within the 'high stakes' testing, performance-driven, surveillance culture in which educators in all sectors in the UK and (increasingly in Australia and the US) have to operate, learners are 'hustled from one skills based task to another' (Marsh and Millard 2000: 61) and given dwindling opportunities for risk-taking or creativity. In such a marketplace, English teachers increasingly deal in knowledge rather than meaning-making (Kress et al. 2004). To develop this scenario further, it seems to me that teachers are increasingly urged to take learner-consumers on whistle-stop package tours of texts and help them to assemble flat-packed (specification compliant) framework responses. But is resistance to this managerialist culture possible? Is there another way which can open students' eyes to the full potential of literature rather than merely enabling them to admire (and perhaps reassemble) the view?

Rosenblatt revisited: experiential and personal responses to texts

To move us forward, Alexander returns to Rosenblatt's work on reading response and asks if the balance has tipped too strongly towards 'efferent' (Rosenblatt 1978: 24) readings of texts at the expense of the aesthetic. An efferent reading is primarily concerned with information retrieval rather than how words are written on a page or the rhythms and associations they might have. With an aesthetic reading, the reader's relationship with the text *and what they bring to the text in the event of reading*, is of central importance. Rosenblatt's work continues to have implications for the reading of 'literary' texts in schools, especially poetry. Researchers observe the efferent nature of responses demanded by some teachers during their students' reading of poetry (Dias and Hayhoe 1988) with the result that teaching becomes devoid of emotional response: ticking off 1,001 poetic forms without experiencing a single poem (Hull 2001);

teaching limericks without laughter or throwing depth-charges into poems to find similes lurking beneath their surfaces (Dymoke 2005). Misson and Morgan explore this efferent approach further by arguing for a pedagogy that embraces corporeal response to aesthetic texts through such activities as work on rhythm and performance, in contrast to an 'anaesthetic' (2006: 130) pedagogy which suppresses bodily feeling.

Post-structuralist theories of reading can appear to challenge the validity and authority of the personal response which Rosenblatt's approach invests in individual readers (McGuinn 2004). We read, write, view, speak, listen and teach in a post-structuralist world where 'text bobs like a cork upon the sea, driven by winds of the immediate context of situation, while out on the horizon lurk the vast influences of different ideological and institutional systems of society and culture'(Burgess 2002: 33). This world is riven by dominant political discourses in which literary texts have to 'earn' (McGuinn 2004: 71) their place *among* other texts rather than assume kingship by divine right. The place of personal response within such a world can appear in opposition to a more radical social justice agenda of critical literacy. However, do they need to be viewed as such separate perspectives? In this book, and in *Critical Literacy and the Aesthetic* (2006), Misson and Morgan aim to reconcile these two positions. In their view, reader response and critical literacy both stress the provisional nature of readings and the multivalency of texts. Furthermore, if readers respond to an aesthetic text emotionally, they remain aware of its deliberate construction for a specific purpose. While the reading of such a text is a personal experience it cannot be regarded as separate from the social because the social contributes to the construction of the personal (Misson and Morgan 2006).

These arguments provoke us to consider whether literary study in schools is currently too concerned with identifying strategies for torturing a text 'to find out what it really means' (Collins 1998: 58) rather than exploring the relationships which are formed between different readers, texts and writers when the 'event' of reading occurs? Should teachers be encouraged to focus more on exploring *how* varied interpretations of texts are formed and arrived at? By developing an understanding of *how* different perspectives are created and actively experiencing the aesthetic at work through their own performances and creative tasks, could students engage more critically and fully with values and arguments embedded within texts and, at the same time, learn *how to express these arguments for themselves* in creative ways rather than learning how to identify aspects of their construction?

Enjoyment

Enjoyment is a key feature of an aesthetic reading. Yet where are the opportunities within current curricula or research agendas for enjoyment or analysis of what it means to enjoy a literary text? Enjoyment is not a readily assessable response to a text (and therefore is not a word which is widely used in assessment criteria). Neither is it a term which can be easily measured (and therefore enjoyment is not a major priority for research funding in a time of high-stakes testing). Although it must be virtually impossible to 'enjoy' every text, surely young readers need to enjoy some of their encounters with texts? Reading for pleasure can help young people to develop their criticalities about a range of texts and refine their own reading preferences whether these be in computer games, lyrics, podcasts or Young Adult Fiction. Ofsted reports teachers' concerns that teaching reading is no longer a 'fun' activity in classrooms (Ofsted 2005). Where once reading a whole text was a shared experience involving personal response and engagement, now the text appears to be treated like a 'manual' (Ofsted 2005: 26) selected with reference to its purpose rather than its quality. How can this situation be redressed and the fun brought back? Are there examples of readers enjoying literature or initiatives which can inform the development of pedagogy in this field? At policy level, slimming down the curriculum and its stifling assessment structures would be major steps forward to providing potential space for enjoyment within the timetable. In the most creative and resistant schools there has always been time for enjoying texts but it is important to be reminded of what this enjoyment can look like. In two secondary schools I visited earlier this year, the enjoyment of texts was a highly visible priority. Both were situated in challenging environments and facing significant behavioural issues yet they resisted the temptation to use five minutes private reading time as a control mechanism at the beginning of lessons. Instead, enthusiastic librarians and English staff were spreading the word about enjoyment of reading. Their activities included: an annual whole-school 'book grab' where students swapped previously read books: senior school book group meetings; corridors lined with posters of quirkily disguised teachers caught in the act of reading their favourite texts. If ever there was a time for more teachers to model themselves as enthusiastic readers in order to promote a hunger for reading in their classes, it is now. When planning their working with texts, teachers need to resist the reference-book approach to literature and ask these and other questions about established practices:

- Could we not read aloud and savour this whole poem/chapter/script several times together before we dismantle it?
- Do I always need to ask students to complete a grid after a reading?
- Does every reading always have to end in a written PEE[1] response?
- Can I build in time to see where the discussion goes?
- Can I ask the students what they would *like* to read?
- Can we share our choices of texts and ask each other why we enjoy them?

How texts are shaped

Metaphor

One aspect of reading which can be neglected within a critical literacy approach to texts is consideration of how texts are shaped. All three chapters look for different ways to explore form to enable students to arrive at a greater depth of understanding about how texts work. Alexander and Misson and Morgan focus on the centrality of metaphor within literary texts (especially poetry texts). For poet Robert Frost, metaphor is what gives poetry its distinctive quality (Frost 1930). A metaphor demonstrates thought in action: the compressed use of language encapsulates an idea in a succinct and often memorable form. If young readers and writers are to genuinely engage with literary texts, they need to go far beyond trope spotting and participate in activities which develop their understanding about the deep structures within a writer's work more fully. Common methods of stimulating greater interaction, shared exploration and deeper textual comprehension of texts are DARTs (Directed Activities Related to Texts *pace* Lunzer and Gardner 1984). When used well, DARTs can be extremely motivating. Misson and Morgan suggest the idea of replacing metaphors with alternatives in order to arrive at an understanding of the impact of the original metaphors within a text. Two reconstructive DARTs strategies frequently used when exploring metaphor are *cloze*[2] and *sequencing*[3]. A carefully structured discussion, centred on reasons for students' own choices of metaphor in a cloze activity (or, alternatively, their ideas for an extended metaphor structure in a sequencing task) could lead to a much greater understanding of *how* and *why* a text has been shaped in a particular way. Ultimately the interaction and discussion which such activities stimulate should be of primary importance rather than the dogged pursuit of correct answers. But, how often are students genuinely given the chance to explore the structure of thought within texts? How often are DARTs used as they were originally intended? How often, perhaps because of time pressures, are they now used in a quick attempt to elicit student response about metaphor before the serious business of teacher-led note-making begins? In addition, how are students encouraged to think about writers' thought processes and think like real writers? Which methods might be the most effective and which simply take the reader further away from the text rather than deeper in to it? These seem to me to be key questions for us all.

Narrative

Fox provides a stimulating example of how students can develop their understanding of narrative structures through reading of comics and graphic novels. In interacting with these texts, young readers' understandings of such aspects as duration, proximity, narrative voice and repetition can be deepened. Fox's comments on the compression of thought structures within texts such as *Maus* (Spiegelman 1987 and 1992) and use of repeated frames seem to suggest strong links with poetry. There is an opportunity here to explore the potential crossover between these seemingly discrete genres.

Visual and verbal

The relationship between visual and verbal as exemplified in comics, graphic novels and picture books is an aspect of English which is given scant attention in mainstream curricula. Influential work by Graham (1990), Lewis (2001), Styles and Arizipe (2002), Johnston and Mangat (2003) has explored the importance of picture books in literacy learning and has investigated how such texts are constructed and how ethnic groups are represented within them. Styles and Arizipe (2002) have shown how young (primary-aged) readers can interact with images in ways which were not predicted by less observant adults. Nevertheless, assessed opportunities for discussion of the relationship between visual and verbal within secondary school curricula tend to concentrate on their relationship in the layout of print media texts such as advertisements or magazine covers. Why is this? What does this avoidance of hugely popular complex and demanding texts tell us about official notions of what constitutes literature? At a time in the UK when National Curriculum English is finally beginning to acknowledge multimodal texts within its programmes of study (QCA 2007), surely it is appropriate to recognize issues regarding visual grammar (Kress and van Leeuwen 1996) much more fully within text selection, classroom learning and, even, assessment?

Making, collaborating and listening

In the previous chapters, reading literature appears to be the foremost aspect of literary engagement. However, the authors also acknowledge, albeit more briefly, the making of texts as an important element of aesthetic response. I have argued elsewhere that if students are to fully engage with how texts work then they need to have opportunities to take creative risks with forms and experiment with the different composition processes involved in their production (Dymoke 2003). In terms of their textual construction, comics, graphic novels and many other text types are often produced through collaboration between writers and artists. For example, Burn and Buckingham's study of creative game authoring demonstrates how textual production can involve students in collaborative composing processes which combine aesthetic and cultural choices and enables the development of thinking skills at a conceptual level (Burn and Buckingham 2007).

Collaborations of all kinds, whether between artists working in different media or the more personal private collaboration between reader, text and writer, should involve participants in listening to the text. Literary texts require us to be attentive to language. For Alexander, listening is reading with the ear. Listening is arguably a neglected art, the poor cousin of speaking and often a very distant relative of reading and writing. Some might argue that listening is more at home with viewing. Perhaps it is only when engaging with visual texts that students are enabled to reflect fully on the impor-tance of sound in the construction of meaning. Web-based initiatives such as the UK's Poetry Archive, the New Zealand Electronic Poetry Centre and Poets Org in the USA[4] have made it much easier to bring writers' voices in to classrooms but we need to think further about the 'new effort of attention' (Lawrence 1929: 255) which literary texts demand of us and ask what role listening could play in pedagogical practices.

Engaging with culture and society

Texts can transform what readers know about the world. As Fox and Misson and Morgan have outlined, texts enable students to develop their understanding of values and critical engagement with social, political and/or personal issues. Developmental comics are drawn and written by collectives of cartoonists and writers all over the world. Fox cites examples of comics created for the new South African democracy by Esterhuysen's team. In recent times, Clark has collaborated with other artists and writers to produce a series of six UNICEF comics designed to raise awareness about aspects of the United Nations Convention on the Rights of the Child (Clark et al. 1998–2003). Circulated free, these comics have reached over 500,000 young readers. Graphic novels which first emerged in the mid-1980s, drew on the traditions of development comics and American DC comics. Comics and graphic novels present their stories in more accessible (but frequently no less subtle) ways than conventional literature and perhaps open themselves up more readily than other texts to a range of interpretations from young readers. Although comics feature in media studies teaching, their use in English classrooms is less common. Should, therefore, comics and graphic novels by Spiegelman, Satrapi and others remain on the fringes of literature when they could be used more widely in classrooms to enable young readers to reflect on social or political issues? Or does this fringe positioning actually make them attractive to readers and allow their writers freedom to subvert and question the status quo in ways that inclusion in the mainstream would diminish?

Conclusion

Alexander, Fox, Misson and Morgan have given us plenty of food for thought about literature. If textual encounters are to be meaningful, then journeys taken in the course of twenty-first-century literary study must be ones in which travellers draw out points of connection between texts and ask questions about what they read, view, listen to and create so they can develop new affective understandings of themselves and others. Furthermore, their readings of print, visual and multimodal texts should be enjoyable, active experiences which ensure that their relationships with literature are life-long rather than school-long. If literature is to do more than just survive in our curricula we must be prepared to resist the manual, take risks, reinvigorate the aesthetic and continue to ask challenging questions about classroom practices, enjoyment and the complex nature of texts.

Section 3

Language(s), multiple literacies and the question of 'English'

I have crossed an ocean
I have lost my tongue
From the root of the old one
A new one has sprung

Grace Nichols,
'Epilogue'

Certainly if writing is to have a future it must at least catch up with the past and learn to use techniques that have been used for some time past in painting, music and film.

William Burroughs,
'The Future of the Novel'

Chapter 10

The New Literacy Studies and Multimodality: implications for the subject and the language 'English'

Brian Street

We need to build 'learning environments devoted to problem identification and solution, argumentation, and public discourse opportunities' via 'the long history of the tight ties between deliberative discourse and visual and performative channels.'

(Shirley Brice Heath; 'Deliberative Discourse: The lost companion of democracy and literacy'; Keynote paper to International Standing Conference for the History of Education, Umea, Sweden, August 2006)

Shirley Heath suggests that we need not separate out the tradition of engaging with 'the word', for which English as a subject has generally been concerned, from the recognition of other channels of communication, such as the visual and performative, with which English as a subject now has to engage, more perhaps than before. What Kress and others currently refer to as 'Multimodality' and also what Horner and Lu, and also Brutt-Griffler and Collins, in chapters in this section of the book, refer to as language diversity and globalization, are all themes that English has now to come to terms with. In doing so, can it maintain its critical and reflexive concern for 'the word' or will it be simply absorbed into these other subject areas and lose its distinctiveness? I will argue in this chapter that for English to encompass the full range of communicative and linguistic practices is not the same as just 'adding some new technologies or websites' to the array – it is deepening and broadening what counts as 'English' while maintaining the critical and reflexive tradition to which the contributors to this volume refer and which Heath describes as 'deliberative discourse'. By this I take her to mean something akin to Tony Burgess' comments earlier in this volume regarding the 'intellectual project' of 'English'. The phrase by Shirley Heath fits with Burgess' approach by broadening the critical stance to include not only the written texts traditionally associated with English as a subject in the curriculum but also visual and other kinds of text, of the kind indicated by Kress in the term 'Multimodality'. In the present case 'deliberative discourse', then, involves critical and reflexive consideration of such texts in classroom contexts. I will offer some examples of what this means after firstly mapping out the conceptual terrain.

I shall briefly explore what literacy studies and Multimodality, as traditions that have recently come closer together, have to contribute to this agenda. I will argue that if we were to adopt an ideological model of literacy, as it has been expressed through New Literacy Studies in the past two decades, allied to an ideological model of Multimodality, as it is emerging in new approaches to the range of communicative modes, then we will be in a stronger position to answer the question 'Why English?' In doing so we will have resisted the technical (and mode) determinism and reductionism that worried the editors in Chapter 1 of this volume, as the decks fill up with new technologies, at the same time as extending the critical tradition of English beyond its sometimes narrow remit in selected genres of the word.

New Literacy Studies (NLS)

What has come to be termed New Literacy Studies refers to a body of work that for the last twenty years has approached the study of literacy not as an issue of measurement or of skills but as social practices that vary from one context to another (Barton and Hamilton 1998; Heath 1983; Gee 1990; Street 1995). In policy circles, on the other hand, dominant voices still tend to characterize local people as illiterate (currently media in the UK are full of such accounts, cf. Street 1998), while on the ground ethnographic and literacy-sensitive observation indicates a rich variety of practices (Barton and Hamilton 1998; Heath 1983). A similar process can be identified in educational contexts, where literacy is often seen as a simple set of technical skills to be conveyed, transposed, deposited in learners who will then have all of the advantages of the fully 'literate' person. From the perspective of New Literacy Studies, with its emphasis on social practices, such a position is narrow and potentially damaging to learners' opportunities. Research, then, has a task to do in challenging such dominant stereotypes and myopia and making visible the complexity of local, everyday, community literacy practices and how they might be built upon in educational contexts. In a recent volume entitled *Literacies across Educational Contexts* (Street 2005) a number of practitioners and researchers addressed this agenda by working across home/school boundaries in a variety of contexts in many different countries. In the Introduction to the above-mentioned volume I argued:

> a social practice approach to literacy in use pushes us towards recognizing the considerable overlap across boundaries as people, texts and practices track through different settings and scenes: children move between home and school; teachers and facilitators bring 'sedimented' features of their background and 'habitus' to bear on their educational practice; schools and other formal institutions of education bring in moving image media, perform-ances and cultural models from outside of the school walls; whilst projects involving literacy, rap music, oral and visual performance may bring in features of schooled education. (Street 2005: 1)

It is such complex teaching and learning practices that 'English' will need to address as it engages with the new worlds of Multimodality and of linguistic diversity. In order to do so, it will also need to engage with appropriate theoretical perspectives that have not, perhaps, been in the traditional canon of 'English' studies or of 'language arts'. I shall briefly indicate some of the concepts that have been developed in other fields and that might help 'English' teachers come to terms with the changes described here.

In trying to characterize new approaches to understanding and defining literacy, I have referred to a distinction between an autono-mous model and an ideological model of literacy (Street 1984). The autonomous model of literacy works from the assumption that literacy in itself, autonomously, will have effects on other social and cognitive practices. The autonomous model, I argue, disguises the cultural and ideological assumptions that underpin it and that can then be presented as though they are neutral and universal. Research in the social practice approach challenges this view and suggests that, in practice, dominant approaches based on the autonomous model are simply imposing Western (or urban) conceptions of literacy onto other cultures (Street 2001). The alternative, ideological model of literacy offers a more culturally sensitive view of literacy practices as they vary from one context to another. This model starts from different premises than the autonomous model. It posits instead that literacy is a social practice, not simply a technical and neutral skill, and that it is always embedded in socially constructed epistemological principles. The ways in which people address reading and writing are themselves rooted in conceptions of knowledge, identity and being. Literacy, in this sense, is always contested, both its meanings and its practices, hence particular versions of it are always ideological; they are always rooted in a particular world-view often accompanied by a desire, conscious or unconscious, for that view of literacy to dominate and to marginalize others (Gee 1990). The argument about social literacies (Street 1995) suggests that engaging with literacy is always a social act, even from the outset. The ways in which teachers or facilitators and their students interact is already a social practice that affects the nature of the literacy learned and the ideas about literacy held by the participants, especially new learners and their positions in relations of power. It is not valid to suggest that literacy can be given neutrally and then its social effects only experienced or added on afterwards.

Before addressing educational responses to these new perspectives I would like to signal one other theoretical framework that I argue can be helpful in considering the issues associated with literacy practices in the new conditions in which they operate in the contemporary. The perspective known as Multimodality is particularly associated with the work of Günter Kress in the UK and focuses on the mixed modes through which meaning is communicated, of the kind indicated in the above extract in the comment regarding educators engaging with 'moving image media, performances and cultural models from outside of the school walls; whilst projects involving literacy, rap music, oral and visual performance may bring in features of schooled education' (Street 2005: 1).

Multimodality

Kress (2003) argues that educational systems in particular and Western societies more broadly have overemphasized the significance of writing and speech as the central, salient modes of representation. It has been assumed that language is the primary site for meaning-making and therefore educational systems should concentrate on speech and writing in training new generations. The work of Kress and his colleagues (cf. Jewitt 2006; Kress and van Leeuwen 1996; Kress et al. 2005) has attempted to redress this emphasis in favour of a recognition of how other modes – visual, gestural, kinaesthetic, three-dimensional – play their role in key communicative practices. As he and I say in the

Foreword to a book significantly entitled, *Travel Notes from the New Literacy Studies: Case Studies of Practice* (Pahl and Rowsell 2006):

> So one major emphasis in work on Multimodality is to develop a 'language of description' for these modes that enables us to see their characteristic forms, their affordances and the distinctive ways in which they interact with each other. [Just as] those in the field of New Literacy Studies (NLS) have attempted to provide a language of description for viewing literacy as a social practice in its social environments [so, in Multimodality] there is an intent to change many emphases of the past – especially in educational contexts of the most varied kinds – from literacy as a static skill and to describe instead the multiple literacy practices as they vary across cultures and contexts. (Kress and Street 2006: viii)

Kress explicitly links his theoretical and research interest in the nature of signs and the shift towards more multimodal understandings, with broader concern for social change of the kind indicated by other authors in this volume as they refer to globalization (cf. Bruce Horner and Min-Zhan Lu (Chapter 11)). He argues that there is now a burning need to link 'issues in representation and communication with the profound changes in the social, cultural, economic and technological world, issues for which there are as yet no answers' (Kress and Street 2006: ix).

The kinds of questions this approach opens up for those interested in education and its role in what some refer to as 'new times' include: What is a mode, how do modes interact? How can we best describe the relationship between events and practices? and How do we avoid becoming the agents producing the new constraints of newly described and imposed grammars? These questions are different from those often being asked in schools, but they may be more relevant to the age we live in than the kinds of questions that arise from the autonomous model of literacy. On analogy with literacy studies, then, those working with different modes may need likewise to develop an ideological model of Multimodality. If we can begin to find answers that will serve us for educational purposes then, I argue, they may arise from having posed the questions in this way.

Educational responses using NLS and MM

I will provide some examples of curriculum work that has taken account of these theoretical shifts and ask whether it satisfies the concern of Shirley Heath (see opening of this chapter and Afterword) and of others for maintaining the traditional values of the 'English' curriculum. Cowan (2005), in a paper in *Literacies across Educational Contexts* (in Street 2005), shows how a pupil at a Hispanic Academic Program in California, who later became an artist, deployed 'a semiotic narrative that uses cultural icons to tell where he came from' but that Cowan as a teacher at first missed the significance of what the student was doing in a way that might look increasingly familiar in the 'English' classroom. Cowan writes:

> We had asked the HAP (Hispanic Academic Summer Program) students to submit two or three pieces of writing and any artwork that they wanted. Joaquin submitted just one short piece of writing but two pieces of artwork, including a full-page drawing that used distinctive iconography: an Aztec pyramid, an Aztec warrior, a mythological god in the figure of a feathered serpent, and a Mexican flag. This kind of artwork, most often created by Latino adolescents in the United States and identifiable by its use of distinctive iconography like Mesoamerican pyramids, figures from Aztec and Mayan mythology, lowrider cars (FN1), *cholos* and *cholas,* is commonly called 'lowrider art' because *Lowrider* magazine and *Lowrider Arte* magazine publish drawings sent in by readers.
>
> (For details of the images referred to and explanations of Lowrider Art see Cowan 2005: 145–69.)

Cowan explains that he asked Joaquin about how he chose what to submit. He replied:

> 'I really didn't know how to use certain words and use certain styles of writing to express everything. But I knew how to draw it and put it out there. ... It's the same sort of thing, like when they found the first drawings in the caves. It was just the bison and people hunting, they didn't have written language but right there they were saying, we were hunters, we survive, we did it. So just by looking at that you read off of it.'

Some years later Cowan (2005) comments on this student's response:

> When he was twelve, Joaquin felt better able to express his meanings visually than through his writing. He sees drawing as an ancient, efficient means of making meaning, that a viewer has only to see an image and 'read off of it' to apprehend its meaning.

I asked Joaquin what he would have said about this drawing in 1994.

Joaquin replied:

'Back then, I just would have been like, oh I like Aztecs so I put these here. And I like pyramids, they're here ... I would have said these were things that make up me. ... I could have probably said something like that's actually me [Aztec warrior], that's actually my house [pyramid] and that's what I believe [feathered serpent] and that's where I come from [flag of Mexico]. It was that simple ... I had an idea of what I wanted to do ... I was like, man I should draw an Aztec pyramid because that's what I like, Aztecs, you know, people, structures, something to do with not really religion but faith and stuff like that ... This is a very early example of it, but nowadays I can pretty much tell a story in one picture.'

Cowan comments with the benefit of hindsight:

Joaquin is now a skilled artist striving to become a film-maker, confident of his visual abilities and developing his writing abilities to translate his visions for films into screenplays. In the summer of 1994, Joaquin created a memorable text, a drawing that 'pretty much tell[s] a story in one picture,' a semiotic narrative that uses cultural icons to tell where he came from, and that was worth keeping. He 'put' his cultural heritage 'out there' so that any reader of the anthology could 'read off of it.' But I couldn't read or comprehend it until years later, because I saw it as an elaborate doodle, not as a visual text communicating a particular meaning. Unbeknown to me when I was teaching HAP students, Joaquin and his peers were communicating messages about their cultural heritage through visual texts that they created and that we published.

Joaqin's teachers had to learn how to 'read' this production since at first they saw it just as 'doodling': only later did they recognize that 'Joaquin and his peers were communicating messages about their cultural heritage through visual texts that they created and that we published'. In providing an ethnographic account of such productions, Cowan is obliged to situate them historically and culturally: 'In Latino visual discourse, drawings feature icons from Mexico, from indigenous Amerindian cultures, and from expressions of pachuco/a, cholo/a, and Chicano/a cultural identities that get invested with meanings that represent the experiences of Latino youth who create and circulate them' (Cowan 2005: 167). In this and the other cases now becoming familiar in the curriculum, the combination of mode awareness and learning is indeed suggestive for future curriculum and pedagogy.

Likewise, Pahl and Rowsell (2006), in the *Travel Notes* volume cited above, call upon a combination of New Literacy Studies and Multimodality to describe the potential for educators to build on children's home knowledge in school. They cite Heath's classic study of the literacy practices of two different communities in the Carolinas (Heath 1983) and Kenner's study of bilingual children that revealed many different sorts of texts being produced by children at home.

Pahl and Rowsell provide a vignette of a five-year-old Turkish boy, Fatih, as he crossed home/school sites:

> His mother, Elif, was Turkish, and had come to the UK from Turkey when she was a teenager to be married. Elif had another child, Hanif, 8. Fatih was having some difficulties with school and was only attending part-time. Elif, Fatih and Hanif lived in a public housing estate in a busy street in North London. Fatih liked to draw, model and make birds at home. He also made bird models at school, and was observed in the classroom pretending to be a bird. He used model materials to make birds, and frequently drew or made birds at home and in the family literacy class he attended. He described how he loved chickens, and when he visited his home village, he liked to chase the chickens. The meaning of the bird slowly became clear. Elif was stroking the head of her other son, Hanif, saying 'little bird'. 'Bird?' I said. 'Yes,' she said. 'I call them 'Bird', 'Kus' in Turkish,' she said. As the research study progressed, over a two-year period, I watched how Fatih extended his interest in birds across the two sites of home and school. (Pahl and Rowsell 2005: 60–1)

Pahl and Rowsell commented on this example in ways that link the various themes raised here, concerning the implications for educational practice of changes in home/school relations, in communicative practices and in linguistic diversity. They note, for instance, the ways in which Fatih kept his interest in birds across the two sites of home and school, and even developed the bird theme when at school, a theme evoked by other researchers such as Hull and Schultz (2002) and Street and Street (1991) who have commented on how it is important to look at the continuities between home and school, rather than the discontinuities. In this example, the crossover between home and school can be seen in the form of Fatih's bird-making practices. This episode shows how texts become artifacts that acquire meanings across sites. By understanding that process, the nature of the home–school boundary can also be rethought. While it is perceived by parents and teachers as a point for separation, the school–home border can be bridged. Fatih was able to duplicate text-making at home and at school successfully. Texts operate as external artefacts, but as 'tools of identity', they bridge gaps (Holland et al. 1998). Text-making was one constant Fatih had between home and school. In both spaces he had access to paper, pens and scissors. By making texts across sites, he is able to make the bird fly into the classroom. (Pahl and Rowsell 2005: 61)

The image of the bird/text flying into the classroom is an appropriate one with which to consider how everyday literacy practices and visual images can be seen to overlap, interweave and bridge the traditional home/school divide. It is also an appropriate place to begin to answer the question posed throughout this volume: How do we describe and teach the forms of knowledge, skills and values people need for 'new times' and what are the implications of this for the 'English' curriculum? I suggest, in commenting on this image in another context:

> If we can follow the flight of different literacies as they soar across different sites and are embedded in different practices, then, drawing upon the rich insights by researchers and practitioners signalled above, we might begin to see how we could learn and teach the new (and the old) literacies we will need for the developing century. (Street 2006: 33)

Pahl has also provided an account of the work of 'Creative Partnerships' (CP) in the UK in which she as a researcher collaborated with teachers and artists to facilitate and make explicit exactly the kind of multimodal engagements that Cowan and his colleagues at first missed but that the teacher she describes in UK did take into account as Fatih's bird flew into her classroom (cf. Street et al. forthcoming; Pahl 2007). Pahl locates the CP project in the UK Labour government's concern to respond to criticisms that its National Literacy Strategy marginalized 'creativity'. In 1999, the National Advisory Committee on Creative and Cultural Education published *All Our Futures: Creativity, Culture and Education*, which argued that a national strategy for creative and cultural education was essential to unlock the potential of every young person. Following this report, in 2000 the Qualifications and Curriculum Authority (QCA) commissioned a review of creativity in other countries, and developed a creativity framework, part of a three-year project designed to advise schools on how to develop pupils' creativity (QCA 2003). 'Creativity' writes Pahl 'began to be seen as both a way of boosting the UK's economic regeneration and a good way of delivering learning' (Pahl 2007).

The challenge for Pahl as a researcher was to see how such a focus on creativity within the classroom could significantly open up spaces where mainstream schooled literacy practices were in some way altered, developed or brought in new practices and identities, in just the way that the chapters in this section have been considering. She became involved in a research project commissioned by Creative Partnerships in the Yorkshire towns of Barnsley, Doncaster and Rotherham to study the impact of collaboration with a group of creative artists on teaching and learning in a Barnsley school. The research aimed to look at ways in which the impact of the artists in the school enabled different kinds of literacy and language practices to take place. Pahl was particularly interested in ways in which teachers 'took hold' of the practices initiated by creative artists. What did teachers do with the art practices when developing curricula for their students? How were art practices discursively constructed in the classroom? How did teachers, having worked with artists, then develop their own understandings of art practices, and integrate them into the curriculum, after the artists themselves had withdrawn, including curriculum to do with writing and reading of the kind traditionally associated with the subject English?

Here, I summarize a slice of data from the research project. The data included 18 teacher interviews, eight classroom observations, interviews with children from the class, and interviews with the creative artists involved. Pahl focused on the concept of the multimodal event, and the multimodal practice, as a lens from which to look at instances of practice. She also looked at ways in which teachers' talk instantiated ideologies connected to concepts of creativity. By focusing on practice, as a heuristic for creative activity, it was possible to pinpoint ways in which both teachers and pupils instantiated what had been creative practices in their work.

Pahl draws upon the work of Heath, cited at the beginning of this chapter, in making the link between literacy and creative arts, arguing that focusing on the visual enables children to push their creative and critical thinking and thereby develop their capacity for metaphorical language (Heath and Wolf 2004). In the study of the impact of a group of artists within a school, Pahl was interested in the relationship between literacy practices and events, and the way creative practices stretched these events and practices with the theoretical perspective that practices were observable and could be traced within texts (Street 2000; Pahl and Rowsell 2005). She traces examples by which an idea initiated by an artist was taken hold of by a teacher and then became part of classroom practice. She used interviews and discussions to try to trace back how the material practice was conceived, and probe the meanings such practices had for participants. This theoretical and methodological apparatus also then made understanding of the concept of creativity more focused, and specific.

The particular practice analysed here involved the procedure by which children were sent home with a disposable camera to capture their favourite toy or person and then these visual images were used to stimulate story-making, both oral and written. The final result was a magazine, *My Home, My School, My Barnsley*, which included many of the images, as well as writing by the children about their social worlds. One of the key aspects of the project was that it was not defined as being about literacy; although literacy practices were embedded within the activities, the final focus of the project was on a magazine, which was produced jointly by the teachers, the children, the parents and the artists involved in the project. Might this be the shape of the 'English' classroom in this new multimodal age?

Pahl interviewed one of the teachers in the project, Jenny, who described how she had developed an environment box project, as a result of the activity within the school. She wanted to develop teamwork with the children, and also to develop a learner-focused approach to teaching. She described the benefits of the project to Pahl in an interview:

it gives them all the skills of cooperating and working as a team and speaking to each other and communicating and listening, so I think that it's definitely benefited them, this notion of speaking with a partner and consulting with a partner ... (Interview, Jenny, 8 March 2006)

Pahl writes in conclusion that this kind of goal, that of 'collaboration and oral discursive skills', was identified as being one of the key outcomes of the Creative Partnerships intervention in a recent inspection report by Ofsted in 2006 (Pahl 2007).

One theme of direct interest to the present volume is that Pahl noted that while the teachers focused on multimodal events and practices in the first instance,

> their talk turned quickly to wider goals of collaboration and learning which they had identified as stemming from the art practices. They moved from practices to values and skills instantiated within the practices, wider goals which were for them critical to the development of the creative learning they wanted to achieve in the school. Creativity, in this instance, was harnessed to the greater good of curricular outcomes, including literacy. By analysing the spread of the practice, its changes and developments can be tracked. The teachers took hold of the project with wider aims for the children, and the art practices were a way to achieve wider goals of collaboration, independent learning and decision-making. In this way 'literacy' became embedded in broader learning issues than just encoding text or 'reading', for which the earlier National Literacy Strategy was criticized. (Pahl 2007)

In a recent paper on the project for the UK Literacy Association Journal *Literacy* (Pahl 2007) she sees the way teachers took hold of the project as a way of defining 'creativity'. In this sense creativity involves 'notions of possibility and pedagogy – posing questions, play, allowing time and space and standing back' and of 'agency – risk taking, being imaginative, innovative and self-determination' (p. 85). Again linking teacher practice with research traditions, in ways that the authors in this section have continually endeavoured to do, she sees such pedagogy and agency as drawing upon the notion of events and practices developed in New Literacy Studies.

Bronwen Low (2005), in the *Literacies across Educational Contexts* volume, brings many of these themes together in relation to a theoretical frame derived from cultural studies. She describes classrooms where pupils' own performance, in rap and other musical styles, combining verbal play with musical improvisation, provides 'a resource of creative, provocative literate practices' for all children, both those already successful in schooled literacy and those whose out of school literacies have not been recognized. The combination by Low of cultural studies approaches with those from New Literacy Studies signals another key dimension of this discussion, the crossing of disciplinary and field boundaries as well as those of content areas such as in and out of school and of print literacy and Multimodality.

Conclusion

How, then, are English subject teachers to respond to this new hybrid array of traditions and of communicative practices associated with them? In a previous era some could be seen to pull up the drawbridge and asserted a barrier between 'English' and such newcomers as 'cultural studies', although there is probably now more accommodation especially with the tradition represented by the Centre for Contemporary Cultural Studies in the UK. But in the present era that accommodation may need to be more immediate. As literacy takes on new dimensions and at the same time multimodal forms of communication begin to dominate the lives of children before they even reach the classroom; and as new theoretical approaches recognize both the variety of 'practices' associated with reading and writing, and the relationship of language to other 'modes', then it may be harder and less valid for English teachers to remain aloof. As Heath argues and as the ideological model of literacy indicates, the 'critical' dimension of English as a subject, highlighted in this volume by Burgess and other contributors, in fact offers a space in which English can indeed meet these new forms and theories. An English curriculum and pedagogy attuned to new literacies and Multimodality may indeed hold a key place as the curriculum adapts to the changes that authors in this volume have been tracking and this may provide a very contemporary answer to the old question 'Why English?'

Pahl and Rowsell (2006: 8) describe the importance of bringing together the two fields briefly summarized above:

> What the New Literacy Studies brings to multimodality is that it avoids the essentializing of visual and linguistic forms. It sees them as in-process. Texts are constantly moving and changing ... They cannot be seen as static forms to be considered in isolation, but they move in a web of significance. We need the multimodal in the New Literacy Studies in order to understand texts as material objects. Multimodality gives an analytic tool to understand artifacts such as children's drawings, and to recognize how literacy sits within a much wider communicational landscape.

The question we might pose here is can the 'English' curriculum handle such complex literacies and Multimodality and the language diversity indicated in such contexts? As Brutt-Griffler and Collins and Horner and Lu, in this section, make clear, children are indeed being socialized into a multilingual world, not the monolingual environment characteristic for many elites in an earlier period and at the same time, as Pahl and Rowsell and Kress make clear, that world also involves hybrid use of communicative modes, visual, three-dimensional, linguistic and non-linguistic. There is more entailed here, then, than 'shifting the deckchairs' – the new communicative environment both in a linguistic sense and in the sense of modalities will require of teachers and their pupils more critical reflexivity about these languages and modes themselves. If traditionally 'English' has tended to use its critical powers to reflect upon the 'word' in specific genres of text, it will now be required to move beyond those genres but it may, as Heath advocates, still claim to be offering a critical and reflexive stance less evident in other areas of the curriculum. This perhaps is what Heath meant by 'deliberative discourse' and what Burgess envisages as the wider 'intellectual project of English'.

My own prognosis for the future is that, in doing so, English as a subject will need to be able to handle the kinds of issues raised by the telling examples above – Joaquin's concern for cultural icons and identity; Fatih's interest in birds as, likewise, indexing cultural identities across time and space; Low's use of cultural studies to interpret and work with pupils' interest in rap and other musical styles; Pahl's accounts of children taking hold of artists' inputs and moving from photographs to storytelling and reading. That will involve more complex theoretical awareness, as in the New Literacy Studies and Multimodality traditions signalled here and in other traditions, such as Cowan's 'transculturation' and Low's cultural studies. Whether that hybrid continues to be termed 'English' is perhaps less important than that it maintains the tradition of critical reflexivity for which English at its best has been recognized.

Chapter 11

Resisting monolingualism in 'English': reading and writing the politics of language

Bruce Horner and Min-Zhan Lu

In this chapter, we inflect the question 'Why English' to signal the possibility of questioning the dominant monolingualism of a school curriculum focused on literacy – the teaching of reading and writing. This monolingualism is signalled both by use of the term 'English' to name that curricular area and by the pedagogical treatment of languages and language relations within (as well as outside) that area. Because this curriculum fails to recognize the actual heterogeneity of language practices within as well as outside the USA and UK and denies the heterogeneity of practices within English itself, it has been charged that it effectively constitutes a tacit policy of 'English Only': only reading and writing practices in English are recognized, and only a limited, 'educated' set of practices with English are accepted as legitimate (Horner and Trimbur 2002; Lu 2006). This tacit policy of 'English Only' is usually defended either in terms of ideologies linking reified notions of language and national identity, or in terms of the 'globalization' of a monolithic, uniform English as an international language of communication (see Harris et al. 2002: 38–9). For example, English is sometimes treated as a fixed entity fluency with which is deemed a valid mark of national identity – as in the dictum, 'Speak English, this is America'. Alternatively, the teaching of only standardized forms of English is advocated as providing students access to English as an International Language (EIL), the lingua franca of the globalized economy, despite other arguments regarding EIL as in fact variable (see Jenkins 2003; McKay 2003). In these formulations, students are figured either as in need of assimilation to 'American' or 'British' national culture, or as potential players in that global economy and its fast capitalist ways, or both.

English-only arguments arise in response to the contradictory pressures of a globalizing economy (see Cohen 2001, Chapter 6). They are a reaction to perceived threats to the national identity and economy posed by the twins of outsourcing and immigration, and they anticipate a linguistically homogeneous global future in which, instead of the presence of a plethora of shifting and interacting world Englishes as well as other languages, it is imagined that everyone will speak and write something termed 'standard English' to ensure efficiency in the worldwide conduct of economic transactions. English-only instruction is restricted to addressing only two questions: What counts as correct usage in the eyes of those in positions to withhold educational and job opportunities? How might I best learn to work English strictly according to such rulings? Both questions treat ambivalence towards US or UK standardized uses of English as an interference to personal and national development.

Against English-only instruction, we pose the question of how we might best go about problematizing English-only rulings on the uses and users of English. We pursue this from the perspective of our own immersion in the field of composition studies. While composition studies as a field roughly parallels and intersects in significant ways with the field of 'academic literacies' (cf. Lea and Street 1998), it is indigenous to the USA, tellingly associated with what is currently called 'English studies', and it has from its inception been linked with a tacit policy of English Only (Horner and Trimbur 2002). Drawing on the scholarship on world Englishes as well as on recent developments in composition studies, we argue for a pedagogy that both recognizes and makes use of the full linguistic range within which literacy practices take place: that is, both the variations within any particular language and, more controversially, cross-language relations and interactions that subject languages to writers' purposes and desires beyond, even other than, achieving certification of possessing either a fixed national (or other) identity or fluency in only the 'English' language skills valued in a globalizing 'free market'.

Linguists' scholarship on world Englishes and the variety of different sets of established practices with English effecting its pluralization into 'Englishes' has problematized treatment of any one set of conventions as posing a universal definition of 'English' (see Jenkins 2003; Kachru 1990; Widdowson 1994). At the very least, this scholarship has led to reformulating the question of who 'owns' English to, or at least adding to it the question of, *which* English is being considered for use, where. Further, work in the linguistics of contact has effectively redefined the norms of communicative situations to be not those of linguistic homogeneity but linguistic heterogeneity (Brutt-Griffler, this volume; Pratt 1987), and it has called into question standard reifications of language, approaching all languages and language varieties as inevitably in flux, their defining borders as at best porous and constructed (Gal and Irvine 1995; Pennycook

2003: 528, and Pennycook 2004). If recognition of the plurality of Englishes has sometimes accepted a problematic reification of particular varieties of English tied to particular nations (as in 'Australian English'), the linguistics of contact has challenged the stability of even those varieties, insisting on their subjection to change and intersection with other languages and language varieties (see Pennycook 2003: 516–22; Parakrama 1995), and highlighting the politics of standardizing such varieties and the privileging of the language practices of English Native Speakers (ENS) over those of speakers of English as a Second Language (ESL), the practices of both over those of speakers of English as a Foreign Language (EFL), and 'native' over 'indigenized' and creolized Englishes (see Nayar 1997; Pennycook 2003: 520; Singh 2000).

Just as these developments in linguistic scholarship may be understood at least in part as effects of some of the phenomena named 'globalization', so recent trends in composition scholarship on how to handle differences in the writing of first-year post-secondary students enrolled in required college composition courses may be understood as responses to the contradictory effects of globalization: specifically, the increasing commodification of higher education and the increasing heterogeneity of students' language practices. The increasing commodification of higher education is manifested by a redefinition of its instructional charge to be the production of commodified skills for exchange on the global marketplace (Slaughter and Rhoades 2004, Chapter 11). In this redefinition, the job of the college English teacher is to produce in students, or give them, the skill of writing standardized English to help them, and the nation, compete in the global market of skilled workers (Downing et al. 2002; Ohmann 1996). The increasing heterogeneity of students' language practices can be understood as a consequence of shifts in populations immigrating to the USA and UK, urbanization and increased competition for both 'native' and international students resulting from the privatization and commodification of higher education. If at times in the past colleges and universities could treat the heterogeneity of students' language practices with neglect, benign or malign, the increasing competition for students requires that schools at least recognize that heterogeneity, whatever the form that recognition takes. In the USA, typically, programmes charged with teaching required first-year composition courses (often including courses in ESL composition) are assigned the task of responding appropriately to this heterogeneity. Yet they find that they can no longer assume that students wish simply to acquire the skill of producing Edited American English (EAE) or Standard Written

English (SWE) to meet dominant demands. That is, in light of the fact that the majority of speakers of English now reside outside the USA and UK, college composition teachers can no longer assume a monopoly on what constitutes appropriate standards of English. Nor can they assume that all students from outside (or inside) the USA and UK have as their primary aim meeting the demands of dominant speakers of English (though many do).[1] 'New times' call for responses in composition alternative to English Only.

In the teaching of US first-year college composition courses, three common approaches to difference in student writing respond to this situation by reinforcing a tacit politics of English Only. Table 11.1 presents these – the 'eradicationist', 'second-language acquisition' and 'accommodationist' approaches – as well as a fourth, emerging approach we term 'multilingual'. (For other models categorizing approaches to difference in writing, see Bizzell 2000: 4–5; Canagarajah 2006b: 589–91; Lea and Street 1998; Smitherman 2000: 346–9. For a review of somewhat analogous responses in sociolinguistics, see Pennycook 2003: 515–22.) These approaches differ in the status assigned to perceived differences between students'

Approach	Status given difference	Explanation of difference	Pedagogy aims and means	Value assigned EAE
Eradicationist	• Error	• Ignorance • Indifference	• Eradicate error • Eradicate error maker	• Correct writing
Second-language	• Interlanguage	• Mediation of writing • Idiosyncratic rules • Proofreading habits	• Diagnose and treat idiosyncrasies • Teach editing	• Correct • 'Target' language
Accommodationist	• Discourse clash	• Ambivalence to dominant Discourse • Discourse interference	• Translation from unprivileged to privileged Discourse	• Dominant • 'Power' Discourse
Multilingual	• 'Code-meshing' • Discourse-blending	• Strategic design to create new discourses	• Development of language and languages	• False ideal • Contingent

Table 11.1

language practices and EAE/SWE; the corollary explanation offered for those differences; the aim and means of the writing pedagogy espoused; and the value assigned to EAE/SWE. Despite differences between the first three approaches, all three reinforce a tacit English-only policy insofar as they not only assume that all students will be writing in and only in English but also support beliefs underlying the politics of English Only: specifically, the beliefs treating language and identity as fixed, linked and uniform, and that treat fluency in standardized English, thus understood, as either a valid mark of national identity or a key that unlocks the doors to global opportunity.

As Table 11.1 indicates, the first three approaches support, in one way or the other, a fixed notion of English as EAE/SWE. To the extent that students' writing differs from what are imagined to be the fixed conventions of EAE/SWE, it is seen as somehow 'in error', though the approaches offer different valuations to and explanations of such error and, consequently, advocate different pedagogies in response. The eradicationist approach, which perpetuates a traditional practice uninformed by research on language and writing development, views any perceived difference from what is imagined to be EAE/SWE as error. It explains error as the result of students' ignorance and carelessness, and it adopts a pedagogy aimed at eradicating either these or the students themselves from the classroom (see Smitherman 2000: 346–7). Eradicationists hold EAE/SWE to represent 'correct' language. While this approach currently has few advocates within composition scholarship, we suspect that it remains dominant in the USA and elsewhere, hence our inclusion of it in this chapter (see Connors 1987; Finegan 1980; Rose 1983).

What we call the second-language acquisition (SLA) approach follows a model drawn from theories of second language acquisition associated with error analysis. This approach views most of students' deviations from conventions of EAE/SWE to be the result of their efforts to follow a set of idiosyncratic rules for spelling, punctuation, vocabulary, syntax and formatting – called an 'interlanguage' – that they have developed in an attempt to approximate the conventions of EAE/SWE (see Bartholomae 1980; Hull 1986; Kroll and Schafer 1978). Through close analysis of patterns in the students' writing – such as inserting a comma before every use of the word 'and' or inserting 'in' before every use of 'which' – and through interviews with and observations of the students and consideration of the context of their writing, instructors taking this approach work with students to develop an understanding of the students' idiosyncratic rules constituting the interlanguage and to develop proofreading skills to identify deviant marks in the students' writing that do not represent their efforts to follow such rules – such as missing words or letter reversals within words. Particular aspects of writing – such as the physical processes of transcription and proofreading – and the roles of genre, writer familiarity with topic, and context of composing are also understood to mediate the students' language. The aim of this pedagogy is to improve students' abilities as proofreaders and their fluency in transcribing and to guide them to replace their idiosyncratic rules for writing with standardized rules that, if followed, are assumed to lead students to the production of writing in conformity with the conventions of EAE/SWE, still understood primarily as simply 'correct' writing and the 'target' language.

The accommodationist approach attempts to accommodate both the legitimacy of students' home languages and what is deemed to be their pragmatic need to master EAE/SWE. Unlike the SLA approach, it elevates the status of students' writing from 'interlanguage' to 'home language' or 'home discourse'. To accommodationists, differences between students' writing and EAE/SWE represent differences in discourse(s), usually between home and school, tied to specific social identities, such as being African-American. Students are seen as either ambivalent towards adopting EAE/SWE and abandoning their home discourse, or their home discourse is thought to interfere with their adoption of EAE/SWE (Gee 1989). Writing itself is viewed as the repository of discourse rather than a mediating factor in its production: thus accommodationists ask whether or not students should be allowed or invited to write 'in' their home languages or should be required to write only 'in' EAE/SWE. Most commonly, accommodationists argue for a pedagogy in which students write 'in' their home discourses during the early drafting stages and then translate the writing into a final draft that follows conventions of EAE/SWE (see, for example, Bean et al. 2003; Elbow 1999). This is thought to free students to develop their ideas more easily, avoid ambivalence towards adopting an alien discourse, and even improve the likelihood of their ability to write fluent EAE/SWE (see Elbow 1999; Smitherman 2000: 164–91). Students should ultimately translate their writing into EAE, accommodationists argue, not because EAE/SWE is somehow inherently superior to other forms of writing as 'correct' but because it is seen as the 'language of power', and all students, it is argued, should be given access to that language (see Bean et al. 2003; Delpit 1988 and 1993; Elbow 1999).

Despite their significant differences, all three approaches are aligned with a monolingual 'English Only' policy in the limited degree to which they acknowledge heterogeneity in language practices and in the reifications of language and identity they support. First, all three share the aim of enabling students to produce writing recognized as conforming to EAE/SWE conventions. While the accommodationist response does grant legitimacy to different varieties of language as something other than mistakes to be eradicated or stages in writing development, it simply argues for substituting, rather than eliminating, those varieties with EAE/SWE – a strategy that reinforces, by understating, the role of power relations in determining what may or may not show 'competence' in using language 'appropriate' to a given situation, and according to what and whose interests a particular practice is deemed 'appropriate' (see Dubin 1989; Fairclough 1992; Leung 2005: 131–2; McKay 2003). The possibility of promoting interaction between varieties in ways that change them all is not considered.

More troubling, all three responses tend to assume the stability of particular language varieties. While the 'eradicationist' response may be understood as motivated partly by concern about the possible 'deterioration' of Standard English, it assumes at least as an ideal the fixed character of EAE/SWE conventions. Likewise, the SLA approach takes EAE/SWE as its 'target' language, and the accommodationist approach treats all language varieties – the student's 'home' discourse as well as 'school' discourse – as fixed, varieties into and out of which writers can 'translate' their ideas without altering what is imagined to be the discrete nature of each. Finally, all three pose a stable image of the student and his or her desires and purpose for writing. The only motivation these imagine for post-secondary (as well as primary and secondary) students within and outside the USA to learn EAE/SWE, and the only relevant concern they pose for teachers, is to improve students' individual career prospects in the capitalist global market. The eradicationist and SLA approaches assume students are fixed and uniform in their desire to master EAE/SWE conventions as a means first to join the academic community on their way to becoming effective players in the fast capitalist ways of the globalizing economy. The accommodationist approach likewise posits students fixed in their desire to acquire the language of power, if ambivalent towards what such acquisition might imply about their equally fixed identification with a 'home'. The possibility is not entertained that students might be pursuing contradictory desires and purposes including, say, the desire to change power relations, the 'language of power', or even the dominance of fast capitalist ways.[2]

What we have termed the multilingual approach is radically distinct from these other approaches in its assumptions about languages, identities, power relations and the relationships between all of these. Perhaps most obviously, multilingualism rather than monolingualism, and a global rather than national perspective, are taken as the norm. In Lu's argument on the work of composition (2004), for example, she draws her examples from the language practices of not only so-called 'mainstream' Anglo-American middle-class students but also a range of other writers, including Toni Morrison, Gloria Anzaldúa and the anonymous Chinese writer of the sign 'Collecting Money Toilet'. Canagarajah's examples of writers 'shuttling' between languages and 'code-meshing' include not only African-American language scholar Geneva Smitherman but also Sri Lankan scholar of Tamil and drama A. S. Canagarajah (2006a, 2006b). For multilingualism means acknowledging as normal and appropriate the full heterogeneity of language practices available to students and on which they might draw, including students' possible familiarity with not only particular prestigious and non-prestigious varieties of English common to the USA and UK but varieties of English common in other parts of the world, as well as varieties of other languages (see Brutt-Griffler, this volume; Harris et al. 2002).

A corollary to recognizing as normal students' familiarity with a range of language practices is the recognition of the complex and fluctuating character of identity in relationship to language. More specifically, there is increasing recognition of students (and others) whose language affiliations defy ordinary monolingual attributions – students, for example, who identify themselves 'as in between [linguistic] worlds', affiliating with a language that 'exists in their minds but not in their tongues', contradicting standard identifications of students as either ESL or NES, immigrant/international or 'native' (Chiang and Schmida 1999: 85, 87, 90; Harklau et al. 1999; see also Canagarajah 1999: 74–6 and studies cited there; Harris et al. 2002; Leung et al. 1997: 556–7 and *passim*; Milanés 1997; Pennycook 2003: 528 and *passim*; Valdés 1992). Identity itself is viewed as performed, constructed in language use rather than expressed or revealed through language, and hence fluctuating and contingent. Students' desires are seen as equally complex, fluctuating and contingent. These desires are understood to include not only a potential desire to become more 'marketable' by acquiring a commodified (and thereby marketable) skill in producing EAE/SWE but also the potential desire to intervene in that market by contesting power relations involved in the construction of EAE/SWE and its status as the 'power' language (Canagarajah 1999: 168–9, 175; Lu 1999).

The belief that students are in fact capable of intervening in such ways highlights the significant difference between the multilingual approach and the three monolingual approaches to difference. First it treats students as possessing agency as writers to draw from among a variety of languages. This shares with the SLA approach the ascription of intentionality to differences in students' writing. However, rather than treating those differences as evidence of an idiosyncratic 'interlanguage' to be abandoned as the writer comes to master conventions of the target EAE/SWE language, or as evidence of interference from the student's 'home discourse', as accommodationists might have it, the multilingual approach treats these differences 'as a strategic and creative choice by the author to attain his or her rhetorical objectives' (Canagarajah 2006b: 591), as 'matters of design' (Lu 2004: 26). In keeping with the findings of work in academic literacies, writing itself is understood as the site of a clash of shifting expectations and beliefs about writing (Ivaniĉ 1998; Lea 1994; Lea and Street 1998; Lillis 2001; Street 1995). Thus, any confusion readers experience with differences is treated 'as resulting from [*their*] lack of know-how or effort to make sense of how and why individual users of English might have come up with specific redesigning of standardized designs ... requiring the same close analysis' typically lavished on canonical texts (Lu 2004: 26–7, emphasis added; see also Matsuda 2002: 193). While this close analysis is similar to that encouraged in the SLA approach, it reads the differences such attention identifies not as evidence of the development of the *writer* towards fluency in a 'target' language but rather as evidence of the potential development of the *language* – not, of course, in the sense of development towards some imagined utopian form but in the sense of change through the active participation of users in response to, and in an attempt to shape, particular conditions of use.

This treatment of difference rejects monolingualist reifications of language as either adequate accounts of their status or as the goal to be pursued in teaching. Lu, for example, asks that we recognize the possibility of students attempting to use English in ways 'that *rework* or *blur* the borders protecting the division and hierarchy of competing languages, englishes, and discourses' (2004: 37; emphasis added; see also Gilyard 1997; Guerra 1997). This parts with the treatment of EAE/SWE by the other three approaches as a fixed 'target' language to be mastered because of its presumed status as either correct or the 'power' language. Instead, as is shown by research on 'academic literacies in UK universities, the constitution of such "target" language practices varies both within and across disciplines as well as over time' (Lea and Street 1998; see also Lees 1989; Williams 1981).

In rejecting such reifications, the multilingual approach challenges both the power of EAE/SWE and the sociopolitical relations maintaining its status as either correct or the 'power language'. If the accommodationist response seems to accept hierarchies among Englishes as, for all practical purposes, givens, and hence requires, however regrettably, teaching a commodified notion of standardized English as the 'power' language with global linguistic currency, the multilingual approach rejects the stability, legitimacy, as well the inherent value of the commodity of EAE/SWE itself (see Matsuda 2002: 192; Bizzell 2000: 6). Attempts to teach a fixed 'power language' are thus viewed as misleading, based on inaccurate accounts of both power and language. Consequently, instead of focusing on what distinguishes one discourse from another, the multilingual approach focuses on the process and power relations involved in marking any utterance as an instance of either mainstream or alternative discourse, academic or vernacular, standard or non-standard, acceptable or not, and it explores how these markings, and the power relations underpinning them, might be contested. The actual 'market' value of EAE/SWE is recognized as contingent on writers' possession of other forms of capital.[3] And while it is understood that writers desire to have their language 'accepted', it is also understood that what constitutes acceptable language is neither fixed nor determined but negotiated.

Thus, rather than attempting to 'give' students 'the language of power', as those adopting an accommodationist approach call for, and hence, presumably, 'access', those adopting the multilingual perspective aim at teaching students about the role of power relations in language and ways of negotiating those relations and thereby changing what constitutes 'powerful' language.[4] In recognizing students' agency as writers in changing language, their familiarity with a variety of practices with a variety of languages, and the contingent identity and status of these practices as 'languages', the multilingual approach rejects the politics of English Only to engage a progressive politics of language focused on valuing difference and fostering change. It shifts our focus from an emphasis on the power of standardized languages to an emphasis on the agency of language users, and it shifts our aim from accommodating current power relations to joining our students in changing those relations in the interests of all. 'English' is treated as a variable and varying set of language practices, making 'Why English?' a question for teachers to pursue with their students through collaborative investigations of the variety of ways 'English' as a school subject has been, is, and might be defined, practised, and valued.

From this perspective, the ideal user of English is not only acutely aware of the pressure to comply with 'English-only' rulings but also attentive to the capacities, rights and necessity of change in all living things: people, their life, society, culture, the world, and the language itself (Lu 2006: 608). As Widdowson reminds us, language is 'essentially protean in nature, adapting its shape to suit changing circumstances ... its vitality and its communicative and communal value [otherwise lost]' (1994: 384). From the perspective of the multilingual approach, English is kept 'alive' by many different ways of using it, active attempts informed by and informing specific, different and dynamic historical and social conditions cogent to the day-to-day existence of individual users. A 'proficient' user of what we term 'Living-English', then, is someone who, as Widdowson (1994) states, treats it 'as an adaptable resource for making meaning', someone who 'possess[es] it, mak[es] it [one's] own, bend[s] it to [one's] will, assert[s] [oneself] through it rather than simply submit[ting] to the dictates of its form' (p. 384; cf. Leung 2005: 134).

As Lu (2006) argues, in pursuing such an ideal, learners and teachers of English pursue four lines of inquiry consistently blocked by English-only projections but critical to the teaching and learning of 'Living-English'. *Line One*: Whereas English-only instruction promises to ensure access to wider communication and better educational and job opportunities, living-English users measure what English-only instruction claims it will do *for* them carefully against what such training has historically done *to* them and to peoples, cultures, societies and continents whose language practices do not match standardized English usages. Chinua Achebe, for example, notes that in countries like Nigeria, adopting English as a 'national' language as well as a 'world' language includes recognizing that it represents a 'package deal' that includes the 'atrocity of racial arrogance and prejudice which may yet set the world on fire' (Achebe 2000: 430).

Line Two: Living-English users also measure the promises made by English-only instruction against what standardized usages alone can *not* do: their inability to articulate meaningful connections across experiences, circumstances of life, social relations relevant to users' day-to-day existence that those very usages discredit. Achebe warns that while 'the English language will be able to carry the weight of [his] African experience ... it will have to be a new English, still in communion with its ancestral home but altered to suit its new African surroundings' (1975: 62; quoted in Widdowson 1994: 384). Living-English users keep deliberate track of the experiences and circumstances that specific standardized usages, unaltered, cannot bear the weight of. In so doing, they better understand these usages as voluntary or involuntary efforts to fix the contexts and purposes of using English, efforts not always in the interests of all its users and certainly not on all occasions. To Achebe, the 'value of English as a medium of international exchange' or a 'universal language' depends on its ability to 'carry the peculiar experience' of its diverse users rather than its ability to universalize the language practices of all its users according to the logic of global business. When employing a standardized usage on a particular occasion, living-English users, such as Achebe or ourselves, would refuse to treat the difficulty or ease they and others experience as a sign of their lack or possession of the 'language of power'. Instead, they approach their own and others' different experiences with the same usage from the perspectives of the particular but different social, historical conditions and relations each user is interested in articulating. Teaching the subject of English as a 'living' language would thus redirect the focus of 'close reading' practices towards questions of what is gained by writers' use or deviation from standard conventions in their texts (literary or otherwise), and how readers might account for their own responses of ease or unease in encountering such practices: what and who is subjected to what through what use of 'English' (see Lu 2006: 612–16).

Line Three: Living-English users understand their task to be one of creatively using, rather than imitating, reality to express their particular experiences. As Widdowson observes, 'English is called upon to carry the weight of all kinds of experience, much of it very remote indeed from its ancestral home.' Hence 'new Englishes' have been and continue to be created 'to carry the weight of different experience in different surroundings' (Widdowson 1994: 384–85). The difficulty here for learners is their need to *unlearn* the fear, encouraged by English-only instruction, that any attention to the need and right to transform standardized usages will interfere with rather than make it possible for them to 'learn' English (Lu 2006: 610).

Line Four: Living-English users develop strategies for tinkering with the very standardized usages English-only instruction encourages them to simply imitate as 'proper'. We see such a strategy operating in the twist Achebe gives to the standardized pronouncement, 'The price non-native English speakers (or non-standard English speakers) must be prepared to pay for better education and job opportunities is to learn the English of wider communication.' Achebe retains the familiar sentence pattern of 'the price such and such must be prepared to pay is to do such and such' but revises it to state, 'The price a world language must be prepared to pay is submission to many different kinds of use' (2000: 432). In so doing, he names standardized English rather than its so-called non-native, non-standard users as the party that must pay the price. Further, by replacing the word 'submission' for the verb 'to learn', Achebe emphasizes the subjugation that is the end objective of any instruction underwritten by the fantasy of a world using one standardized language. He highlights the agency of users by depicting them as submitting English to many, and many different, uses.[5]

In a critique of multilingual perspectives, Pennycook has argued that we need to 'disinvent current notions of language in order to be able to reinvent them for use in a new politics of language studies', warning that many arguments associated with multilingualism 'operate with a strategy [of] pluralization rather than a questioning of the inventions at the core of the whole discussion' and hence 'reproduce the same concept of language that underlies all mainstream linguistic thought' (Pennycook 2004: 7). In the remainder of this chapter, we examine how residual reifications of language and motive can resurface in pursuit of the 'multilingual' approach we have been advocating. We will also be suggesting particular pedagogical strategies that might follow from analysis of these dangers. First, as several proponents have cautioned, in advocating hybridization of discourse, there is the danger of hypostatizing and fetishizing hybridity as well as, again, EAE/SWE (Dobrin 2002: 46; Bizzell 2002: 3). For example, hybridity, or 'mixing' or 'meshing' of discourse, may come to be pursued for its own sake rather than as a strategy enacted in the context of particular needs, desires and conditions. This tends towards the aestheticization of discoursal forms aligned with the same formalist orientation that would reject particular forms as 'in error' (while lauding others as 'elegant' and 'correct'), failing to take into account the contextual and contingent understanding of what is 'hybrid' and not. The hypostatizing of hybrid discourse can also leave unchallenged the reified notions of academic and other mainstream discourse, or EAE/SWE that literacy researchers have shown to be inaccurate (Lea and Street 1998; Petraglia 1995). In seeking to insert or 'mesh' elements of other discourses into mainstream discourse, the always already 'mixed' and fluctuating character of the privileged, mainstream varieties goes unrecognized, contributing to support their ongoing privileged status as 'pure' and fixed entities.

We can see this problem arising in the question of what texts students are to be assigned to read. It is common among those adopting a multilingual approach to recommend assigning recognizably 'hybrid' texts (see, for example, Lisle and Mano 1997; Mejía

2004; Milanés 1997). The logic here is to resist the pressure of the canon and the homogeneity of its language and to thereby encourage students to experiment themselves with producing more linguistically heterogeneous writing, following the example of the assigned texts. Thus it is recommended that students read texts in which mixtures of the vernacular and mainstream are deployed (in work by such writers as Achebe, Anzaldúa, hooks, Hughes, Morrison, Smitherman) to contest enforced homogeneity of language practice, and that the composition course construct can be used as a 'safe house' where students can experiment, 'interrogate, negotiate, and appropriate new rhetorical and discursive forms without fear of institutional penalties' (Canagarajah 1997: 191; see also Elbow 1999; Gilyard and Richardson 2001; Guerra 1997; Lisle and Mano 1997; Lovejoy 2003; Lu 1999, 2004).

It is clear that the reading of texts by non-mainstream authors and discourses thereby marked *as* non-mainstream can expand students' sense of who can be a 'writer', the kind of writing that might be produced, the non-mainstream purposes that might be pursued, and the various linguistic means of pursuing them. At the same time, there is a danger that these examples may be idealized as models to be imitated rather than examined for how and why the writers might be reworking available forms in response to specific contingencies, as well as for prompting examination of the contingencies affecting how and why individual students or teachers as readers might respond to their reworkings of those forms. Further, there is a danger that attention to examples already 'marked' as alternative will leave unchallenged discourse that would not appear to be so marked, whether it is canonical literature or 'standard' texts from mainstream media or bureaucratic texts. Contrary to myth, such mainstream discourse is not 'pure' but 'hybrid' in the language resources deployed (see Travis 2005/6: 55), its invisibility an effect of canonization. However, simple etymological investigation can challenge the 'pure' monolingual character of such writing (leaving aside the frequent 'borrowings' common especially in academic texts). And comparison of examples of officially 'correct' writing from different historical periods and across genres and disciplines can challenge the static character of canonical standards. Thus, to avoid slipping back into reifications of EAE/SWE and other discourses, it seems appropriate to ask students to investigate not only the 'hybridity' of texts marked as deviant but also the hybridity of those that come with the imprimatur of being 'standard', how the hybridity of only certain texts and not others is commonly recognized, and, further, how the standards themselves have fluctuated over time and space, subject to reworking in response to the contingencies of specific material social circumstance.

To work against the abstraction of language practices, pursuit of such strategies will need to include, and indeed will need to define particular practices in terms of, material conditions, resources and practices with these. For example, students can be asked to examine how use of conventional and unconventional notations in transcribing language can change the discourse within which the writer is ostensibly writing (see Lo Bianco 2000: 101–3; Kandiah 1995: xxxiii; Parakrama 1995). Those attempting a multilingual approach can avoid the hypostatizing of 'hybrid' discourse by attending to the material micro-processes by which any discourse is (re)produced, including attention to writers' and readers' orientations to text that scholarship adopting the SLA approach has shown to produce what writers themselves would identify as 'error'. And it can attend to the particular mixing of not just 'discourse' but of media and genres, and the effects of these on the (re)production of writer identity and discourse in any utterance.

We have been arguing that currently dominant tacit 'English only' policies in the teaching of literacy practices represent responses to a globalizing economy and that alternatives to these policies can likewise be understood as responses to effects of that globalizing – not just changes in immigrant populations and student demographics, but also increasing recognition of the pluralization of English, its interactions with other languages, and a consequent de-linking of language with nationality. The common argument aligned with a tacit policy of 'English only' heralds EAE/SWE as the global lingua franca, the now common linguistic coin of international exchange. However, while what we have termed the multilingual approach rejects the reification of English and the occluding of Englishes that this yields, there is also a danger that multilingualism itself might be abstracted into a competing commodity for global exchange. We can see this risk in some of the appeals made on behalf of adopting a multilingual approach. For example, Canagarajah argues that 'in order to be functional postmodern global citizens' who can negotiate differences transnationally, 'even students from the dominant community (i.e., Anglo American) now need to be proficient in negotiating a repertoire of World Englishes' (2006a: 591). Bizzell makes a similar argument in observing that 'success in school' now requires that students learn discursive resources other than 'standard English and traditional academic discourse' (2000: 5–6). Likewise, Matsuda warns that because 'the audience of scholarly communication is no longer limited to native speakers of dominant varieties of English', 'everyone in the US academy needs to reassess their assumptions about discourse practices in the academy' (2002: 193–4).

While such claims about discourse practices are valid, there is a danger in yielding to the temptation to sell a commodification of such practices as, say, 'multilingual skills', especially in light of the pressures on schools brought on by the privatization of education (cf. Heller 2002, 2003). Aside from supporting that process of privatization, such a move would elide the concrete labour involved in those practices, claiming for situated practices the status of abstract skills that, as situated practices, they do not possess, and leaving unchallenged the conditions and ideologies of fast capitalism making demands for such commodities. In other words, like the false, if frequent, claims made that composition courses will somehow equip students with a general, all-purpose skill in producing EAE/SWE applicable to and exchangeable in all situations (see Petraglia 1995), claims that schools can equip students with the skills of multilingualism needed for their individual economic improvement and the improvement of national economies would cede the resistance to the same commodifications of language skills, and those ostensibly possessing them, that the move towards a multilingual approach was intended to counter. While we can defend the potential use value of students engaging ways of working within and across languages in their writing (and reading), practice in such engagements will not in itself yield improvements in students' individual economic plights (see Heller 2002: 59–61), and framing their work in such terms will likely reinforce the ideologies that would have us believe so and that would posit a restricted, uniform sense of students as having such pursuits as their only aim. We can better equip our students for working to improve both their economic situations and their world by acknowledging the range of forces that contribute to the value and effects of their efforts and engaging them in negotiating the power relations within and through which their writing is produced, in pursuit of a variety of aims.

By rejecting reified notions of language, identity and nationality, and the ideologies linking these to one another, a multilingual approach makes possible a return from abstract ideas of language to language as living 'constitutive activity', what Raymond Williams has called 'a persistent kind of creation and re-creation … a constant regenerative process' (1977: 31–2). By recognizing the plurality of Englishes and other languages, their fluctuating character and the agency of writers in reconstituting these, a multilingual approach both honours the work in which students already engage and encourages them to take up that work more consciously as active participants in the creation and re-creation of language and its constitution of their world. In so doing, we will redefine English from a 'subject' to a question: not the question of what English is, nor even the question of which English will be used, but what we and our students will make of it and use it for, and why.

Chapter 12

English as a multilingual subject: theoretical and research perspectives

Janina Brutt-Griffler and James Collins

The present chapter suggests that part of the task of rethinking English in schools involves *managing the linguistic diversity* that manifests itself as *English as a multilingual subject*. In non-English-speaking nations, managing linguistic diversity involves choices around the incorporation – or conscious exclusion – of English from the curricula of various schools, a range of policy options that Brutt-Griffler (2002, 2005) has shown to often revolve around questions of class affiliation. This discussion is, however, directed to the context of English-speaking nations, where the issue takes on the obverse content: what is to be done with the myriad languages pupils now bring with them into the classroom? What is their relation to English in English-dominant nations becoming increasingly multilingual and whose borders are becoming increasingly porous? We will suggest that one of the central justifications for English as a subject is the increasingly multilingual nature it has assumed in the classroom – that English education has become (or has the potential to become) the foundation of multilingual literacy.

When we step outside the charged ideological debates about the spread of English around the world and the threat to English in English-speaking nations, we face the fundamental recognition that for a large and constantly increasing number of students and teachers, what we have traditionally conceived as English education is a *multilingual subject* taking place in a bi- (or multi-)lingual classroom.

There are three important implications that follow from this conclusion.

1. It needs to be recognized that we must transcend the binary of English *versus* other languages in the classroom and recognize the growing reality of *English as bilingualism.*
2. Methods within English education must be tested on bilingual students – a large and growing proportion of all students taking English as a subject in the schools.

3. There is, therefore, a need for scholars in English education and those in second-language acquisition to collaborate.

This chapter discusses each of these propositions, adducing quantitative and ethnographic data from an ongoing research study.

1. The transnational bilingual classroom

We start with an illustration from what Brutt-Griffler (2006a) has called *the transnational bilingual classroom* – the increasingly multilingual educational experience concomitant with globalization. In a science class in an urban elementary school in southern Africa, a teacher conducts a lesson on the danger of lightning. The first thing the researcher observes is the multiplicity of languages that make up the medium of instruction. In multilingual classrooms such as those found in southern Africa, the presence of students from different language backgrounds, social classes and countries of origin, poses a tremendous challenge to language teachers. Most teachers find themselves unable to converse directly with all the students they are teaching because they may not necessarily share a common language with all of their students. In such a context, language teaching is mediated by other students. For example, the teacher may be proficient in Tswana and English, while there are students from Tswana, Zulu, Sotho and Afrikaans backgrounds. The teacher's instruction is initially targeted at students who understand Tswana and another African language. The student who understands Tswana and Sotho might then mediate between the Sotho and Zulu students and the Sotho/Zulu students may then mediate between them and Sotho and Afrikaans students, and then chained instruction continues until everyone is included through a strategy of mediated instruction. These are more and more the actual conditions of learners and teachers in the transnational bilingual classrooms.

This interaction represents some of the potential consequences. One student, in translating the English the teacher uses for another who does not understand it, mistranslates the object of the lesson, leading to the second student's conclusion that the teacher is telling them that 'lights can kill'.

1. T: Our lesson today is on lightning. What is our lesson on?
2. Ss: (in unison): Lightning
3. S1: Lightning – *zvinoreveyi?*
4.   (Lightning – what does it mean?)

5. S2: *Magetsi*
6. (Lights)
7. T: Lightning can kill
8. S2: *Magetsi anogonakuuraya*
9. (Lights can kill)

(Brutt-Griffler 2006a: 26)

At first glance, this classroom interaction appears to embody the worst fears of the educational dangers of what Phillipson (1992) has famously called English linguistic imperialism in contexts such as southern Africa. But that is not what actually makes this exchange so illustrative. The example illustrates, rather, the ease with which the effects of transnationalism can be misunderstood – or misrepresented, by being oversimplified. This classroom interaction illustrates the larger phenomenon of the effects of transnationalism, also known as globalization, on English education, suggesting the need to better understand the new linguistic diversity emerging in urban centres and its implications for English language and language arts curricula.

1.1 Language diversity revisited

A decade or a decade and a half ago it was almost taken for granted in the field of applied linguistics that transnationalism, 'globalization', was producing linguistic homogeneity. There were a large number of books like Nettle and Romaine's *Vanishing Voices* that predicted that 'smaller languages are dying out due to the spread of a few world languages such as English, French, Chinese, and so on'. They cited the spread of English as 'leading to the top-down displacement of numerous other tongues' (2000: 144). The danger was from a common medium; the solution lay in mother-tongue education (Skutnabb-Kangas 2000).

With their attention diverted by what turned out to be a phantom threat – a predatory English language – applied linguists were slow to recognize a fundamental reality: transnationalism has produced linguistic diversity on a scale that no one could have imagined. Brutt-Griffler (2006a) argues that the process of linguistic globalization so often blamed for threatening language diversity has actually proved, on the contrary, productive of it. She writes:

The notion that 'linguistic diversity' is *decreasing* due to globalization ... rel[ies] on a very particular set of assumptions – that language diversity consists of many more or less uniform language-using communities each speaking its own language –

hence, on the number of discrete languages that can be counted and recorded.... Two other, perhaps equally significant, measures of linguistic diversity are *increasing*: the numbers of multilingual speakers – or the range of linguistic proficiencies of individual speakers – in many parts of the world and the number of languages represented in most of the large cities of the world. (p. 8)

That these languages are present in ever growing numbers is apparent throughout the English-speaking world. In the USA, the proportion of 5 to 17 year olds who use a language other than English at home ranges from 35 per cent (Minneapolis) to 72 per cent (Miami). While Miami represents a predominantly Spanish-speaking context, the variety of the languages in Minneapolis is both remarkable and more typical of the diversity found outside Florida and Texas: about one-third Spanish, another one-third Hmong, with the remaining one-third made up of unspecified African languages (15 per cent), Vietnamese (3.6 per cent), Laotian (2.5 per cent), Arabic (2 per cent) and 26 other languages and undifferentiated language groups (Modern Language Association 2006). For Great Britain, a recent study reports that 30 per cent of London schoolchildren use a language other than English at home, with a total of more than 300 languages represented (Baker and Eversley 2000). And the 2001 Canadian Census found that the mother tongues of 39.9 per cent of the population of Toronto were languages other than English and French, with the corresponding number for Vancouver coming in at 37.6 per cent. The census returned more than 100 different mother tongues in use nationwide (US Census Bureau 2006).

   As Brutt-Griffler notes, the results of these processes are eroding the imaginary normative notion of use of national and ethnic languages by largely monolingual speech communities, 'intact communities of practice inhabiting compact geographical spaces' (2006a: 8). Demographic shifts and technological advances in telecommunications, as Graddol (2004) has argued, are combining to produce profound effects on language use that may redefine how we think of languages (as local, national, regional, or world) as early as the middle of the twenty-first century. This was in evidence in a recent *New York Times* article, for example, that called attention to how taxi drivers carry on international cell phone conversations in a wealth of languages (Elliott 2003) – languages that can thus no longer be said to be local or regional. If international languages are constructed so as to include linking diasporas to mother countries, most of the world's larger languages could thus already be said to be international in an age of increasing transnational migrations.

This reconfiguration of linguistic space, Brutt-Griffler (2006b) shows, has galvanized would-be guardians of the old order into political and scholarly action. On one side, critics of what they term the *linguistic imperialism* of English decry the spread of that language as a contributor to, in the oft-cited words of Nettle and Romaine, 'the extinction of languages … as part of the larger picture of worldwide near total ecosystem collapse' (2000: 17). But it is equally significant that another set of language ideologues are raising the alarm about an altogether different spectre – that of the disappearance of English from large sections of the major English-speaking nations at the expense of another set of encroaching languages. What these activists have in common is the concern that languages are migrating from where they allegedly belong to foreign territory where they do not, threatening a natural order of *one people one language* that is variously conceived as social (ethnic/national) or even, in a few cases, evolutionary/ecological in a biological sense.

For some time, there have been conflicting imperatives within the field of applied linguistics. Ever since Robert Phillipson wrote his *Linguistic Imperialism* in the early 1990s and the language endangerment movement took hold soon thereafter, there has been much attention to the plight of languages and language groups. Their goals of preserving languages and safeguarding the rights of the speakers of minority languages are certainly laudable and important. But there was also a certain tendency within some of the work to dismiss the goal of maximizing opportunities for the L2 learner as secondary. At its most extreme, it manifested a tendency to replace the speaker as the unit of applied linguistic analysis with the language – so that protecting languages was seen as something very different from promoting the goals of speakers. Indeed, the very goals of speakers (if, for instance, it involved learning English with native-like proficiency) were viewed by some as a residue of cultural and linguistic imperialism and thereby something to be countered via consciousness-raising about the culturally imperialist agenda motivating English spread.

In contrast, Brutt-Griffler (2002, 2005) has issued a strong challenge to the reductionist notion that English spread is a simple and straightforward function of cultural imperialism. She has insisted on an analytically more rigorous and nuanced approach that investigates, alongside of ethnicity, such social variables as class and gender. She underscores the reasons English learners themselves gave for seeking English proficiency, and put forward an alternative account of English spread that emphasized their agency. She has engaged in empirical analyses that, joined with the work of linguists like Salikoko Mufwene and Alamin Mazrui, debunked the myth that English spread was endangering languages in Africa (Mufwene 2004; Muzrui 2004).

Such an approach also means taking seriously Guadalupe Valdes's (2004) emphasis on the importance of academic literacy for L2 learners faced with a world that requires it for access to higher education. It means focusing attention on the high-stakes tests they take in school. As Carrasquillo et al. (2004) note, 'The immediate academic achievement and future (employment) success of these students depends significantly on how successfully they acquire spoken and written English proficiency'(p. 3). Alongside the rightful concern directed by language professionals to the plight of the world's thousands of endangered languages, we must muster equal attention and help for the world's tens of millions of L2 learners, like those in the USA, as Carrasquillo et al. remind us, for whom 'the most crucial challenge is the expectation of local, state, and national educational agencies that they score at grade level on state and national standardized tests, especially in the area of English language arts and mathematics' (2004: 3, see also Burgess, this volume). We must advocate for them as effectively as the language endangerment movement has raised consciousness on the disappearance of languages, and find ways to serve their needs, especially the 66 per cent enrolled in US elementary schools.

This emphasis foregrounds the aspirations and needs and educational goals of L2 learners, rather than dismissing them as a function of someone else's ideological hegemony. The implications for education of linguistic diversity in the era of globalization are profound. Fitzgerald (2006) argues cogently, 'When children are suddenly immersed in new language cultures and classrooms in which their native languages are not supported, second language writing ability looms large in students' academic development. In such situations, second-language composing is critical to educational advancement' (pp. 351–2).

It is not just in southern Africa that students in the transnational bilingual classroom often underperform in comparison to their monolingual peers, sometimes lagging quite significantly (though experience is very uneven in this respect across different groups). Snow estimates that there are 5 million K-12 students in the USA with limited English proficiency, who 'arrive with high home-language literacy skills and no English, or with a history of failed and interrupted schooling and no English' (quoted in Guensburg 2006: 36).

As Fitzgerald emphasizes, multilingual writing must be given 'priority attention'. In her state-of-the-art evaluation of multilingual writing, Fitzgerald points out that while we have a rich and an 'advanced state of research and theory on native-language composing of school-age students, it is surprising to find the paucity of research on multilingual composing at school-age levels' (2006: 350). As the school system places demands on their literacy skills, so too must applied linguists shift some of our focus from the more heavily studied and better understood realms of second-language acquisition to areas like second-language writing, which, as Fitzgerald notes, has been 'rooted in the study of college and adult students', and for which we still lack a comprehensive theory (p. 350).

2. Educational challenges: the English-language classroom and the bilingual writer

The last two of the implications of *English as a multilingual subject* with which this chapter begins are responsible for the innovative collaboration of the co-authors of this chapter, Brutt-Griffler, a specialist in second-language education, and Collins, an expert in English education, discussed in the next section.

2.1. *Putting English education to the test for bilingual students: Writing Intensive Reading Comprehension Study*

Over the last three years, James Collins has directed a major experimental study called Writing Intensive Reading Comprehension (WIRC)[1] sponsored by the US Department of Education. The study's working hypothesis has been that bringing reading and writing together, especially by helping students write to generate, organize and express ideas about reading while they are reading and discussing literary selections, will improve reading comprehension and writing performance among low-performing urban school students. Findings from this large experimental evaluation generally support the claim that school-based writing-about-reading interventions contribute to academic achievement. At the same time, the results challenge several related aspects of writing-to-learn cognitive theory: that writing is more suitable as a mode of learning for higher ability students (the WIRC students are generally poor readers and writers and are all in low-performing schools); that self-regulation is a key component of writing-to-learn (WIRC relies on assisted writing in the form of thinksheets and classroom discourse); and that writing-to-learn is best used to learn course content (WIRC focuses instead on grappling with content to learn reading and writing skills and strategies). In contrast to a 'read first, write later' approach currently popular in

US schools, WIRC's intervention and learning method are designed to break down large reading and writing tasks into manageable components, and subsequently guide the students to transform their knowledge about the reading in the context of writing. WIRC's approach is grounded in a *sociocognitive* theory of writing (Collins 1998, and Collins et al. 2006; Wertsch 1991; Vygotsky 1978, 1986) and a cognitive/social practice view of print literacy development (Purcell-Gates et al. 2004; Hull and Schultz 2002).

Low-performing urban school students include both native English-speaking and bilingual students. Outside of English-speaking countries English has long been a multilingual subject. But now English is also becoming a multilingual subject for a large proportion of learners in English-speaking countries. Nowhere is this more true – and nowhere are the stakes for learners higher – than among the at-risk population of urban bilingual elementary school aged learners. This has come through in the effort to develop effective instructional interventions for reading and writing among low-performing urban students.

A key component of this study is the opportunity to compare the impact of this method on learning among first- and second-language students. Students in fourth and fifth grade in seven schools in the Buffalo public schools which were identified as failing to meet performance standards as specified by the State of New York have participated in the study. In 2004–5, the second year of the study, the total number of students was 866 students comprising 44 class-rooms. Of the total number of students, 17.4 per cent were English Language Learners (ELLs), whose first language is predominantly Spanish. The L1 Spanish students are enrolled either in English mainstream classes or bilingual classes; in the latter case they receive some instruction in Spanish. WIRC's intervention is accessible to them in either English or in Spanish, with the exact content being translated by the WIRC team. The study uses statistical methods to compare experimental and control groups for reading and writing achievement gains measured by standardized assessments in September and May, that is, before and after the experimental inter-vention which assists students writing about 30 literary selections during the school year. In addition, the research team has systemat-ically been collecting qualitative data via classroom observations and videotaping classroom instruction.

This chapter is not concerned with giving a full statistical account of the results of the study, but rather to present some quantitative data and findings from our classroom ethnography that are suggestive of the implications of English as a *multilingual subject*. Two classroom excerpts demonstrate the transcendence of the binary of English *versus* other languages in the language arts classroom, underlining the growing reality of *English as a multilingual subject.*

Classroom discourse: excerpt 1[1]
At the beginning of a 30-minute lesson in English language arts, a fifth-grade teacher is filling in a graphic organizer that she has drawn on the blackboard to help students organize their knowledge of a literary text entitled 'Summer of Fire', a literary selection in the Harcourt *Trophies* series. The teacher interacts with the students and includes their input as she fills in the Venn diagram on the blackboard. Students have the same graphic organizer in front of them and write information in it. However, not all concepts that the students encountered in the readings are familiar to them. One of them is the word 'vital'.

1. T: ... so dangerous but vital job, okay, vital from vita, what's vita in Spanish?
2. S1: I don't know
3. T: Vida? Que es vida?
4. S1: ((xxx))
5. S1: Oh life
6. T: Que es vida?
    ]
7. S1:   Life
8. T: No la vida loca, but vida
    ]
9. S1:   Life
10. T: Right. So vital, if it comes from vida, means something that is what?
11. S1: Necessary?
12. T: Necessary, yes, something like as necessary as your life. So vital that's what it means. It's important, yes.

(Fifth Grade Classroom Ethnography, February 2007)

Meanwhile in another classroom in the same school, a bilingual fifth-grade teacher works with students on a language arts curriculum lesson. While Spanish dominates as the language of instruction and of learning among the students, English is also used by the bilingual teacher and students, underscoring the bi/multilingual context that English as a subject is increasingly assuming.

Classroom discourse: excerpt 2
Students are working on a story entitled 'Everglades', another literary selection in the Harcourt *Trophies* series. The teacher is walking around the classroom helping students answer the questions they are working on. Like the previous except, this one has been taken from a videotaping session as part of a classroom ethnography.

1. T: Esos son ejemplos de… pero ¿dónde esta la palabra multitudes? **Did you find it again?** Yeah, pero otra vez está ahí. Creo que sí, no está en amarillo, pero creo que si hay más ejemplos. **Elyanis, come on honey, come on.**

2. S1: (Student shows the teacher the evidence that she has found in the book)

3. T: **So, where did you find it?** ¿Qué dice?

4. S1: Hay muchas cantidades de islas, una multitud de ellas en el Caribe…
    (Teacher is looking at the student's page as student is reading the answer)

5. T: **OK, so, let's stop right there.** Hm, so, ¿cómo es que en está oración que está aquí en el principio (pointing at the beginning of the question), cómo es que esta oración que me estas leyendo va con la palabra multitudes?

6. S1: hmm…

7. T: **What do you happen to know multitude means?**

8. S1: ((xxx))

9. T: ¿Aquí que dice?

10. S1: Una multitud de panteras, venados y mapaches, y otros animales vinieron al río.

11. T: So, entonces ¿qué significa esta palabra multitudes?

12. S1: Multitudes son los animales que vinieron al río y…

13. T: **Let's look at the sentence again, I'll read it to you OK?**
    (Teacher is distracted by another student that comes to get her approval of the answer he has written down on his thinksheet, causing the session with the other student to be interrupted).

(Fifth Grade Classroom Ethnography, February 2007)

These two classroom excerpts help us understand the concept of English as a multilingual subject. They demonstrate the transcendence of the binary of English *versus* other languages in the language arts classroom and underscore the growing reality of English as bilingualism. Secondly, they underscore the changing nature of English education. We have argued that English education has become (or has the potential to become) the foundation of multilingual literacy. In the following section, we address the implications arising out of English as a multilingual subject for carrying out research.

2.2 Putting English education to the test for bilingual students: WIRC's impact

The empirical study of Writing Intensive Reading Comprehension has been concerned to test its effectiveness directly on English language learners. Data from Year 2 in WIRC's study show higher gains among ELLs on the post-test, as compared to students who were never ELLs. These preliminary findings might be considered in light of bilinguals having greater cognitive advantages. Researchers have compared monolinguals and balanced bilinguals on a variety of measures of divergent thinking, which includes a person's fluency, flexibility, elaboration and originality of thinking. The findings point to the higher scores of bilinguals on these measures. Arnberg (1981) suggests that the further the child moves towards balanced bilingualism, the higher the cognitive gains they achieve. Cummins (1977) introduced the notion of a threshold, a developmental stage in bilingual development that might constrain its cognitive gains:

> There may be a threshold level of linguistic competence which a bilingual child must attain both in order to avoid cognitive deficits and allow the potentially beneficial aspects of becoming bilingual to influence his cognitive growth. (In Baker 2003: 146)

Evidence suggests that bilinguals score higher on tests on metalinguistic awareness, i.e., the ability to 'reflect upon and manipulate the structural features' of language and treat it as an 'object of thought' (Tunmer and Herriman 1984: 12). At the same time, Galambos and Hakuta (1988) point out that metalinguistic awareness is tied to the degree of the child's knowledge of the two languages. Carlisle et al. (1999) claim that the degree of bilingualism either constrains or enhances metalinguistic performance. The students who were classified as 'formerly ELLs' no longer seemed to be constrained by the linguistic competence and potentially they might have built more successfully on their bilingual knowledge.

Findings from Year 2 of the WIRC study are consistent with findings from the other studies just reviewed. As we said earlier, the WIRC research is testing the hypothesis that adding assisted writing to classroom activities involving the reading and discussing of literary selections will improve reading comprehension and writing performance in fourth and fifth grade classrooms to a greater degree than in similar classrooms where students only read and discuss the same literature. The assisted writing in the WIRC experimental classrooms involved thinksheets designed to help students generate, organize and write about ideas from their reading. These thinksheets were completed with teacher and peer assistance for all literary selections. The assumption throughout the WIRC study is that writing is an activity that shapes cognition during the act of reading. When students simultaneously write and read, the physical and cognitive actions of writing upon students' thinking while reading were expected to enhance reading comprehension.

The Year 2 findings generally support the WIRC hypothesis. Students in both fourth and fifth grade classrooms benefited from the WIRC intervention, outpacing their counterparts in the control group. Results were consistently strong, furthermore, for English language learners. ELLs in Grade 4 in the WIRC study reached higher gain scores (differences between pre-test and post-test achievement levels) for reading comprehension on a short constructed reading comprehension response, and higher gains on essay writing than did their counterparts in the control classrooms. The total gain score on all writing tasks combined was also higher for the experimental group as opposed to the control group.

In Grade 5, we observe a similar trend. ELLs reached higher total gain scores in comparison to students who were never ELLs and higher gain scores on the remaining four other measures of reading and writing, the same measures just reported for Grade 4. Experimental ELLs groups in Grade 5 performed better in comparison to ELLs in control groups on all but two variables. It is important to point out that we observed the highest gains among students who were classified as 'formerly ELLs' and now are placed in regular mainstream English classes.

The general conclusions we draw from this analysis of the WIRC findings are these:

- Writing does indeed help to shape cognition during the act of reading.
- Integrated, assisted writing during the study of literary selections can positively influence the development of reading and writing abilities.
- These effects are even more pronounced for English language learners.

3. WIRC's impact: bilingual students' voice

To further investigate the impact of the study's curriculum, we held student group interviews as part of our classroom ethnography. Data reveal that ELLs students in the study are becoming metacognitive about the stages of the writing process. They demonstrate a growing awareness of writing as 'process'. In the interview in lines 1–14, they use the metaphor of a puzzle to articulate their understanding how the earlier steps in the writing process, reflected in the scaffolding of the study's intervention, help them arrive at the finished essay. Thus significantly they do not see the different activities that the WIRC curriculum asks them to engage in as isolated from one another. One of the goals of this methodology is to push students to *transform* the newly acquired knowledge rather than simply retell the facts (Collins et al. 2006).

Classroom ethnography: student interview 2
1. I: Okay. Did doing the thinksheet help you with the story?
2. S: Yeah.
3. I: How did it help you?
4. S1: If you read the story it would give you like *questio:ns* ((xxx))
5. I: So answering the questions helped?
6. S1: ((xxx))
7. S1: It's fun too because, um, like if you write down the different ones then when you start writing you gotta like put the pieces together.
8. I: You have to put the pieces together?
9. S1: Like a puzzle.
10. I: What does that mean? Can you show me on your thinksheet? What you mean by that?
11. S1: Like I have different stuff written on here, (≤ .2) these papers [the student shows the thinksheet] so then when its time to do this I try to like grab some information from here and then
12. S1: Put it all together
13. S1: Put them all *together*, make it make sense ((xxx))

14. S1: It's like this. It's like this, *puzzle*, but it's all *together*, and we build a *new* puzzle and then we try to build it.

(Fifth Grade Student Group Interview, January 2007)

Another group of students in their group interview articulates that when they have to write an essay, the graphic organizer, which is an important component of the intervention, acts as a plan for them.

Classroom ethnography: student interview 2
1. I: Mhmm. When you write the paper? So which part of the thinksheet helps you *write* the *most*? When you get to, when you have to write the essay which part of the thinksheet do you use?
2. S1: ((xxx)) [student indicates the middle part]
3. I: Which one? The middle part? Can you show me the middle part?
    [Interviewer is interrupted. Tells someone to watch out for the camera]
4. I: The graphic organizer? Is that what you're showing me?
5. S1: This one [indicating the graphic organizer]
6. I: Okay. How does it help you *write*?
7. S: (3.0)
8. I: How does it help you write the essay? ((xxx))
9. S1: Because the graphic organizer you like write *stuff*, informa:tion. And when you're gonna write the story you get some *informa:tion*, you get the stuff that you write in organizer ((xxx))
10. I: So it, it helps you, how?
11. S1: Like, you don't *forget* stuff. Like you got it all right all ((xxx)).
12. I: I see. So, when you sit down to write your essay, does your, your graphic organizer already has, it's your plan then?
13. S1: Yeah
14. I: Okay
15. S1: It like your plan what you're gonna write.

(Fifth Grade Student Group Interview, January 2007)

The data suggest that that ELLs respond positively to 'structured reading-writing' instruction. The findings seem to support Gomez et al. (1996), who found that fifth-grade native Spanish speakers showed significant growth in writing for analytic and holistic overall quality scores in the context of structured writing instruction (in Fitzgerald 2006).

Conclusion

The educational implications of the growing linguistic diversity found in the urban (and increasingly other) schools in English-speaking nations – and the world – are profound. These realities pose a formidable challenge to the pedagogical goals of simultaneously facilitating maintenance of heritage languages and developing English literacy(ies). In the context of the type of sociocognitive approach adopted by WIRC, bilingualism need not be a disadvantage to the growing number of bilingual students entering the classrooms of English-speaking nations relative to their monolingual peer groups in urban schools. Such a finding can help take us forward in generation of knowledge on effective educational practice to promote advanced levels of language and literacy among language learners. That step constitutes a critical component of the larger task of investigating how the second-language learner and the language teacher are influenced by transnational processes, and how these processes shape the kinds of bilingualism and language proficiencies we observe in the world today.

The findings are potentially relevant to monolingual English speakers as well. In a world increasingly shaped by the need for bilingualism, inducing increasingly strident calls for more effective bilingual education in both the USA and UK (cf. Brutt-Griffler 2007), the English/language arts classroom presents a vastly under-utilized educational space for encouraging greater societal bilingualism. The current focus on 'mainstreaming' many ELLs, therefore, provides an interesting opportunity to test whether *English as a multilingual subject* might provide a useful avenue towards that goal for at least the portion of English monolingual students who end up in mixed native speaker/ELL classes. In such settings, the considerable resources that the bilingual students bring to the classroom could be used to partially offset the 'disadvantages' of monolingualism, just as the native proficiency of the non-ELLs is used to offset the 'disadvantage' of non-mother tongue English proficiency. Perhaps then it will emerge that the development of English as a multilingual subject represents a stage in the larger transition to societal bilingualism in an increasingly transnational world.

Resources
The Writing Intensive Reading Comprehension Website at the State University of New York at Buffalo:
www.gse.buffalo.edu/ePortfolio/view.aspx?u=wirc&pid=407

1 See transcription conventions used in the study.
S1 is used to indicate any one of the 3 or 4 students who spoke, one at a time.
S indicates a group response.
: indicates a vowel stretch.
___ indicates emphasis or volume.
((xxx)) indicates speech that cannot be understood due to background noise or too many voices at the same time.
(h) indicates laughter.
(≤ .2) indicates a micropause, all other pauses are indicated in seconds in parenthesis.
[ ] Brackets indicate overlapping talk.

Chapter 13

The multiple languages and literacies of English: a response to Section 3

Suzanne M. Miller

Since literacy for everyone became a goal across Western nations about 150 years ago, controlling the uses of literacy in schools has been 'an enduring political and religious preoccupation' (Collins and Blot 2003: 3). This move to confine what counts as English and literacy education appears across the globe, which the recent case of the National Reading Panel (NRP) report in the United States can serve to illustrate. Using narrow definitions of literacy and of research, reviewing a relatively small set of studies, and over-generalizing the 'findings' (e.g., extensive focus on alphabetic decoding) to all literacy instruction, the ideological NRP report distorted views of literacy and then inserted them uncritically into the No Child Left Behind (NCLB) legislation (Allington 2002). By many accounts, almost every public elementary classroom in the nation is being negatively impacted by the resulting restrictive literacy and accompanying high-stakes standardized tests, leaving many children behind (Johnson and Johnson 2005; Meier and Wood 2004).

The chapters in this section argue that the intellectual agenda of English studies must be reclaimed from such efforts to limit what counts as schooled literacy to a tidy set of techniques with predictable outcomes. This version of literacy, what Street here (also 1984) calls the 'autonomous model', masks the underlying ideology of what is presented as a neutral and universal (Western) approach to narrow technical skills with print text. In contrast, in the social spaces of the twenty-first century, new literacies and technologies and within-nation language diversity have emerged and are emerging through everyday literacy practices by human beings who now move constantly across real and virtual borders. In diverse contexts, socio-cultural variations in uses of texts, languages, communicative purposes, values, modes of representation – all point to literacy as plural, that is, to multiple literacies or 'multiliteracies' (Street, this volume; also, New London Group 1996), that is, producing and understanding multiple, representational print and non-print forms deeply embedded in new social practices and contexts.

As the contributors suggest, English studies now need to address this question: How should the contemporary changes in uses of literacy and users of English in the world influence the discipline, if at all? In their arguments Street, Horner and Lu, and Brutt-Griffler and Collins, raise issues that, taken together, provide some compelling answers and pose new questions.

Bridging the school/out-of-school divide

In nations around the world students enter local English classrooms with hybrid languages, multimodal literacies and other funds of knowledge (Moll et al. 1992). Even if we ask them to, they do not leave their knowledge outside the door, as Gee (2004) puts it, like guns in the old west. In their embodied presence, students bring to school with them what they know and can do. The chapters in this section examine the implications of students' changing funds of knowledge for teaching and learning the subject of English.

For one thing, bilingual or multilingual students can, with teacher and other students' support, use their strong oral languages to help them learn English academic literacies (Brutt-Griffler and Collins, this volume): in this study of elementary school students, use of home language and social mediation provided tools for new English learners to understand unfamiliar writing practices in English. These social interactions are also practices which can influence the nature of what students learn and their ideas about what counts as literacy. In these instances they are positioned in school as possessing strength with a home language they can draw on, a solid strategy for ongoing literacy learning.

Horner and Lu explore US college composition courses, where a mythic, fixed, Standard English is dissolving into new norms of 'linguistic heterogeneity', appearing through the presence of international multilingual students speaking 'Englishes'. The authors propose giving status to these students' diverse home and community language practices through a 'multilingual' approach that takes a global perspective and multiple languages as the norm. Street's account of ethnographic work revealing that diverse texts 'acquire meanings' at home which may be brought to school suggests that wider social networks enter school with students, too, and can be resources for literacy learning. Research provides evidence that young children bring to school rich literacy practices related to popular culture which can enable learning to write – if teachers appreciate home practices and allow such texts into school literacy (Dyson 2003).

Bridging the divide between home/community literacy practices and school in ways that honour students' competence with out-of-school languages and literacies, however, does require conscious expansion of what counts as English and literacy education in school (Street, this volume; also, Hull and Schultz 2002). Over the past two decades, the social and cultural contexts for new technologies *have* produced a shift in the professional concept of literacy from the conventional sense of reading and writing *only* print text to an enlarged sense of reading and writing multiple forms of 'non-print' texts, as well (e.g., International Reading Association 2001; National Council of Teachers of English 2003). More students are arriving at school with facility in creating, understanding, and using print-mixed texts embedded in new technologies. Instead of drawing on such digitally afforded literacy practices in school learning, though, teachers focused only on print may not even notice what students know and can do (King and O'Brien 2002).

At this point in the argument for rethinking English, Street quite rightly poses an essential question: 'How do we describe and teach the forms of knowledge, skills and values people need for what some refer to as "new times" and what are the implications of this for the "English" curriculum?' His answer is also instructive: to inquire into these questions we need to engage with new theoretical perspectives, a familiar form of regeneration in English studies.

Theoretical frameworks for change

The chapters in this section take up the issue of aims and values that can sustain the discipline as we rethink and renew English as a subject. All authors point to the need to turn to new theoretical frameworks that call for expanding our concepts of literacy, help to explain needed changes and guide English educators towards complex practices of teaching and learning.

Theoretical perspectives provide a stance to direct the many competing attentions of the field. For example, theorizing student funds of knowledge helps us to attend to and enable the powerful way that student literacies, languages and current understandings mediate (Vygotsky 1978) new learning. However, the exponential accumulation of new literacies embedded in new technologies (e.g., from blogs to zines and beyond) seems a reasonable objection to importing them all into the English curriculum as they emerge. As Street points out, though, the problem of change is *not* one of how subject English should be *constituted*. Instead, he suggests using New Literacy Studies/Multimodality theoretical perspectives that contest the ideology of the single, predetermined, print-only version of school literacy (Street; also, Kress 2000). Similarly, emerging interdisciplinary linguistic theories challenge notions of 'Standard' forms of English with hybrid ones that expand ideas about what should enter the English classroom (Horner and Lu, this volume; Brutt-Griffler and Collins).

The field of New Literacy Studies is particularly helpful in that it brings together thinking across several disciplines to theorize the notion of literacy as *literacy practices* that are embedded in social relationships and differ as enacted across time and space (Gee 1990; Street 1995). In this sociocultural approach, literacy is not singular, 'autonomous' or neutral (Street 1984) – as it is portrayed by NCLB and much curricular material – but rather contextually purposeful and shaped by power issues and identities. These social literacy theories foreground the importance of everyday literacy practices. They also attend to the limitations of the social, and the need for the agency of individuals as actors who author their worlds (e.g., Gee 2000).

Each of the three chapters addresses the goal of rethinking English by foregrounding the personal, social, cultural identities, development and agency of students, *rather than* specific content. Brutt-Griffler and Collins contest the approaches to English learners that treat *their* personal goals for language learning as secondary. Horner and Lu critique the approaches in the composition classroom where, routinely, 'students are figured' as objects for cultural assimilation or pawns in the spread of English in fast capitalism. Instead, they argue for attention to these students' purposes and desires as readers and writers and they envision students mixing Englishes and languages as potential critique, a desirable outcome. Street demonstrates that a child creating all sorts of texts about birds at home and at school bridges the gap between them and suggests implications for the child's self-understanding through school literacy. In short, treating literacy practices as identity-making endeavours respects student agency to draw from multiple modalities, languages and texts in making and remaking their lifeworlds (Holland et al. 1998).

This formulation works against the reduction of human dignity and value in this era of new capitalism where human worth is too often defined by business in terms of profits (Horner and Lu; Gee 2004). But what exactly is the role of English classes, then? Besides a focus on social practices of language and literacy, the field needs to focus sharply on 'critical reflexivity' about languages, literacies and modes (Street) and develop their uses more consciously (Horner and Lu). The move towards critical deliberation on multiple kinds of 'texts' (Street) builds on traditions in the field, but expands their scope beyond print and into the world.

Through these theoretical lenses, additional questions arise as ongoing reflexive projects for English education: How can we understand local literacy practices with attention to the global context? (Street). How might English become a multilingual subject? (Brutt-Griffler and Collins), and what will we and our students make of English, what will we use it for, and why? (Horner and Lu). If, as these authors argue, English is a dynamic field evolving through use, then these questions can guide us into the future.

Another effort at reconstructing English education

The central focus of this volume – the need to rethink and renew English in schools at the level of its social and educational purposes – was taken up in part in the USA by the Conference on English Education (CEE – the organization within the National Council of Teachers of English for professionals who prepare English and language arts teachers). In response to contemporary national policies that narrow and distort literacy, CEE met in 2005 at an invitational Leadership and Policy Summit to reclaim what counts as English education (Miller and Fox 2006).

The initial response by the inquiry group tackling the slightly different question, '*What* is English Education?', noted the historical reality of the gulf between what we know in the discipline and what government educational policies promote. The centralizing and homogenizing tendency of NCLB is relatively new to the USA, which has always had, in theory, locally controlled school curricula. Neo-conservative proponents have used NCLB federal funding as a lever to instantiate nationally an ideology of literacy as a neutral, rule-based, universal set of skills with accompanying high-stakes tests in elementary schools. The so-called 'standards and accountability' movement has made its way through the states to secondary schools, as well.

In this national context and the global one, as well, CEE was moved by the call for attention to needed change:

We need a broad and thoroughgoing rethinking of the very intellectual field that we are supposed to profess ... [We need to] demand more than canonical and reproductive machinery for the production of lists of outcomes, competencies, and skills, or required textbooks. But this shift will require some working principles for how we define profession, work, and field. (Luke 2004: 85–7)

In response, participants functioning in small thematic inquiry groups at the Summit negotiated sets of consensus belief statements to begin defining 'working principles' (available at www.ncte.org/groups/cee/featuredinfo/122844.htm).

Like the authors in section 3 of this book, the Cee group pursuing the question also turned to critical literacy theory as a means of moving away from canonical content and towards literacy practices that develop habits of mind. Among others, they foregrounded Paulo Freire (1970), whose theories provided a vision of problem-posing dialogue and inquiry to develop the power of agency through literacy (Alsup et al. 2006). The stance towards learning English, then, was 'characterized by questions, inquiry, and uncertainty' by students *and* teachers, rather than fixed answers or a canon of texts (Fecho 2004, this volume).

Another CEE Summit group exploring culturally and linguistically diverse learners called on English educators to conduct inquiries into cultural lives (of themselves and their students) as a means of understanding and enabling the funds of knowledge students bring to school. They argued that drawing on diverse students' resources in culturally responsive teaching is necessary, but not enough: 'For critical multicultural educators, it is necessary to see and engage students as both intellectuals and producers of knowledge' (Boyd et al. 2006; Morrell 2005).

Street argues that 'the combination of mode awareness and learning is suggestive for future curriculum and pedagogy'. But how will pedagogical practice shape these proposed expansions of literacy in schools? If English education is to take on the transformative agenda outlined in these chapters and at the CEE Summit, the field needs images of innovative English teachers working in these new ways. In the last section I provide an illustration of how the above-mentioned theoretical frameworks for English studies might look as curriculum and pedagogy in action.

Digital video composing as multimodal literacy practice

The City Voices, City Visions (CVCV) Digital Video Composing Project offers professional development to urban teachers in using digital video composing as a literacy practice and learning tool for students in Grades 5–12. The funded project has placed digital technologies into under-resourced schools, and provides teachers with ongoing professional development and support in their classrooms (Miller and Borowicz 2005, 2006).

The term DV composing aims to conceptualize and emphasize the knowledge-assembling and communicative functions of this quintessential multimodal literacy practice. DV composing is an authentic, high-status, social and cultural practice with powerful attention-getting qualities and expert versions in the real world. The connection to youth-media culture (music videos, movies, vlogs, clip culture[1]) is strong, making it a high-interest endeavour that draws on student (explicit and implicit) out-of-school knowledge.

The project brings together many of the themes discussed in this section through a theoretical framework that integrates New Literacy Studies, multimodal literacies, practice theories of identity (Holland et al. 1998) and critical literacy. A growing body of research situated in CVCV classrooms examines both teacher learning and subsequent changes in student engagement, learning and school performance (summarized in Miller and Borowicz 2006).

Teachers and their students participating in their own knowledge creation saw purpose and agency in their work. They redefined themselves as social producers of meaning who moved out of passivity, alienation and powerlessness (e.g., Miller and Borowicz 2005, 2006). Across CVCV classrooms students drew on social and cultural funds of knowledge that included youth media practices, home and peer languages, vernacular history and urban life experiences to connect to and make sense of curriculum from what they already knew. This interweaving of modes and knowledges for meaning-making mediated student understanding of the school curriculum, and also served social and personal agendas of students, particularly those perceived to be struggling academically.

In making a poetry video, for example, the teachers and then their students performed their interpretations by orchestrating multimodal resources. Curriculum concepts such as perspective, theme, audience became deep conceptual knowledge, learned in the context of multimodal meaning-making. (For examples, see a teacher's poetry interpretation of 'Introduction to Poetry' by Billy Collins at cvcvenglish.blogspot.com. Access a student poetry video on her own poem at www.gse.buffalo.edu/org/cityvoices/ prod_v19.html.)

A few stories from this research illustrate student responses in the dynamics of DV classrooms. In a high school class a student named Darrius, who was constructed in school as non-responsive and a troublemaker, created a DV story in response to a novel to depict his vision of the importance of loyalty among friends. In a noticeable change, he came to class early and often stayed late, sometimes giving up his lunch period to work on his movie, focusing his attention on curriculum in an intense DV design experience. His next movie centred on a hip-hop poem he had written commemorating the deaths of his brother and cousin. In such performances, Darrius was repositioned in school as an active creator making sense in/of English class.

In an eighth-grade English class students in small groups made a DV representing each chapter from *The Outsiders* with a tableau, using body placement, gestures and facial expressions to capture a significant aspect of the text. These students enacted a new DV genre when they added a TV reality-show 'confessional', with students looking into the camera and speaking in character, to construct motives, pose questions and sound themes in their interpretations. In each case, students engaged in a process of aesthetic response and reflection, interpreting print text, their lives and the world through orchestration of multimodal resources for meaning-making.

In the chapters from this section of the book – and in the research reported from the CVCV project above – the critical turn was made through theoretical lenses that propose a broader and deeper version of English and school-based literacy education by bringing out-of-school into school, repositioning students as competent, creating designers of multimodal meaning instead of just consumers, allowing for composing tied to students' purposes and desires, and *providing mediational tools for critique* of texts, practices, worldviews.

In all, the subject of English needs to broaden and deepen through reflexive action on theory and practice – *despite of* and *because of* efforts to control the uses and users of literacy in schools. All of the authors promote the idea of transformed pedagogies in English classrooms that move away from wrong-headed notions of a universal literacy. As we re-envision what it means to teach English, we must also attend to embodied teacher learning, school change, policy manoeuvres. The debates about language and literacy are ongoing. We must find ways to bring our funds of knowledge to civic disputes about teaching English at all levels. Most of all, as Freire argued, we must insist on drawing on the critical human capacities for curiosity and agency of our students: teaching and learning must occur with 'the conviction that change is possible' (Freire 1998: 72).

Culture is ordinary: that is the first fact. Every human society has its own shape, its own purposes, its own meanings. Every human society expresses these, in institutions, and in arts and learning. The making of a society is the finding of common meanings and directions, and its growth is an active debate and amendment under the pressures of experience, contact, and discovery, writing themselves into the land.

Raymond Williams,
'Culture is Ordinary'

Chapter 14

More than 'soldiering on': realizing the potential of teacher education to rethink English in schools

Viv Ellis

In this final chapter, I focus on the potential of teacher education in the process of rethinking English that the contributors to this book have identified as so important. Teacher education has been an important underlying theme in many of the preceding chapters and my intention here is to give it some explicit attention. My title comes in part, as a quotation, from an article on teacher education from a special issue of the National Council for Teachers of English (NCTE) journal *English Education*, itself an outcome of the Conference on English Education's (CEE) summit on 'Reconstructing English Education for the Twenty First Century' (see Miller, this volume). The authors of the article point out that teacher education is often characterized by tension between the 'theoretical' academy and the 'practical' school experiences of pre-service teachers, whereby educational 'ideals' from the university are typically 'thwarted in the field':

> And yet we soldier on, making the effort to inculcate ideals, even if far too much evidence from research on teacher education reveals that the values of the schools ultimately trumps those of the university for most preservice teachers. (Dickson et al. 2006: 318)

The argument of this chapter is that the potential of school-based, university-supported teacher education in the rethinking of English is actually profound if it is conceptualized in ways that stimulate development in *all* of the multiple settings for teacher learning and provide participants with the conceptual tools for understanding and working on the change process. Realizing the potential of teacher education will require partnerships between universities and schools that view knowledge as relational and systemic (Greeno et al. 1996;

Engeström and Miettinen 1999; Ellis 2007) – rather than a thing that is 'delivered' – and also understand learning as situated – socially, culturally and historically (Lave 1988; Vygotsky 1986; Cole 1996). In essence, this means building relationships that enable the active exploration of the conditions for teachers' and students' learning – the capacity for accessing, engaging with, and developing new knowledge *in the school setting*. This is not simply a call for unspecified 'close links' between schools and university education departments nor is it about (as Bullough suggested nearly twenty years ago) 'bring[ing] the student into contact with the best educational practices' in schools for fear of being 'miseducative' (Bullough 1989: 148–9). Rather, it is a call for joint work on understanding the object-motive of the activity of English teaching, paring away at the extent to which this object is shared by participants, exposing tensions, conflicts and contradictions along the way so that, fundamentally, English teaching can be seen as an interesting intellectual problem that can be actively worked on by its participants. It is about *expanding* English teachers' and teacher educators' learning. So, in this chapter, I give two illustrations of efforts within my own programme – the Oxford Internship Scheme – to do more than 'soldier on'. I should add that I am not presenting these brief instances of practice as exemplars and certainly not as generalizable solutions – nor do I think they are indicative of any sort of completed process of renewal. Rather, they represent two ways in which I have tried to begin some of the work suggested by the contributors to this book within my own institutional setting and with the aim of contributing to the rethinking of English in the schools with which I work.

Setting the scene: pre-service teacher education in England

It is worth briefly providing some context for pre-service teacher education in England so that it is possible to have some sense of how local circumstances both enable and constrain the work described. Pre-service, secondary (high school) teacher education at the graduate level in England has been essentially school-based (24 out of 36 weeks) since 1992. This direction was set by government as part of major educational reforms and this particular reform also established the notion of partnership teacher education in which universities and schools entered into formal relationships focused on the provision of school-based mentoring by experienced teachers (DfE 1992). Within my own institution, this kind of one-year, graduate programme had been operating with some success since 1987 and it is sometimes suggested that the Oxford Internship Scheme (along with another notable scheme at Sussex University) has been highly influential on the 'national experiment' of school-based teacher education in England (Benton 1990; Furlong et al. 2000).

Pre-service teacher education in England is also highly regulated by the state. There are national teaching standards for the award of Qualified Teacher Status (QTS) and these are defined by a government agency known as the Training and Development Agency for Schools (TDA). There are national, online tests in the 'skills' of literacy, numeracy and the use of ICT that all prospective teachers must pass. All teacher education programmes are inspected on at least a three-year cycle by the Office for Standards in Education (Ofsted), the same government agency that inspects school effectiveness. On the basis of inspection results, funding decisions are made by the TDA and universities (or, to use the jargon, 'providers') are ranked as category A, B or C. 'Non-compliance' with TDA regulations and a failed Ofsted inspection can lead to punitive measures and, ultimately, the withdrawal of funding for the course by the TDA. To this extent, teacher education in England is funded differently to the rest of the university sector. Additionally, from 1998 to 2002, the TDA specified in minute detail (in 'Initial Teacher Training National Curricula') the 'essential subject knowledge' and approved teaching methods for primary and secondary English, mathematics, science and the use of ICT. Although these requirements are no longer legally enforced, their residue (in terms of teacher education practice) has often become institutionalized.

It is also worth noting that schools in England are subject to regular inspection by Ofsted to ensure compliance with the latest policies, that there is a National Curriculum (specifying subject 'content') and also National Strategies (specifying approved 'methods'). Students in Engalnd's schools also take more 'pen and paper' examinations than anywhere else in Europe at ages 7, 11, 14, 16, 17 and 18. On the basis of their results, school league tables are constructed to inform parental 'choice' and performance management techniques used by school managers to reward individual teachers.

I provide this brief background not to secure readers' sympathy but to give some sense of what teaching and teacher education in England has to work within. These factors inevitably inform how participants perceive freedom of movement within the activity systems of English teaching. Providing this information may also help to contextualize the two brief examples that follow.

Voices: expanding understandings of learning and literacy

> The world according to a sixteen year old. I get up, start running
> to my right. There are stereos blasting. Big, dark, rush. Within
> a half an hour there's a cop car, skidding, I see it. Scared. Flashing
> lights. I hear the voices. The world according to a sixteen year
> old.
> The world according to a sixteen year old. But immediately the
> mood change. Running for lives. Dark, rough, blood lines, lying
> on the ground. The world screaming – according to a sixteen year
> old.
>
> (Ama's opening monologue)

Ama escaped the Rwandan genocide with her family and settled in
Oxford. At home, her first spoken language was Kinyarwanda,
although she spoke English with her friends and at the local comprehensive school. She lived with her family on a housing estate in East
Oxford, an area pretty much like any other town in England (Attlee
2007). Ama was recommended by the Social Services department to
join a local youth theatre and she had grown in confidence and
expertise over several years. My pre-service teacher education
students (known in the Oxford programme as 'interns') and I met
Ama – and other young youth theatre members – through our
efforts to expand our understandings of learning and literacy by
working in non-school settings. We have undertaken this work every
year for the last five years and we have recently started to work in
other settings such as hostels and education centres for young
homeless people.

During our collaboration in 2003–5 on the youth theatre's 'Voices'
project, we worked with the education coordinator (who also teaches
part-time on the university-based programme), a digital film-maker,
and a playwright (Ellis 2005). The youth theatre's work was funded
by grants from the Arts Council, the local authority's urban regeneration budget, and the Social Services department. Our contribution, as a teacher educator and intern English teachers, was to
work with the young people in workshops and rehearsals, devise an
education project that could be offered alongside the production
itself, and document the development process (to gain some insight
into the young people's participation and learning) through ethnographic methods. In the teacher education programme, work in the
non-school education settings is combined with an early emphasis
on investigating young people's cultural worlds in the intern teachers'
school placements. The purposes of this aspect of the overall

programme for English interns are threefold: first, to encourage them to build relationships with young people on the basis of common interests and shared cultural pursuits; second, to develop the capacity to observe and understand learning in more informal settings and to bring these understandings to bear on their work in schools; and third, to stimulate English interns' appreciation of young people's own cultural worlds and the ways in which they participate in the social, meaning-making practices of talk, reading and writing outside school. The aim is that by expanding under-standings of learning and literacy, the interns will be more responsive to their students and also be able to think more conceptually about what constitutes 'good English teaching'.

Within the university programme, our work began (as it still does) with a workshop on Robert Browning's poem 'My Last Duchess', one of the most common 'set texts' for schools in England due to its position in an anthology published for the GCSE[1] examination by the largest examinations board, the Assessment and Qualifications Alliance (AQA) (AQA 2007). Many interns are familiar with this text through their own studies, usually at university as part of a Victorian poetry survey course. As Britzman noted some time ago, however, beginning English teachers 'often expect to teach what they have been taught' and often on the basis that a particular text has been 'deemed great and timeless' (Britzman 1992: 253). So it was that some of the interns (though by no means all) were surprised when the foci in our workshop were the concept of voice and the commodification of culture, the latter foregrounded in the characterization of the Duke at various points in the poem, from his opening gesture to his 'last Duchess painted on the wall' to his closing, apparent digression as he accompanies a visitor down his palace's main staircase:

> ... Notice Neptune, though,
> Taming a sea-horse, thought a rarity,
> Which Claus of Innsbruck cast in bronze for me.
> (Browning 1849/2007)

After an investigation of the Browning text that built knowledge of dramatic monologue as a poetic form, the interns then wrote their own texts, focusing particularly on the first-person voice, the dramatic situation and its unheard voices, and the implied interaction between the speaker in the poem and the non-speaking listener. Following the workshop on Browning's poem, we moved on to a reading of Ron Koertge's *The Brimstone Journals* (Koertge 2001), specifically chosen as an example of award-winning adolescent literature, and a narrative about an averted high school massacre constructed through a collection of dramatic monologues. Initially, my dialogue with the interns had to be focused on what some of them perceived as the inferior quality of Koertge's poetry compared to Browning's. To understand the purpose of the reading as more than a ranking exercise in which Browning would always come out on top was sometimes difficult. But a compromise was effected that allowed us to move on to look more conceptually at how narratives are constituted by different voices.

Our work in the youth theatre setting started with observations of the playwright beginning to develop an original script with the youth theatre members, some of whom had read *The Brimstone Journals*. The ultimate outcome was to be a digital video film. The playwright worked with transcripts of a web-based, asynchronous message board to show how narrative was realized in the intersections of the various 'threads'. We observed as he also shared with the group extracts from writing he himself found exciting and influential. In particular, he focused on the anti-realistic stance and the percussive, associative language of writers such as Carol Churchill and Claire Dowie. The digital film-maker also showed the young people how to develop a character 'from the outside in', using physical artifacts as well as their own bodies to shape a persona. Provocatively for some of the English interns, he also authorized the young people in their use of non-Standard English; indeed, in examples of his own writing, he scrupulously avoided capital letters and used the language of SMS (text) messaging. This was a small part of our wider purpose in pursuing 'living-English work' (Lu 2006: 611). Over the next few months, as the interns made intermittent visits to the youth theatre project, the dramatist, the education coordinator and the digital film-maker worked with the young people to prepare their own group narrative constituted by different voices and presented in the form of dramatic monologues that would be performed and filmed. 'Reflections on the Phoenix' was the challenging outcome, a film that explored, from diverse narrative perspectives, how a violent act on a housing estate eventually led to the renewal of the communities who called it home. The film was shown at an East Oxford arts festival near to the end of the teacher education programme and an accompanying educational package offered to local schools and youth organizations that included workshops on the language of the film and the concept of voice.

At the same time as beginning to work on the youth theatre project, and with similar purposes in terms of learning outcomes, the interns were also beginning to investigate the cultural worlds of small groups of students in their own placement schools. The aim of this activity was to try to understand how English teaching in a particular setting might take account of young people's 'funds of knowledge' (Moll et al. 1992) and meaning-making practices outside school and build upon their existing cultural expertise. A second aim was to help the interns work with the language data generated in interviews and other interactions with the subtlety and critical awareness they were used to bringing to bear on literary texts. In other words, this activity – particularly as it was framed as an assignment for the pre-service teachers – was also conceptualized as a tool in their development as teachers *and* educational researchers.

In similar work undertaken this year, Sarah, a pre-service teacher, interviewed a group of teenage boys in her placement school who wrote and performed their own songs. Sarah was interested in how they worked as a band and how they situated their own work within particular musical subcultures. She was also interested in how the kinds of literacy practices they were participating in outside school might link with the kind of English curriculum she wished to develop for them during her student teaching. One boy, Ray, told her:

'When I started doing English here, it did make me appreciate written text more (.) because I'd look at it literally and think (.) yeah, OK, that means that. And then I'd look at it more metaphorically and think yeah, actually it does mean that but on a deeper level it has more to say. I think that got me interested in writing music more as well.' (Stewart 2006: 13)

Sarah (and Ray) perceived an important potential contribution for English in the development of the tools of textual analysis. Good music for Ray involved multiple layers of meaning in the lyrics and he seemed aware that his capacity to interpret (and to produce) these had been developed, in a significant way, through engaging in English work.

These efforts to expand understandings of learning and of literacy in pre-service teacher education are not intended to make deterministic points about the inevitable irrelevance of formal education for young people. Rather, through this kind of teacher education, the intention is to show how work in English can contribute to young people's and teachers' personal, social and cultural development while also, pragmatically, making progress towards national assessment benchmarks within the prevailing policy context. Significantly, this kind of teacher education work also interprets culture as a *verb*, as meaning-making practice in context, and shows how 'tradition' in terms of literature might be interpreted as a dynamic and democratic process rather than a conservative fiat. It is an attempt to challenge what Britzman (1992) described as the 'monolithic view' of what constitutes English, a view of culture and language that

> shuts out consideration of the more complex problem of what kinds of social relationships are possible when culture is synonymous to a museum of western artefacts and when those encountering this grand structure are positioned as spectators to the meanings of others. (Britzman 1992: 253)

Becoming more than a spectator 'to the meanings of others' has long been a goal of some versions of English teaching. But more is needed. Through the sort of integrated work I have described here – combining close attention to learning and literacy practices out-of-school with a complementary focus on subject concepts (such as voice, narrative and metaphor, etc.) – we can encourage pre-service teachers and their students to explore what English might have to contribute to their development. Working in informal educational settings and investigating young people's own cultural worlds can provide an opportunity to explore the evolving relationship between what Vygotsky called scientific (or 'academic') concepts and spontaneous concepts (Vygotsky 1986; Burgess, this volume). Through this kind of teacher education work, pre-service teachers can identify the potential of the activity of English teaching to bring learners' spontaneous concepts (developed in the everyday environment and having immediate significance) into contact with the scientific concepts of schooling (evolved in the specialized interactions of classroom instruction and having cultural and historical significance) with the goal of developing mature concepts. It is vital to recognize that the goal is mature concepts – rather than the obliteration of the capacity for spontaneous concept formation and the objectification of scientific concepts – as it reveals the historical, dynamic process through which a subject like English can develop and continue to be worth working in. It is within the zone of activity, of social practice, that the possibility for the development of mature concepts and – ultimately – the development of new scientific concepts exists. This recognition, with its combined emphasis on pedagogy and development, demonstrates, as Burgess (this volume) argues, the continued relevance of a Vygotskyan perspective on English teaching.

Working in the field: developing knowledge in practice

As Dickson et al. (2006), Grossman et al. (2001), and others have suggested, in teacher education programmes, 'the values of the schools ultimately trump those of the university' (Dickson et al. 2006: 318). This is a process Smagorinsky describes as 'the tendency for teachers to gravitate to the norms of the school' (Smagorinsky 2007: xii). In these circumstances, the examples of efforts to expand understandings of learning and literacy I have offered above might simply be dismissed as a university-based teacher educator's attempt at a critical inoculation of individual pre-service teachers against the conservative practices of schools. Rather, I have suggested that these efforts were designed to bring English interns into contact with young people in order to participate in cultural activity and with the aim of positively informing the interns' broader understandings of learning and literacy. Nevertheless, I recognize that working with individual pre-service teachers alone will not necessarily make it easier for them to access and engage with the knowledge distributed across the school settings in which they are learning to teach nor will it necessarily guarantee that practice in those settings is at least adequate, never mind exemplary. For this reason, over the last two years, a pilot project within the Oxford Internship English programme has stimulated work with our partner English departments on the development of these settings as learning environments for pre-service teachers and for a form of continuing professional development. Designed as participatory, interventionist research within the framework of activity theory-informed Developmental Work Research (DWR) (Engeström 1991, 1999), the DETAIL project (Developing English Teaching and Internship Learning)[2] has focused on leveraging and supporting the development of subject knowledge in practice. Fundamentally, DETAIL has sought to make English teaching an interesting intellectual problem that can be worked on by its participants (experienced teachers, pre-service teachers, a university teacher educator – and students) collaboratively.

There were three aspects to the DETAIL intervention: first, an increase in the number of intern teachers in the pilot school English departments from two to four (this was intended to disrupt further the potential for a conservative apprenticeship to a single mentor teacher)[3]; second, a greatly increased emphasis on collaborative planning and teaching between the four interns and all members of the English department (so that the diverse knowledges experienced teachers bring to bear on the activities of planning and teaching might

be exposed for interns' examination); and third, each of the participating English departments identified an aspect of practice that
they wished to develop and that could be worked on jointly with the
intern teachers over a long school placement. The purpose of this
third aspect of the intervention was specifically to raise teachers'
subject knowledge as a collective and relational phenomenon and to
identify and develop the forms of subject knowledge distributed
across or, in Lave's formulation, 'stretched over' (Lave 1988), the
participating department's English teachers and aspects of their
environment. It is this third aspect – collaborative professional
inquiry (Street and Temperley 2005) – that I will focus on here and
which I am suggesting, after Alsup et al., is an important responsibility for English teaching as a field (Alsup et al. 2006: 288).

Identifying an aspect of English teaching practice that the departments (as groups of diverse individual teachers) wished to develop
was a difficult and somewhat unusual process. English teachers and
heads (chairs) of departments often feel that they are told what to
do and have very little freedom of movement when it comes to
thinking about and developing their practice. Work with the schools
on preparing the ground for this aspect of the intervention and then
identifying areas of practice to develop and then thinking about
questions that might guide their professional inquiry took the best
part of a year. Very often, the starting points were very instrumental
and related to Ofsted inspection reports or self-evaluation documents
or the pressure to raise grades across the all-important D/C boundary
at GCSE.[4] It was necessary to work with this instrumentalism and
to engage with real problems in the settings in which the interns
would be learning to teach. Fortunately, the schools participating in
the pilot recognized the reciprocal relationship between working with
beginning teachers on their learning and the continuing development
of their experienced teachers and also saw the potential benefits in
terms of students' learning.

So, in one location, a large, mixed comprehensive school with a
relatively stable staff (many of whom had worked there for up to ten
years), the English department decided that they wished to work on
the development of young people as critical and independent readers
of extended whole texts at Key Stage 3.[5] The rationale for this quite
specific focus might be apparent to readers in England: recent policy
has emphasized coverage of key authors from the National
Curriculum and this has sometimes led to students being drilled in
extracts for examination purposes. In this school, the English teachers
felt that their teaching of reading was not as good as it had once been,
that students were not enjoying reading in English (either in terms

of 'diet' or instructional methods) and that their students were unprepared for the kinds of reading required by examinations further up the school (at GCSE and, especially, post-16) and in their own lives outside.

When a group of four interns arrived at this school placement at the beginning of the new academic year, part of their programme was to collaborate with the teacher mentor (redesignated as 'local tutor' for the pilot) to design and carry out a systematic inquiry into the chosen area of practice and, eventually, to come up with recommendations for action to present to the department as a whole. My role in the intervention as a university-based teacher educator was to support the department (principally the local tutor and interns) in the collaborative inquiry as well as supporting the working of the teacher education partnership. For the intern teachers, the process of inquiry was given assessment significance by becoming the ground for two of their three assignments: the first, a report of the process of the inquiry leading up to the research-informed recommendations; the second, a reflective evaluation of the implementation of some of the recommendations in their own practice in this setting and, subsequently, in their second placement school.

The desire to understand how young people might be developed as critical and independent readers of extended whole texts led this particular school's interns to: search the literature; interview experienced teachers; survey whole cohorts of students and construct samples to interview from the results of this survey; observe lessons systematically; and physically investigate the various stock rooms, cupboards and hallways in which English department stock and resources were stored. At the end of the first phase, the interns had several recommendations for their host English department. Of these, one was particularly interesting. Through their reading of the literature and their work in the university, the interns had come across the work of Harvey Daniels on literature circles (Daniels 1994). Literature circles as a pedagogic tool are designed to encourage independent learning, where students 'set their own goals, pursue their own questions, conduct their own inquiries' (Daniels 1994: 10) in relation to texts. This strategy seemed highly appropriate for their department in terms of the goal of students' critical and independent reading. As they investigated the English stock cupboards, however, they found what appeared to be the resources for a literature circles programme: small sets of adolescent fiction now covered in dust. In discussions with some of the longer-serving teachers, it emerged that the teachers thought they had once tried something like literature circles in practice but that it had been abandoned as being too resource intensive, endless worksheets being produced with questions and activities tailored to the texts in stock. Through further interviews and reading, however, the interns were able to show the department that what they had tried (group reading of small sets of novels) was *not* a literature circles programme as their aim at the time had not been independence. Rather than teaching students how to operate independently in the circles and, fundamentally, how to establish certain patterns of critical interaction around a text, the department had simply spent an awful lot of time devising teacherly questions specific to each novel.

What was interesting to observe in this school was the way in which the collaborative inquiry activity uncovered knowledge that already existed within the English department, 'stretched over' the personal memories of experienced teachers and physical artefacts in stock cupboards. But exposing the department's historical practice was followed by work on the contradictions and tensions inherent in their different understandings of 'literature circles' that led to new collective knowledge being developed within that setting.

Broadening out the active work of teacher education to the school department setting also had benefits that were sometimes less empirically based. One of the texts the interns found to be influential on their thinking about the teaching of reading and one that they shared with their department was Denis Sumara's *Private Readings in Public: Schooling the Literary Imagination*. Sumara's distinction between the reading teacher as 'tour guide' and the teacher who 'dwells' in the text (Sumara 1996: 184) became a powerful conceptual tool for the department more generally in the way that they interpreted the object of activity – the teaching of critical, independent reading. Sumara's conceptualization of omniscient, 'tour guide' reading teachers and passive, recipient, 'tourist' students was disturbingly close to the situation as it was perceived by the department's teachers themselves at the outset. For the experienced teachers and for the interns, the importance of 'unmasking' the teacher (ibid.: 232) as a reader with a personal response was renewed (or initiated) during this process, leading an intern like Rachel to consider her own practice and prospective identity as an English teacher and how the setting in which she had been learning to teach had both afforded and constrained her development:

Reflecting upon the classes I have observed and taught, I would also question how 'comfortable' the study of English is at my school, and whether there is room to stretch the relationship between teacher and students. Sumara notes that it is common for beginning teachers to attempt to remain neutral towards their classes, and indeed it is important to maintain a professional teacher–student relationship. Nevertheless, it is his challenge to expose a personal response to classes which has been most important for me during this inquiry ... I would further suggest that, if the teacher is willing to expose their personal response to the text, students are provided with an occasion not to just emulate but 'springboard' from. As Coleridge, and others before him acknowledged: 'The dwarf sees farther than the giant, when he has the giant's shoulders to mount on'. (Beaumont 2007: 14–15)

In its focus on active work in the key settings for teacher development – schools – the DETAIL project has suggested how pre-service teacher education might contribute to the rethinking of English. Primarily, this work conceptualizes English teaching and its associated subject knowledges as an interesting intellectual problem to be worked on, a system within which experienced teachers and interns have the potential for agency. Above all, projects like DETAIL demonstrate the importance of the development of social relationships and collaborative work and have the potential to be transformative at the level of the individual *and* the community.

From dissent to practical shaping: renewing our estate

The two examples of teacher education practice I have been discussing are illustrative of the potential of teacher education to contribute to the rethinking of English in schools. In terms of the institution of teacher education as a whole, however, I recognize they are no more than gestural. Also, there are undoubtedly many other opportunities to take up and new relationships to form; in the USA, NCTE has taken an important step in this direction in its activities as a subject teaching association (Miller, this volume). But, in this chapter, I have tried to show where teacher education, as a structurally important institution, might figure in the renewal process. I have offered, perhaps, an activist reconceptualization of what teacher education is required to do at present by policy, but precedents clearly do exist in the early experiments in school-based teacher education in England and in the Professional Development School movement in the USA (Furlong et al. 2000; Hoyle and John 1998, Teitel 2003). Moreover, both of the examples discussed were funded from within existing resources and have been sustained and developed in the intensively monitored environment of pre-service teacher education in England.[6]

The renewal of English in schools – as both a process and an outcome of the kind of informed rethinking we have tried to engage in and stimulate with this book – is urgent and overdue. The possibility of renewal, however, is ever-present and inevitable as long as young people are among the subject's intended participants. Young people will continually press for a new and constructive stage for English (as many of our contributors have shown) which will be achieved through the kinds of 'open discussion, extending relationships and practical shaping' that Raymond Williams wrote about over forty years ago (Williams 1965: 383). Practical shaping, as several of our contributors have also shown, is concerned with what we *can do* rather than describing what we can't. It is an activity that English teachers inevitably engage in every day, with the aim of shaping the best outcomes for their students. But countering the directive interventions of policy in many national contexts requires that we work much more collectively (as, perhaps, we once did) and consider how our local practice in English can contribute to the development of the field, the renewal of the estate of English in schools. It will mean thinking once again about the subject as an intellectual project. And we will have allies in this endeavour. For as long as young people like Ama want to use literacy and literature to make sense of and actively work on their own lives, then rethinking and renewing English will be a persistent obligation we are challenged to address:

> You said our world always screams. Well not according to this voice. It's not just one body in a second cage. The shadows on the ground, perhaps. But the tulips they give birth. And they didn't call our estate the Phoenix for nothing. And they didn't give birds wings without a cause. And the Phoenix wings are still beat, beat, beating. Heartbeat beat. Not beaten. Hear me. This is the word according to a sixteen year old.
>
> (Ama's final monologue)

Afterword

Shirley Brice Heath

A genre entitled 'afterword' offers at least three possibilities: complement, reiterate or expand prior words of the volume. I attempt all three. My perspective here is that of linguistic anthropologist who has spent most of my academic career teaching in an English Department (Stanford University). Hence, I connect easily with the central question of this volume. In many academic meetings that deliberate variations on the question 'why English?' I have put on my anthropologist's hat and listened with as much detachment as possible. My interjections into these meetings have, more often than not, urged colleagues to attend to what current social science research tells us about how language, oral and written, is being used and valued – particularly among adolescents and young adults. I have also reminded colleagues of the vital role of rhetoric, its attention to oral language, and the values it offers over the instrumental approaches that 'composition' or 'writing' classes so often take in the current push for 'academic discourse.' Here I amplify these points to complement and reiterate the valuable work of the prior three sections.

Points of difference and connection

Several chapters of this volume echo debates about the death of English (such as Spivak, 2003). In these debates, several presuppositions are at work. The first assumes that young people now turn their energies from printed texts to online engagement with virtual objects.[1] A second common proposal asserts performance to be the preferred mode of young people. Another sets forth the centrality of multimodal literacies in communities where access to the internet is consistently available. All these presuppositions are born out by social scientists who study the everyday learning lives of young people in post-industrial nations.

Mattering more than these broad generalizations, however, is the actual nature of young learners' interactions with virtual worlds, performance and multimodal literacies. Chapters in this volume detail brief cases of engagement by the young with performative, visual, and communicative modes in circumstances outside customary academic environments and artifacts. Instances noted here cover relatively short periods of time, feature textual spurts, conversational reference to recent or contemporary events and texts derived from direct lived experience. Since the opening of the twenty-first century, these same patterns have consistently shown up in reports on everyday language interactions of learners which include few elements found within academic study of English: sustained engagement with extended texts, conversational references to written materials and depth of knowledge of literary texts that are fundamental to the cultural history of English.

What then do these reports mean for English classrooms? Many educators argue that classrooms should absorb or at least attend to the nature and substance of the everyday lives and interests of young learners. Social scientists, however, while acknowledging the inevitable need to deal with this issue, provide scrutiny of the nature of English (as well as mathematics and science) used within the everyday interactional work and language of the young. Their findings tell us much about language change and its relation to the potential and the challenge of the core principles noted in Chapter 1 for teachers and teacher educators (cf. Chapter 14 and Section 3). These social science studies suggest how difficult it will be to put these principles into practice and how much more we have to know in order to reconcile values and ideals of English classrooms with current linguistic realities.

Learning and using language in change

Between 2000–5, young people learning in their own time increasingly mixed and layered texts, music, images and interactive technologies to build strong performative frameworks. They did so mostly in collaborative peer work using electronic media and voluntarily undertaking opportunities to learn how to use new software for mixing, editing and producing materials, often for niche audiences.[2]

However, many of these studies show that only those at the top end of technical expertise sustain their involvement – *both productive and receptive* – with the same project or texts over a period of time sufficient for them to move beyond *beginner* stage in more than a few types of productions. Most young people who become *expert* select one or two kinds of frameworks (such as creation and participation with video games, often multi-party types) and stay with these for an extended time. Those who do not have sufficient expertise to *create* with the technological potential of their software or the internet move from topic and type of involvement, generally without achievement of *intermediate* expertise level.[3] The language behaviour of the majority of young learners – those described here as achieving only 'mediocre' or minimal levels of receptive *and* productive expertise – have strong implications for English classrooms.

Though increasing their time in digital space each year, these young learners also spend more time doing smaller bits of interaction in diverse situations. We might say that they were doing more of less and more of the same. Let's look at what this means from the standpoint of language learning and the amount and extent of meaningful practice needed to achieve fluency across a repertoire of genres and styles. Learners of 'mediocre' and minimal expertise in mixing and layering modes and texts gain insufficient practice to master a substantial corpus of specialized vocabulary, meta-awareness of learning strategies, and deep competence in explication of processes. Those at the expert level tend to have these linguistic competencies, though not always for production through both spoken and written language without visual or performative props.

The written language that young learners produce in their interactions with electronic media is characterized by a preponderance of short sentences, with highly redundant chunks of material, and they gain little experience with multi-paragraph arrangement of ideas on the same topic. Their writing reflects a mix of given or previously scripted text, and their inclusion of written language with other media shows substantial borrowing of 'special effects' from their more creative counterparts. As a consequence, in *any* calls for even sustained *receptive* engagement with extended printed or oral language these young people can quickly be characterized as having short attention spans and inadequate comprehension as measured by standard means.[4] They also tend to avoid arguing with academic texts, even when their own empirical evidence suggests that such texts are wrong. In effect, they do not involve themselves sufficiently in the substance of issues raised to bring their own work to bear in oral or written argument (Viechnicki and Kuipers, 2006).

Furthermore, when social scientists look at those occasions where the young engage in extended text interaction on single topics, they find two interdependent features – layering and repetition. Extended linguistic texts, whether oral or written, move in and out of visual, performative and other communicative modes. For example, PowerPoint presentations offer ubiquitous evidence of the urge to 'bullet' in writing what is being said in oral presentations. Moreover, images and other visual means reinforce and repeat concepts from words said and/or written. Visual representations change often and generally remain on screen for a few seconds during a single presentation Even when they can be brought into engagement with a single topic for more than a few minutes, the speech of those who have 'mediocre' or minimal linguistic fluency is marked by short sentences, a narrow range of phrasal units and thin slices of extended talk.

Values of literacies that hold

To be sure, social scientists find that two historically established functions of literacies still hold. The *exchange value* of literacy remains, and the young recognize the value of multimodal literacies, including oral and written of language, for *meeting their own felt needs*. Through all modes of literacy, young people tend to convey and receive information on a just-enough-just-in-time basis. The young value (and talk about) the newest and most recent through narratives that often portray surface acquaintance rather than substantial immersion. For example, in 2006, adolescents and young adults in the United States reported getting most of what they knew about current events through daily programmes on comedy television channels. When questioned, the young report their belief that they can learn what they need when they need it. Their narrative accounts affirm their social membership with their peers around communal knowledge; yet temporal and causal syntactic markers are in short supply. Time collapses into a brief past and short future.

Such a condensation of time co-occurs with language change. Corpora of language show that uses of past perfect and future perfect tenses are declining along with expression of the future tense with auxiliary verbs. In most contexts, the present tense expresses the future (e.g. *this means* rather than *this will mean*). An additional language change comes in the substitution of coordinating conjunctions for causal and temporal connectives, meaning that sentences 'string' together as linear equivalent segments without subordination and complex interlinking. Mental state verbs also show a reduced lexical range. To begin utterances with an expression that has become particle-like in English (e.g. 'I think') has become common, even among media figures.

If we consider the implications of these changes in language use, we come easily to understand how young readers have difficulty and little patience interpreting passages from literary writers of the past. For example, George Eliot's *Middlemarch* is filled with passages such as the following:

> Meanwhile there was the snow and the low arch of dun vapour – there was the stifling oppression of that gentlewoman's world, where everything was done for her and none asked for her aid – where the sense of connection with a manifold pregnant existence had to be kept up painfully as an inward vision, instead of coming from without in claims that would have shaped her energies. – 'What shall I do?' 'Whatever you please, my dear:' that had been her brief history since she had left off learning morning lessons and practising silly rhythms on the hated piano. Marriage, which was to bring guidance into worthy and imperative occupation, had not yet freed her from the gentlewoman's oppressive liberty; it had not even filled her leisure with the ruminant joy of unchecked tenderness. (1963:267).

Here the interior mind moves back and forth across time, with backdrop and foreshadowing. The give and take of past and future provide the essence of meaning here, and such literary texts sit on the foundation of a deep grasp of temporality and causality. The hypothetical underlies all literature in both its syntactic renderings (such as *if-then* propositions) and rhetorical grounding in deliberative discourse. Aristotle's ideas of rhetoric described deliberative discourse as addressing the future through exhortation and dissuasion in consideration of the possible and impossible. Deliberative discourse enables speakers to use language to know ideas as well as to know people.

English and teacher education

Throughout the twentieth century, secondary schools and higher education institutions rapidly replaced rhetoric courses with those devoted to composition and writing. Yet in the first decade of the twenty-first century, academic departments and professional associations of rhetoric increased; university students in the USA, Sweden and Canada demanded more courses in Rhetoric. By 2007, a few secondary schools in the United States were teaching it.[5] Yet no programs of teacher education required substantial study of rhetoric in their preparation of teachers of English.

The same point holds for courses on child language, adolescent language development, and the literature of children and young adults. Most teacher education programmes in universities of the UK offer courses in children's literature. Few teacher education programmes in the USA, Australia, New Zealand and Canada include such courses; emphasized instead are pedagogical approaches to teaching reading through basal readers. A central value in the literature of children and young adults lies in the breadth of lexical, syntactical, stylistic and genre exposure they offer.

I make these points here to indicate the extent to which English education might limit choices and ignore empirical and historical evidence on what should appear as self-evident: English is all about knowing, using and developing language structures and uses. Yet we have a long way to go before English and English education classrooms provide sufficient intensive meaningful language experience to enable learners to move with and beyond the words and experiences of their everyday lives.

What's the point?

In the academic meetings in which I urged colleagues in the humanities to attend to social science research on what is changing in language uses and structures, blank stares and quizzical looks evidenced the unspoken question of 'what's the point?' Of course, there is no single point. But there also cannot be an excess of points or endless repetition of the self-evident compliment that our discussions raise 'new questions' and 'challenging answers.' But where is the something more we all know is needed? To be sure, we must honor the everyday lives of learners, their stories, their social practices and their multi-layering of modes and media. Meanwhile, however, we have to acknowledge that this liberal ideology will not overcome the fact that legal, political and economic leaders –even those under the age of 40 – produce and understand language(s) in complex and intertextual ways that have to be modelled, practised, and contextualized purposefully with young people who want to realize visions of their possible futures.

The young enter our classrooms full of their stories and electronic fascinations. We do them no favour if they leave with these tales and interests validated and with only the same language structures and uses they brought with them. Literary forms, ranging from fiction and drama to position papers and science reports, need introduction and mediation by experts in classrooms who know enough about everyday worlds *and* those unlikely to be in the daily world of young people to integrate the two. Teachers with such expertise know the vital need of all learners for a deep and expansive repertoire of linguistic competence. We can encourage the young to be critically reflective, politically aware and socially astute. Yet if they have not read and heard, as well as practised in meaningful roles with supportive models, the kinds of language they will need to deliberate and contest existing injustices and necessary reforms, they will remain subject to social, economic and political exploitation. Personal narratives and youth theatre telling stories of teen angst, family tensions and strains in peer relation-ships cannot build concepts of the hypothetical in the abstrac-tions of the aesthetic, scientific, political or economic. We cannot depend primarily on learner interest or agency to engage the young with strong models and intensive practice. To add breadth and depth to the linguistic repertoires of the young, teachers need to imagine and enable more and more valid roles through which young people gain meaningful practice with styles, genres and types of language.

Community learning environments offer several examples of engaging roles for young learners that go beyond their immediate interests. As Miller points out in her response to Section 3, some youth groups operating almost entirely beyond the classroom take up political issues in comparative and persuasive terms. As social entrepreneurship opportunities multiply at the behest and ingenuity of the young in communities across the post-industrial world, young people set out goals and take on roles that make pertinent the need to produce and understand wide-ranging written and spoken texts (see Heath & Robinson, 2004 and Heath, 2002). Cosmopolitan culture, economic migration and the global market-place will surely encourage more young people to see the need to go beyond the comfortable language practices of their local communities. Yet they must have guides and mediators. Why not English teachers, who will have to revisit and revalue rhetoric and know much more of structures and uses of language that cut across contexts, uses, genres and professional identities? Just as Section 2 maintains, literatures need to keep a firm place. Yet comparative literature, as well as the literature of children and young adults, should enter the hallowed domain of English literature written for adult readers.

Those of us who care about English have to disturb many common-sense truths that have entered the realm of contemporary folklore. I argue that we can do so by valuing empirical evidence on the critical need the young have for a deep and wide linguistic repertoire. Young learners in English classrooms are not mere students taking our courses but the future citizens upon whom the political and economic realities of democracies depend. We have to be strategic about expanding the funds of knowledge in which the young can and will invest if we are to ensure that their future civic participation will pay off.

Notes

Notes for Chapter 1

1　At the time of writing, the ongoing debate about the suitability of the play as a high school work could be followed at:
www.freewebs.com/voicesinconflict
www.wilton.k12.ct.us/whs
maxzook.wordpress.com/2007/04/13/the-unkindest-cut

2　There have, of course, been very many attempts to confront the problem of English, too numerous to list here. Most, however, focus on 'what' (curriculum as *content*) or 'how' (pedagogy as *methods*) questions. The focus of this volume is the 'why' question – concerning the purposes and rationales for English as a school subject.

3　Overall, across UNICEF's categories of material well-being, family and peer relationships, health and safety, behaviour and risks, educational well-being and subjective well-being, the USA and the UK came bottom out of a list of 21 countries. Although we share concerns that the UNICEF study inevitably could not claim a complex analysis of cultural differences (nor even, necessarily, to compare 'like-with-like'), the survey responses from young people in the UK and the USA reveal an extremely worrying picture of child welfare and disengagement with educational systems.

Note for Chapter 2

1　Vygotsky uses the term 'scientific' concepts widely, with reference to both the social and the natural sciences. In some ways, 'academic' concepts or 'theoretical' concepts conveys more accurately in the contemporary context the breadth of the original argument.

Notes for Chapter 4

1   For a full listing of this series, written under the supervision of
     the Commissioners of the Irish National Schools and published
     between 1831 and the late 1860s, see Akenson (1970: 231).
2   *The Fourth Book of Lessons for the Use of Schools, Printed and
     published by the direction of the Commissioners of National
     Education, Ireland* (Dublin, 1859) Alex Thom & Sons, Printers
     and Publishers. This and others in the series, are in the school
     book collection in The Ulster Folk and Transport Museum,
     Belfast, EL/05/10.

Notes for Chapter 6

1   When we talk about 'we' or 'us' as 'the reader', for the sake of
     simplicity we are referring to an ideal kind of reader – one who
     understands the text and is aligned with its meanings and values.
     Any individual reader's experience of the text will be more
     idiosyncratic, more various.
2   Of course, even when one discourse is dominant in a text, it can
     be said that others are sub-vocal, even when silenced by the text;
     that is, readers can activate these in what the text does not or
     cannot speak of.

Notes for Chapter 7

1   The project ran from 1996–2001 and involved four European
     HE institutions. The published anthologies of war literature
     for children were:
     (a) Annemie Leysen, Carol Fox, Irene Koenders (eds) (2000)
     Kom Vanervond met Verhalen, Belgium, Bakermat (Flemish
     edition).
     (b) Carol Fox, Annemie Leysen, Irene Koenders (eds) (2001) *In
     Times of War*, London, Pavilion Books (English edition).
     (c) Manuela Fonseca, Irene Koenders, Annemie Leysen, Carol
     Fox (eds) (2003) *La Longe, À Paz*, Lisbon, Edições
     Afrontamento (Portuguese edition).
2   Manga is the collective name for Japanese comic books. They
     are fast becoming a world-wide publishing phenomenon. Very
     recently Manga versions of Shakespeare's plays have been
     published.

3   *Viz* is an extremely rude comic, published in the UK on a fortnightly basis, aimed at an adolescent male readership.

4   For example, there is an interesting reflection on the composing of *Maus* on p. 16. Art tells his partner – 'There's so much I'll never be able to visualise. I mean reality is too complex for comics ... so much has to be left out or distorted.'

5   Nearly all the categories of Mood, Tense and Voice, described by Gerard Genette in his *Narrative Discourse* (1972) can be shown clearly through the pictures in *Maus*. The chronology of *Maus* is unusually complex: there are at least four kinds of story time:

(a) The time of the story of Vladek's survival of the Holocaust in the 1930s and 40s.

(b) The time of Vladek telling the story to Art in the 70s and 80s.

(c) The time of Art's composing the book (which is in the text).

(d) The time of our reading Art's composition.

Spiegelman's text weaves in and out of these chronologies and the changes are signalled by framing devices, visual metaphors like the trains which stretch across the tops and bottoms of pages showing transitions of time and place as well as representing the cattle trucks of the Holocaust, and the positioning of speech bubbles and first-person narration within or outside the frames.

Notes for Chapter 8

1   I recall having a minor epiphany while glancing through the Crowther Report (1959). It was so shockingly *readable*.

2   For superb literary satires on the separation of language from life, see the plays of Václav Havel (e.g. *The Garden Party*; *The Memorandum*) in which the Theatre of the Absurd meets Kafkaesque bureaucracy. Noting with approval someone's remark that the main hero of *The Garden Party* is the cliché, Havel apparently added, 'The cliché organizes life; it expropriates people's identity.'

3   In this section I draw quite heavily on Olson's book and its important argument. Crudely put, he argues that schools as institutions have goals which are not the same as those of the individuals of which the institution is composed. While the implications of this are brilliantly analysed, I think the book is less good at proposing ways of reconciling these conflicting agencies.

4   It is relevant to mention that the lesson used Powerpoint; instead of 'chalk and talk' it was 'click and talk'. The effect of the

'textbook on the screen' was to prompt the pupil task of copying down.

5   Compare D. H. Lawrence in his poem 'Thought', where he says that thought is not 'a trick, or an exercise' but rather is 'a man in his wholeness wholly attending'.

6   Or that when Frost's oven bird frames the question 'what to make of a diminished thing', it could be a question for readers of this volume. Books on ornithology say that the oven bird's colloquial name 'teacher-bird' originated from 'its loud and distinctive song, commonly interpreted as *teacher-teacher-teacher*'. Reuben Brower (1963) writes that 'anyone who has walked in dry July woods will remember how the metallic refrain of the oven bird bores into ears and mind'. Oven bird – teacher – managerialist prose – Frye's conference speaker: most of my essay is in Frost's poem.

7   The first text-message?

Notes for Chapter 9

1   PEE (Point, Evidence, Explain) is an acronym widely used in UK English classrooms when teaching students how to structure exam-style essay responses to texts. See Viv Ellis's polemical response to the use of PEE – 'The Classic Dilemma', *Times Educational Supplement* 20 May 2005; available at www.tes.co.uk/search/story/?story_id=2105647 (accessed 24/4/07).

2   Cloze involves blanking out words, phrases, line endings and readers use contextual clues to make or predict a version of the text.

3   In a sequencing activity readers are asked to order single lines, sentences, paragraphs, stanzas, or images to create a text.

4   Website addresses are: www.poetryarchive.org; www.nzepc. auckland.ac.nz/; www.poets.org

Notes for Chapter 11

1   For recognition of this as regards English Language Teaching (ELT), English as an International Language (EIL) and English as an Additional Language (EAL) in a variety of locations, see Leung 2005; Mohan et al. 2001; Jenkins 2003; McKay 2003;

Widdowson 1994. On the worldwide growth in multilingualism, see Brutt-Griffler, this volume.

2 On the mixed views and desires of students, see Ivanič 1998, and Lillis 2001. Delpit's suggestion (1993: 292ff.) that writers might use dominant Discourses (in Gee's [1989] sense) against the dominant is a refinement of the accommodationist position: by mastering dominant discourse (*sic*), she argues, one is in a position to transform dominant Discourse (*sic*).

3 For an illustration of the contingent value of the 'possession' of EAE/SWE, see T. Kandiah's account of the 'refinement' of the text of a job announcement from 'NATIVE SPEAKING, EXPATRIATE ENGLISH TEACHERS FOR FOREIGN STUDENTS' to 'NATIVE SPEAKING, CAUCASIAN ENGLISH TEACHERS FOR FOREIGN STUDENTS' (Kandiah 1998: 79ff.).

4 For arguments advocating pedagogies focusing on such contingencies, see Canagarajah 2006b; Fairclough 1992; Harris 1995; Horner 1999a, 1999b; Lu 1999; Luke 1998.

5 On these lines of inquiry and specific strategies for engaging students in such lines of inquiry, see Lu 2006.

Note for Chapter 12

1 The research reported here was supported by the Institute of Education Sciences, US Department of Education, through Grant PR Award R305G040153 to the State University of New York at Buffalo. The opinions expressed are those of the authors and do not represent views of the Institute or the US Department of Education.

Note for Chapter 13

1 Clip culture refers to an emergent new literacy, 'an internet activity of sharing and viewing a short video'. It was made possible by broadband networks, but has boomed since 2005 when websites for uploading clips emerged on the market, including youtube, Google Video, MSN Video. Sources for clips include news, movies, music video and amateur video shot with DV, digital cameras, webcams and mobile phones. (Adapted from en.wikipedia.org/wiki/Clip_culture.)

Notes for Chapter 14

1   GCSE is the General Certificate of Secondary Education, an examination taken by the majority of young people in British schools at age 16. The examination boards publish in advance an anthology of literary extracts, poems and short stories, on which students are tested.

2   For further information about the DETAIL project, see www.edstud.ox.ac.uk/research/detail

3   Student teachers have usually been placed in pairs in secondary school subject departments within the Oxford Internship Scheme since the late 1980s. The reason given for this innovation at the time was to make student teachers a 'critical mass' within the school as a whole in the hope that this would require explicit attention to teacher education by the school (see Benton 1990).

4   League tables of school examination results are published in England as part of the government's strategy of encouraging competition between schools and informing parental 'choice'. For league table purposes, only the proportion of grades A* to C counts.

5   Key Stage 3 is the description used in England's National Curriculum to describe the 11–14 age group of students.

6   Funding was received from the John Fell Fund to research the DETAIL project but the interventions themselves were supported through existing TDA funding following negotiations between the university and each participating school's headteacher.

Notes for Afterword

1   See, for example, Flood, Heath and Lapp, 2007; Laddaga, 2007; Liestol, Morrison, and Rasmussen, 2003; Wardrip-Fruin and Harrigan, 2004.

2   For a survey of the 'writing' of university students during their college years – in and out of their classrooms, see http://ssw.stanford.edu. Numerous other modes worked along side and often led their writing, and their lives beyond the classroom demanded more writing of them than their class-rooms did. See also Lunsford, 2005.

3   The *Handbook for Literacy Educators: Research in the Visual and Communicative Arts* (1997) drew the attention of language arts and English teachers to the rapidly changing nature of interactions of the young with modes of literacy. The second

volume of this *Handbook* (2007) points out the many ways in which the forecasts made a decade earlier fell short of reality. while other trends and directions in the performative, visual and communicative dimensions of multimodal literacies and language developed. The majority of chapters in the handbook derive from various kinds of collaborative enquiry with young learners and reveal the patterns noted here. Other sources on the changing language of young people include the many articles since 2000 in journals such as *Journal of Linguistic Anthropology, Journal of Youth Studies,* and *Anthropology and Education Quarterly.* Longitudinal examination of the language of young people in community theatre, visual arts, and community service is reported in Heath 2006, 2004, 1996, and Heath and Smyth 1999).

4   These points regarding what it takes to gain fluency in language relate directly to the fact that funders in the United Kingdom and United States, in particular, tend to support short-term or one-off exposures of the young to interactive projects, such as those using the arts. Such projects often stem from the right assumption – that young people enjoy such work, but these projects give no attention to the realities of human development and language learning: sustained time and interaction are needed. Learners have to have sustained meaningful immersion in any mode or medium in order to internalize associated language uses, structures and genres at a level adequate to support transfer into other realms of skill-building. For studies of effects on secondary students and their school environment of work in a multi-year project in the sciences and arts, see Heath, Boehncke and Wolf, 2007.

5   See, for example, a secondary-level textbook on rhetoric; Cognard-Black & Cognard, 2005.

References

References for Chapter 1

Cowan, A. L. (2007) 'Play about the Iraq War divides a Connecticut school', *New York Times*, 24 March 2007, B1–B3.

Department for Education and Employment (DfEE) (2001) *Framework for Teaching English: Years 7, 8 and 9 (Secondary National Strategy)*. London: DfEE.

Department for Education and Skills (DfES) (2006) *DfES School and College Achievement and Attainment Tables*; available at www.dfes.gov.uk/performancetables; accessed 27 April 2007.

Department of Health (DH)/National Health Service (NHS) (2006) *Community Health Profiles*; available at www.community-healthprofiles.info; accessed 27 April 2007.

Earl, L., Watson, N., Levin, B., Leithwood, K., Fullan, M., Torrance, N. with Jantzi, D., Mascall, B. and Volante, L. (2003) *Watching and Learning 3: Final Report of the External Evaluation of England's National Literacy and Numeracy Strategies*. Toronto: Ontario Institute for Studies in Education, University of Toronto.

Ellis, V. (2003) '*Didactus interruptus*; or, why the Key Stage 3 English strand should withdraw (and what should happen next)', *Forum – for Promoting 3–19 Comprehensive Education*, 45 (3), 92–7.

Hardy, T. (1896/1978) *Jude the Obscure*. Harmondsworth: Penguin.

Hunter, I. (1988) *Culture and Government: The Emergence of Literary Education*. London: Macmillan.

Ofsted (2006) *Review of Inspection Evidence 2000–2005: English* London: Ofsted.

UNICEF (2006) *The State of the World's Children 2007: Executive Summary*. Paris: UNICEF.

Wignall, A. (2004) 'The junior judge', *Guardian*, 9 November; available at education.guardian.co.uk/egweekly/story/ 0,,1346137,00.html; accessed 27 April 2007.
Williams, R. (1965) *The Long Revolution*. Harmondsworth: Pelican.

References for Chapter 2

Britton, J. (1970) *Language and Learning*. Allen Lane: Penguin Press.
Daniels, H. (2001) *Vygotsky and Pedagogy*. London and New York: RoutledgeFalmer.
Davydov, V. V. (1990) *Types of Generalization in Instruction*. Reston, VA: National Council of Teachers of Mathematics.
Department of Education and Science (DES) (1975) *A Language for Life. Report of the Commission of Inquiry appointed by the Secretary of State for Science and Education under the chairmanship of Sir Alan Bullock (The Bullock Report)*. London: HMSO.
Department of Education and Science (DES) (1988) *Report of the Committee of Inquiry into the Teaching of English Language under the Chairmanship of Sir John Kingman, FRS (The Kingman Report)*. London: HMSO.
Department of Education and Science (DES) and Welsh Office (WO) (1989) *English for Ages 5–16 (The Cox Report)*. London: HMSO.
Elkonin, D. (1972) 'Toward the problem of stages in the mental development of the child', *Soviet Psychology*, 10(3), 224–51.
Karpov, Y. (2003) 'Vygotsky's doctrine of scientific concepts: its role for contemporary education', in A. Kozulin et al. (eds) *Vygotsky's Educational Theory in Cultural Context* (pp. 65–82). Cambridge: Cambridge University Press.
Kozulin, A., Gindis, B., Ageyev, V. and Miller, S. (eds) (2003) *Vygotsky's Educational Theory in Cultural Context*. Cambridge: Cambridge University Press.
Van der Veer, R. and Valsiner, J. (1991) *Understanding Vygotsky: A Quest for Synthesis*. Oxford, UK and Cambridge, USA: Blackwell.
Vygotsky, L. S. (1986) *Thought and Language*, A. Kozulin (ed. and trans.). Cambridge, MA: MIT Press.
Wertsch, J. (1985) *Vygotsky and the Social Formation of Mind*. Cambridge, MA and London: Harvard University Press.
Zuckerman, G. (2003) 'The learning activity in the first years of schooling: the developmental path toward reflection', in A.

Kozulin et al. (eds) *Vygotsky's Educational Theory in Cultural Context* (pp. 177–99). Cambridge: Cambridge University Press.

References for Chapter 3

Aarons, L. (1996) *Prayers for Bobby: A Mother's Coming to Terms with the Suicide of Her Gay Son.* New York: Harper Collins.

Bakhtin, M. (1981), 'Discourse in the novel', in M. Holquist (ed.) *The Dialogic Imagination. Four Essays,* C. Emerson and M. Holquist (trans.) (pp. 259–422). Austin: University of Texas Press.

Camus, A. (1968) *Lyrical and Critical Essays,* P. Thody (ed.), E. C. Kennedy (trans.). New York: Vintage.

Coles, G. (2003) *Reading the Naked Truth: Literacy, Legislation, and Lies.* Portsmouth, NH: Heinemann.

Darling-Hammond, L. (2004) 'From "separate but equal" to "No Child Left Behind": the collision of new standards and old inequalities', in D. Meier and G. Wood (eds) *Many Children Left Behind: How the No Child Left Behind Act Is Damaging Our Children and Our Schools* (pp. 3–32). Boston, MA: Beacon Press.

Fanon, F. (1965) *The Wretched of the Earth.* New York: Grove Press.

Fecho, B. (2004) *'Is This English?' Race, Language, and Culture in the Classroom.* New York: Teachers' College Press.

Finn, P. (1999) *Literacy with an Attitude: Educating Working-Class Children in Their Own Self-Interest.* Albany: State University Press of New York.

Freire, P. (1970) *Pedagogy of the Oppressed.* New York: Continuum.

Freire, P. (1983) 'The importance of the act of reading', *Journal of Education,* 165(1), 5–11.

Gordon, L. (2000) *Existentia Africana: Understanding Africana, Existential Thought.* New York: Routledge.

Heath, S. B. (1983) *Ways with Words: Language, Life, and Work in Communities and Classrooms.* Cambridge: Cambridge University Press.

Hermans, H. and Kempen, H. (1993) *The Dialogical Self: Meaning as Movement.* San Diego, CA: Academic Press.

Hull, G. and Schultz, K. (2002) *School's Out: Bridging Out-of-School Literacies with Classroom Practice.* New York: Teachers' College Press.

Jensen, D. (2004) *Walking on Water: Reading, Writing, and Revolution.* White River Junction, VT: Chelsea Green.

Laird, J., DeBell, M. and Chapman, C. (2006) *Dropout Rates in the United States: 2004* (NCES 2007-024). US Department of Education. Washington, DC: National Center for Education Statistics. Retrieved 30 March 2007 from nces.ed.gov/ punsearch

Roeder, M. (2004) *Someone is Watching*. Lincoln, NE: iUniverse.

Rosenblatt, R. (1994) 'The transactional theory of reading and writing', in R. Ruddell, M. Ruddell and H. Singer (eds) *Theoretical Models and Processes of Reading* (4th edn) (pp. 1057–92). Newark, DE: International Reading Association.

Rosenblatt, L. (1995) *Literature as Exploration* (5th edn). New York: MLA.

Sanchez, A. (2003) *Rainbow Boys*. New York: Simon & Schuster.

Sartre, J. P. (1956) *Being and Nothingness; An Essay on Phenomenological Ontology*, H. Barnes (trans.). New York: Philosophical Library.

Schultz, K. and Fecho, B. (2005) 'Literacies in adolescence: an analysis of policies from the United States and Queensland, Australia', in N. Bascia, A. Cumming, A. Datnow, K. Leithwood and D. Livingstone (eds) *International Handbook of Educational Policy* (pp. 677–94). The Netherlands: Kluwer Academic.

References for Chapter 4

Achebe, C. (1975) *Morning Yet on Creation Day*. London: Heinemann.

Akenson, D. H. (1970) *The Irish Education Experiment: The National System of Education in the Nineteenth Century*. London: Routledge & Kegan Paul.

Akenson, D. H. (1985) 'Mass schooling in Ontario: the Irish and "English Canadian" popular culture', in D. H. Akenson *Being Had: Historians, Evidence and the Irish in North America*. Ontario: P. D. Meany.

Andrews, J. H. (1975) *A Paper Landscape: The Ordnance Survey in Nineteenth-Century Ireland*. Oxford: Clarendon Press.

Brutt-Griffler, J. (2002) *World English: A Study of its Development*. Clevedon: Multilingual Matters.

Canagarajah, A. S. (1999) *Resisting Linguistic Imperialism in English Teaching*. Oxford: Oxford University Press.

Crawford, R. (ed.) (1998) *The Scottish Invention of English Literature*. Cambridge: Cambridge University Press.

Curtis, B. (1988) *Building the Educational State: Canada West, 1836–1871*. London, Ontario: The Althouse Press.

Eaglestone, R. (2000) *Doing English: A Guide for Literature Students.* London: Routledge.

Goldstrom, J. M. (1966) 'Richard Whately and political economy in school books 1833–80', *Irish Historical Studies*, 15(58), 131–46.

Goldstrom, J. M. (1972a) *The Social Content of Education 1808–1870.* Shannon, Ireland: Irish University Press.

Goldstrom, J. M. (1972b) *Education: Elementary Education 1780–1900.* New York: Barnes and Noble.

Green, A. (1990) *Education and State Formation: The Rise of Education Systems in England, France and the USA.* London: Macmillan.

Misra, B. G. (1982) 'Language spread in a multilingual setting: the spread of Hindi as a case study', in R. L. Cooper (ed.) *Language Spread: Studies in Diffusion and Social Change* (pp. 148–57). Bloomington: Indiana University Press.

Ngũgĩ, wa Thiongo (1986) *Decolonising the Mind.* Nairobi: East African Educational Publishers.

O'Sullivan, D. J. (1999) *The Irish Constabularies, 1822–1922: A Century of Policing in Ireland.* Dingle, Ireland: Brandon Press.

Parvin, V. E. (1965) *Authorization of Textbooks for the Schools of Ontario 1846–1950.* Toronto: University of Toronto Press.

Pennycook, A. (1994) *The Cultural Politics of English as an International Language.* Harlow, England: Longman.

Phillipson, R. (1992) *Linguistic Imperialism.* Oxford: Oxford University Press.

Viswanathan, G. (1998) *Masks of Conquest: Literary Study and British Rule in India* (Reprint of original 1989 Columbia University Press edition). Delhi, Oxford: Oxford University Press.

References for Chapter 5

Barton, D. and Hamilton, M. (1998) *Local Literacies: Reading and Writing in One Community.* London: Routledge.

Barton, D., Hamilton, M. and Ivanic, R. (2000) *Situated Literacies: Reading and Writing in Context.* London: Routledge.

Beard, R. (2001) 'Research and the National Literacy Strategy', *Oxford Review of Education*, 26(3, 4), 421–36.

Britton, J. (1970) *Language and Learning.* Allan Lane: Penguin Press.

Department of Education and Science (DES) and Welsh Office (WO) (1990*) The Statutory Order: English in the National Curriculum.* London: HMSO.

Department for Education and Employment (DfEE) (1998) *The National Literacy Strategy*. London: HMSO.

Department for Education and Employment (DfEE) (1999) *English: The National Curriculum for England*. London: HMSO.

Department for Education and Employment (DfEE) and Welsh Office (WO) (1995) *English in the National Curriculum*. London: HMSO.

Department for Education and Skills (DfES) (2001) *Framework for Teaching English: Years 7, 8 and 9*. London: HMSO.

Earl, L., Watson, N., Levin, B., Leithwood, K., Fullan, M., Torrance, N. with Jantzi, D., Mascall, B. and Volante, L. (2003) *Watching and Learning 3: Final Report of the External Evaluation of England's National Literacy and Numeracy Strategies*. Toronto: Ontario Institute for Studies in Education, University of Toronto.

Ellis, V. (2003) 'The love that dare not speak its name? The constitution of the English subject and beginning teachers' motivation to teach it', *English Teaching: Practice and Critique*, 2(1), 3–14.

Fisher, R. (2004) 'Embedding the literacy strategy: snapshots of change', *Literacy*, 38(3), 134–40.

Goodwyn, A. and Findlay, K. (2003) 'Shaping literacy in the secondary school: policy, practice and agency in the age of the National Literacy Strategy', *The British Journal of Education Studies*, 51(1), 20–35.

Kingman, S. (1988) *Report of the Commission of Enquiry into the Teaching of the English Language*. London: HMSO.

Lewis, M. (2004) 'Editorial', *Literacy*, 38(3), 117–18.

Luke, A. and Kapitzke, C. (1999) 'Literacies and libraries: archives and cybraries' *Curriculum Studies*, 7(3), 467–91.

McKie, J. and Jackson, A. (2006) *Reflections on Teacher Education in the Four Nations of the United Kingdom*. Escalate Higher Education Academy; online publication; escalate.ac. uk/2919; accessed 21 April 2007.

Marshall, B. (2000) 'A rough guide to English teachers', *English in Education*, 34, 24–41.

Marshall, B. (2003) 'The write kind of knowledge in English', *English Teaching: Practice and Critique*, 2(3), 83–94.

Marshall, B. (2006) 'The future of English', *Critical Quarterly*, 48(1), 108–14.

Marshall, B., Turvey, A. and Brindley, S. (2001) 'English teachers – born or made: a longitudinal study on the socialisation of English teachers', *Changing English*, 8(2), 189–201.

Marti, F., Ortega, P., Idiazabel, I., Barrena, A., Juaristi, J., Junyent, C., Uranga, B. and Amorrortu, A. (2005) *Words and Worlds: World Languages Review*. Clevedon: Multilingual Matters.

Martin, N. (1976) *Writing and Learning across the Curriculum 11–16*. Washington, DC: Acropolis Books.

Martin-Jones, M., Ivanic, R. and Chandler, D. (2007) 'Bilingual literacies for learning in Further Education 2005–2007'. available at www.tlrp.org/proj/martin-jones.html; accessed 21 April 2007.

Moss, G. (2004) 'Changing practice: the National Literacy Strategy and the politics of literacy policy', *Literacy*, 38(3), 126–33.

National Writing Project (1990) *Making Changes: Resources for Curriculum Development*. Edinburgh: Nelson.

Ofsted (2003) *The Key Stage 3 Strategy: Evaluation of the Second Year*. London: Ofsted.

Qualifications and Assessment Authority (QAA) (2006) *Functional Skills Draft Standards: English, Maths and ICT*. London: HMSO.

Rosen, C., Rosen, H., Council, S. and Britain, G. (1973) *The Language of Primary School Children*. London: Penguin Education for the Schools Council.

Smith, J. (2005) 'How students' everyday literacy passions (practices) are mobilised within the Further Education curricula', *Journal of Vocational Education and Training Conference*, 57(3), 47–60.

Street, B. (2003) 'What's "new" in New Literacy Studies? Critical approaches to literacy in theory and practice', *Current Issues in Comparative Education*, 5(2), 77–91.

Williams, R. (1983) *Culture and Society 1780–1950* (2nd edn). New York: Columbia University Press.

Xianqiong, H. (2005) 'The sword of Damocles hangs over a multitude of languages. Will it fall? Would this be such a major catastrophe?', *Changing English*, 12(2), 337–45.

References for Chapter 6

Barthes, R. (1977) 'From work to text', in S. Heath (ed.) *Image-music-text* (pp. 155–64). Glasgow: Fontana.

Bourdieu, P. (1977) *Outline of a Theory of Practice*, R. Nice, (trans.). Cambridge: Cambridge University Press.

Butler, J. (1990) *Gender Trouble: Feminism and the Subversion of Identity*. New York: Routledge.

Foucault, M. (1990) *The History of Sexuality: Vol. 3: The Care of the Self*, R. Hurley (trans.). Harmondsworth, UK: Penguin.

Misson, R. and Morgan, W. (2006) *Critical Literacy and the Aesthetic: Transforming the English Classroom*. Urbana, IL: NCTE.

References for Chapter 7

Anderson Ho Che (2005) *King: A Comics Biography of Martin Luther King Jnr.* Seattle: Fantagraphic Books.

Barthes, R. (1970) *S/Z: An Essay*. Paris: Editions du Seuil.

Briggs, R. (1982) *When the Wind Blows*. London: Penguin Books.

Briggs, R. (1984) *The Tin-Pot Foreign General and the Old Iron Woman*. London: Hamish Hamilton.

Briggs, R. (1998) *Ethel and Ernest: A True Story*. London: Jonathan Cape.

Campbell, J. (2004) 'Drawing pains', *Guardian*, 28 August.

Carrier, D. (2000) *The Aesthetics of Comics*. Harrisburg: Pennsylvania State University Press.

Esterhuysen, P. (1991) *The River of Our Dreams*. Johannesburg: Storyteller Group

Esterhuysen, P. (1994a) *Our Time to Choose*. Johannesburg: Matla Trust on behalf of the Independent Forum for Electoral Reform (IFEE).

Esterhuysen, P. (1994b) *Spider's Place* – Volumes 1–4. Johannesburg: Handspring Trust.

Esterhuysen, P. (1996) 'Focusing on the frames: using comic books to challenge dominant literacies in South Africa', in D. Baker, J. Clay and C. Fox (eds) *Challenging Ways of Knowing*. London: Falmer Press.

Fox, C. (1996) 'Introduction to *Focusing on the Frames'*, in D. Baker, J. Clay and C. Fox (eds) *Challenging Ways of Knowing*. London: Falmer Press.

Juno, A. (ed.) (1997) *Dangerous Drawings*. New York: Juno Books.

Levi, P. (1966) *If This Is A Man*. Oxford: The Bodley Head.

Meek, M. (1988) *How Texts Teach What Readers Learn*. Stroud: Thimble Press.

Minear, R. H. (2001) *Dr Seuss Goes to War: The World War 2 Cartoons of Theodor Seuss Geisel*. New York: The New Press.

Sacco, J. (2003a) *Palestine* (Foreword by Edward Said). London: Jonathan Cape.

Sacco, J. (2003b) *The Fixer: A Story from Sarajevo*. London: Jonathan Cape.

Sacco, J. (2003c) *Notes From A Defeatist*. London: Jonathan Cape.

Satrapi, M. (2003) (Translated from French) *Persepolis: The Story of a Childhood*. London: Jonathan Cape.

Satrapi, M. (2004) (Translated from French) *Persepolis 2: The Story of a Return*. London: Jonathan Cape.

Satrapi, M. (2005) *Embroideries*. London: Jonathan Cape.

Sebald, W. G. (2001) *Austerlitz*. London: Hamish Hamilton.

Seuss, Dr (1961) *The Sneetches*. New York: Random House.

Spiegelman, A. (1987) *Maus: A Survivor's Tale, Vol. 1, My Father Bleeds History*. London: Penguin.

Spiegelman, A. (1992) *Maus: Vol. 2, And Here My Troubles Begin*. London: Penguin. (Volumes 1 and 2 of *Maus* are available as one volume.)

Spiegelman, A. (2005) *In the Shadow of No Towers*. London: Viking Penguin.

Tardi, J. (1993) *C'était la Guerre Des Tranchées (Trench Warfare)*. Belgium: Casterman.

Ware, C. (2000) *Jimmy Corrigan: The Smartest Kid on Earth*. London: Pantheon.

Watson, P. and Esterhuysen, P. (1994) *Heart to Heart*. Johannesburg: The Storyteller Group.

References for Chapter 8

Abbs, P. (2003) *Against the Flow*. London: RoutledgeFalmer.

Alexander, R. (2004) 'Still no pedagogy? Principle, pragmatism and compliance in primary education', *Cambridge Journal of Education*, 34(1), 7–33.

Booth, W. C. (1988) *The Company We Keep: An Ethics of Fiction*. Berkeley and Los Angeles: University of California Press.

Brower, R. A. (1963) *The Poetry of Robert Frost: Constellations of Intention*. Oxford: Oxford University Press.

Bruner, J. S. (1966) *Toward a Theory of Instruction*. Cambridge, MA: Belknap Press of Harvard University Press.

Clark, U. (2001) *War Words: Language, History and the Disciplining of English*. Amsterdam: Elsevier.

Costa, A. L. and Kallick, B. (2000) 'Describing 16 habits of mind'; available at www.habits-of-mind.net/pdf/16HOM2.pdf; accessed 8 September 2006.

Donoghue, D. (1998) *The Practice of Reading*. New Haven and London: Yale University Press.

Egan, K. (1999) *Children's Minds, Talking Rabbits and Clockwork Oranges: Essays on Education*. New York: Teachers College Press.

Egan, K. (2005) *An Imaginative Approach to Teaching*. San Francisco: Jossey-Bass.

Frye, N. (1970) 'Elementary teaching and elemental scholarship', in *The Stubborn Structure: Essays on Criticism and Society* (pp. 90–105). London: Methuen.

Frye, N. (1982) 'Humanities in a New World', in *Divisions on a Ground: Essays on Canadian Culture* (pp. 102–17). Toronto: Anans.

Havel, V. (1993) *The Garden Party and Other Plays*. New York: Grove Press.

Heaney, S. (1983) *Among Schoolchildren: A John Malone Memorial Lecture*. Belfast: John Malone Memorial Committee.

Holbrook, D. (1961) *English for Maturity: English in the Secondary School*. Cambridge: Cambridge University Press.

Holbrook, D. (1967) *The Exploring Word: Creative Disciplines in the Education of Teachers of English*. Cambridge: Cambridge University Press.

IAAMSS (1952) *The Teaching of English*. Cambridge: Cambridge University Press.

Jones, K. (2006) 'Part of the main: a project for English', *English in Education*, 40(1), 80–91.

Knight, R. (2001) 'English in a straitjacket: the National Literacy Strategy at Key Stage 3', *The Use of English*, 52(3), 193–203.

Marshall, B. (2004) *English Assessed*. Sheffield: NATE.

Olson, D. R. (2003) *Psychological Theory and Educational Reform: How School Remakes Mind and Society*. Cambridge: Cambridge University Press.

Palmer, F. (1988) 'Skillsology versus culture', in R. Knight and I. Robinson (eds) *'My Native English': Criticisms of an Unnecessary Crisis in English Studies* (pp. 53–60). Bishopstone: Brynmill Press.

Paulin, T. (1992) 'The Great Horn-Handled Jack-Knife: *Great Expectations* as Epic Poem', in *Minotaur: Poetry and the Nation State* (pp. 112–32). London: Faber and Faber.

Rosenblatt, L. M. (1978) *The Reader, the Text, the Poem: The Transactional Theory of the Literary Work*. Carbondale: S. Illinois University Press.

Rosenblatt, L. M. (1995) *Literature as Exploration*. New York: The Modern Language Association of America.

Stevens, D. and McGuinn, N. (2004) *The Art of Teaching Secondary English: Innovative and Creative Approaches.* London: RoutledgeFalmer.

References for Chapter 9

Burgess, T. 'Writing, English teachers and the new professionalism', in T. Burgess, C. Fox and J. Goody *When the Hurly Burly's Done: What's Worth Fighting for in English Education?* Perspectives on English Teaching 1. Sheffield: NATE.

Burn, A. and Buckingham, D. (2007) 'Towards game authoring', *EnglishDramaMedia*, 7(2), 41–6.

Clark, J. S. (ed.) (1998–2003) *Children Have Rights*, 1 (1998); *Children Have Rights*, 2 (1999); *All Children Have Rights*, 3 (2000); *Every Child Has Rights*, 4 (2001); *Cry Me A River*, 5 (2002); *No Secrets*, 6 (2003). London: UK Committee for UNICEF.

Collins, B. (1998) 'Introduction to poetry', in *The Apple that Astonished Paris* (p. 58). Fayetteville: The University of Arkansas Press.

Dias, P. and Hayhoe, M. (1988) *Developing Response to Poetry*. Buckingham: Open University Press.

Dymoke, S. (2003) *Drafting and Assessing Poetry*. London: Paul Chapman Publishing.

Dymoke, S. (2005) 'Wireless keyboards and mice: could they enhance teaching and learning in the secondary English classroom?', *English in Education*, 39(5), 62–77.

Frost, R. (1930) 'Education by poetry', in R. Frost (1995 edn) *Collected Poems, Prose and Plays* (pp. 712–28). New York: Library of America.

Graham, J. (1990) *Pictures on the Page*. Sheffield: NATE.

Harrison, B. T. (1994) 'Freedom within the framework: nurturing the imagination in the National Curriculum', *Curriculum*, 15(2), 104–11.

Hull, R. (2001) 'What hope for children's poetry?', *Books for Keeps*, 126, 10–13.

Johnston, I. and Mangat, J. (2003) 'Cultural encounters in the liminal spaces of Canadian picture books', *Changing English*, 10(2), 199–203.

Kress, G. and van Leeuwen, T. (1996) *Reading Images: The Grammar of Visual Design*. London: Routledge.

Kress, G., Jewitt, C., Bourne, J., Franks, A., Hardcastle, J., Jones, K. and Reid, E. (2004) *English in Urban Classrooms*. London: RoutledgeFalmer.

Lawrence, D. H. (1929) in Macdonald, E. D. (ed.) (1961) 'Preface' for Crosby, H. 'Chariot of the Sun', *Phoenix* (p. 255). London: Heinemann.

Lewis, D. (2001) *Reading Contemporary Picture Books*. London: RoutledgeFalmer.

Lunzer, E. and Gardner, K. (1984) *Learning from the Written Word*. Edinburgh: Oliver and Boyd.

McGuinn, N. (2004) 'Romantic words and worlds', in D. Stevens and N. McGuinn (eds) *The Art of Secondary English*. London: RoutledgeFalmer.

Marsh, J. and Millard, E. (2000) *Literacy and Popular Culture*. London: Paul Chapman Publishing.

Misson, R. and Morgan, W. (2006) *Critical Literacy and the Aesthetic*. Urbana, IL: NCTE.

Ofsted (2005) *English 2000–2005: A Review of Inspection Evidence*. London: HMSO.

Qualifications and Curriculum Authority (QCA) (2007) www.qca.org.uk/secondarycurriculumreview/subject/ks4/english/index.htm; accessed 5 February 2007.

Rosenblatt, L. M. (1978) *The Reader, the Text, the Poem*. Carbondale, IL: Southern Illinois University Press.

Spiegelman, A. (1987) *Maus: A Survivor's Tale Vol 1 My Father Bleeds History*. London: Penguin.

Spiegelman, A. (1992) *Maus II: And Here My Troubles Begin*. London: Penguin.

Styles, M. and Arizipe, E, (2002) *Children Reading Pictures: Interpreting Visual Texts*. London: Routledge Falmer.

References for Chapter 10

Barton, D. and Hamilton, M. (1998) *Local Literacies: Reading and Writing in One Community*. London: Routledge.

Cowan, P. (2005) 'Putting it out there: revealing Latino visual discourse in the Hispanic Academic Summer Program for middle school students', in B. Street (ed.) *Literacies Across Educational Contexts: Mediating Learning and Teaching* (pp. 145–69). Philadelphia: Caslon Publishing.

Gee, J. (1990) 'Orality and literacy: from The Savage Mind to Ways with Words', in *Social Linguistics and Literacy: Ideology in Discourses*. London: Falmer Press.

Heath, S. B. (1983) *Ways with Words*. Cambridge: Cambridge University Press.

Heath, S. B. and Wolf, S. (2004) *Visual Learning in the Community School*. London: Creative Partnerships.

Holland, D., Skinner, D., Lachiotte, W. and Cain, C. (1998) *Identity and Agency in Cultural Worlds*. Cambridge, MA: Harvard University Press.

Hull, G. and Schultz, K. (2002) 'Locating literacy theory in out-of-school contexts' in *School's Out: bridging out-of-school Literacies with Classroom Practice* (Chap. 1, 11–31). New York: Teachers College Press.

Jewitt, C. (2006) *Technology, Literacy and Learning: A Multimodal Approach*. London: Routledge.

Kress, G. (2003) *Literacy in the New Media Age*. London: Routledge.

Kress, G. and Street, B. (2006) 'Multi-modality and literacy practices', in K. Pahl and J. Rowsell (eds) *Travel notes from the New Literacy Studies: Instances of practice*. Clevedon: Multilingual Matters.

Kress, G. and van Leeuwen, T. (1996) *Reading Images: The Grammar of Visual Design*. London: Routledge.

Kress, G., Jewitt, C., Bourne, J., Franks, A., Hardcastle, J., Jones, J. and Reid, E. (2005) *English in Urban Classrooms: A Multimodal Perspective on Teaching and Learning*. London: RoutledgeFalmer.

Low, B. (2005) '"Sayin" it in a different way', in B. Street (2005 edn) *Literacies across Educational Contexts: Mediating Learning and Teaching* (pp. 105–23) Philadelphia: Caslon Publishing.

National Advisory Committee on Creative and Cultural Education (1999) *All Our Futures: Creativity, Culture and Education*. London: DfES.

Ofsted (2006) *Creative Partnerships: Initiative and Impact*. London: Ofsted.

Pahl, K. (2007) 'Creativity in events and practices: a lens for understanding children's multimodal texts', *Literacy*, 41(2), 81–7.

Pahl, K. and Rowsell, J. (2005) *Literacy and Education: Understanding the New Literacy Studies in the Classroom*. London: Sage.

Pahl, K. and Rowsell, J. (eds) (2006) *Travel Notes from the New Literacy Studies: Instances of Practice*. Clevedon: Multilingual Matters.

Qualifications and Curriculum Authority (QCA) (2003) *Creativity, Find it, Promote it!* London: QCA.

Street, B. (1984) *Literacy in Theory and Practice*. Cambridge: Cambridge University Press.

Street, B. (1995) *Social Literacies: Critical Approaches to Literacy in Development, Ethnography and Education*. London: Longman.

Street, B. (1998) 'New Literacies in Theory and Practice: what are the implications for Language and Education?', *Linguistics and Education*, 10(1), 1–24.

Street, B. (2000) 'Literacy "Events" and literacy practices: theory and practice in the "New Literacy Studies"', in K. Jones and M. Martin-Jones (eds) *Multilingual Literacies: Comparative Perspectives on Research and Practice*. Amsterdam: J. Benjamins.

Street, B. (ed.) (2001) *Literacy and Development: Ethnographic Perspectives*. London: Routledge.

Street, B. (ed.) (2005) *Literacies across Educational Contexts: Mediating Learning and Teaching*. Philadelphia: Caslon Publishing.

Street, B. (2006) 'New literacies for new times', *NRC Handbook*. Oak Creek, WI: National Reading Conference.

Street, B. and Street, J. (1991) 'The schooling of literacy', in D. Barton and R. Ivanic (eds) *Writing in the community* (pp. 143–66). London: Sage.

Street, B., Lefstein, A. and Pahl, K. (forthcoming) 'The National Literacy Strategy in England: contradictions of control and creativity', in J. Larson, (ed.) (forthcoming) *Literacy as Snake Oil 2*. Portsmouth, NJ: Peter Lang.

References for Chapter 11

Achebe, C. (2000) 'African writers and English', in L. Burke, T. Crowley and A. Girvin (eds) *The Routledge Language and Cultural Theory Reader* (pp. 427–33). New York: Routledge. Originally published 1975, in *Morning Yet on Creation Day*. London, Heinemann.

Bartholomae, D. (1980) 'The study of error', *College Composition and Communication*, 31, 253–69.

Bean, J., Cucchiara, M., Eddy, R., Elbow, P., Grego, R., Haswell, R., Irvine, P., Kennedy, E., Kutz, K., Lehner, A. and Mastuda, P. K. (2003) 'Should we invite students to write in home languages? complicating the yes/no debate', *Composition Studies*, 31(1), 25–42.

Bizzell, P. (2000) 'Basic writing and the issue of correctness, or, what to do with "mixed" forms of academic discourse', *Journal of Basic Writing*, 12(1), 4–12.

Bizzell, P. (2002) 'The intellectual work of "mixed" forms of academic discourse', in C. Schroeder, H. Fox and P. Bizzell (eds) *ALT/DIS: Alternative Discourses and the Academy* (pp. 427–33). Portsmouth, NH: Boynton/Cook.

Canagarajah, A. S. (1997) 'Safe houses in the contact zone: coping strategies of African-American students in the academy', *College Composition and Communication*, 48, 173–96.

Canagarajah, A. S. (1999) *Resisting Linguistic Imperialism*. Oxford: Oxford University Press.

Canagarajah, A. S. (2006a) 'The place of world englishes in composition: pluralization continued', *College Composition and Communication*, 57, 586–619.

Canagarajah, A. S. (2006b) 'Toward a writing pedagogy of shuttling between languages: learning from multilingual writers', *College English*, 68, 589–604.

Chiang, Y. D. and Schmida, M. (1999) 'Language identity and language ownership: linguistic conflicts of first-year university writing students', in L. Harklau, K. M. Lose, and M. Siegal (eds) *Generation 1.5 Meets College Composition: Issues in the Teaching of Writing to US-Educated Learners of ESL* (pp. 81–96). Mahwah, NJ: Erlbaum.

Cohen, E. S. (2001) *The Politics of Globalization in the United States*. Washington, DC: Georgetown University Press.

Connors, R. (1987) 'Basic writing textbooks: history and current avatars', in T. Enos (ed.) *A Sourcebook for Basic Writing Teachers* (pp. 259–74). New York: Random House.

Delpit, L. (1988) 'The silenced dialogue: power and pedagogy in educating other people's children', *Harvard Educational Review*, 58, 280–98.

Delpit, L. (1993) 'The politics of teaching literate discourse', in T. Perry and J. W. Fraser (eds) *Freedom's Plow: Teaching in the Multicultural Classroom* (pp. 285–95). New York: Routledge.

Dobrin, S. I. (2002) 'A problem with writing (about) "alternative" discourse', in C. Schroeder, H. Fox, and P. Bizzell (eds) *ALT/DIS: Alternative Discourses and the Academy* (pp. 45–56). Portsmouth, NH: Boynton/Cook.

Downing, D., Hurlbert, C. and Mathieu, P. (2002) 'English incorporated: an introduction', in D. Downing, C. Hurlbert and P. Mathieu (eds) *Beyond English Inc.: Curricular Reform in a Global Economy* (pp. 1–22). Portsmouth, NH: Boynton/Cook.

Dubin, F. (1989) 'Situating literacy within traditions of communicative competence', *Applied Linguistics*, 10, 171–81.

Elbow, P. (1999) 'Inviting the mother tongue: beyond "mistakes", "bad English", and "wrong language"', *Journal of Advanced Composition*, 19, 359–88.

Fairclough, N. (1992) 'The appropriacy of appropriateness', in N. Fairclough (ed.) *Critical Language Awareness* (pp. 31–56). London: Longman.

Finegan, J. (1980) *Attitudes toward English Usage*. New York: Teachers College Press.

Gal, S. and Irvine, J. T. (1995) 'The boundaries of languages and disciplines: how ideologies construct difference', *Social Research*, 62, 967–1001.

Gee, J. P. (1989) 'Literacy, discourse, and linguistics: introduction' and 'What is literacy?', *Journal of Education*, 171(1), 5–25.

Gilyard, K. (1997) 'Cross-talk: toward transcultural writing classrooms', in C. Severino, J. C. Guerra and J. E. Butler (eds) *Writing in Multicultural Settings* (pp. 325–31). New York: Modern Language Association.

Gilyard, K. and Richardson, E. (2001) 'Students' right to possibility: basic writing and African American rhetoric', in A. Greenbaum (ed.) *Insurrections: Approaches to Resistance in Composition Studies* (pp. 37–52). Albany: State University of New York Press.

Guerra, J. C. (1997) 'The place of intercultural literacy', in C. Severino, J. C. Guerra and J. E. Butler (eds) *Writing in Multicultural Settings* (pp. 248–60). New York: Modern Language Association.

Harklau, L., Losey, K. M. and Siegal, M. (1999) 'Linguistically diverse students and college writing: what is equitable and appropriate?', in L. Harklau, K. M. Losey and M. Siegal (eds) *Generation 1.5 Meets College Composition: Issues in the Teaching of Writing to US-Educated Learners of ESL* (pp. 1–14). Mahwah, NJ: Erlbaum.

Harris, J. (1995) 'Negotiating the contact zone', *Journal of Basic Writing*, 14(1), 27–42.

Harris, R., Leung, C. and Rampton, B. (2002) 'Globalization, disaspora and language education in England', in D. Block and D. Cameron (eds) *Globalization and Language Teaching* (pp. 29–46). London: Routledge.

Heller, M. (2002) 'Globalization and the commodification of bilingualism in Canada', in D. Block and D. Cameron (eds) *Globalization and Language Teaching* (pp. 47–63). London: Routledge.

Heller, M. (2003) 'Globalization, the new economy, and the commodification of language and identity', *Journal of Sociolinguistics*, 7, 473–92.

Horner, B. (1999a) 'Mapping errors and expectations for basic writing: from the "frontier field" to "border country"', in B. Horner and M. Lu *Representing the 'Other': Basic Writers and the Teaching of Basic Writing* (pp. 117–36). Urbana, IL: National Council of Teachers of English.

Horner, B. (1999b) 'Rethinking the "sociality" of error: teaching editing as negotiation', in B. Horner and M. Lu *Representing the 'Other': Basic Writers and the Teaching of Basic Writing* (pp. 139–65). Urbana, IL: National Council of Teachers of English.

Horner, B. and Trimbur, J. (2002) 'English only and US college composition', *College Composition and Communication*, 53, 594–630.

Hull, G. (1986) 'Acts of wonderment: fixing mistakes and correcting errors', in D. Bartholomae and A. Petrosky *Facts, Artifacts and Counterfacts: Theory and Method for a Reading and Writing Course* (pp. 199–226). Upper Montclair, NJ: Boynton/Cook.

Ivaniĉ, R. (1998) *Writing and Identity: The Discoursal Construction of Identity in Academic Writing*. Amsterdam: John Benjamins.

Jenkins, J. (2003) *World Englishes: A Resource Book for Students*. London: Routledge.

Kachru, B. (1990) *The Alchemy of English: The Spread, Functions, and Models of Non-native Englishes*. Urbana, IL: University of Illinois Press.

Kandiah, T. (1995) 'Centering the periphery of English: towards participatory communities of discourse', in A. Parakrama *De-Hegemonizing Language Standards: Learning from (Post)Colonial Englishes about 'English'* (pp. xv–xxxvii). London: Macmillan.

Kandiah, T. (1998) 'Epiphanies of the deathless native user's manifold avatars: a post-colonial perspective on the native speaker', in R. Singh (ed.) *The Native Speaker: Multilingual Perspectives* (pp. 79–110). New Delhi: Sage.

Kroll, B. M. and Schafer, J. C. (1978) 'Error analysis and the teaching of composition', *College Composition and Communication*, 29, 242–48.

Lea, M. (1994) '"I thought I could write till I came here": student writing in higher education', in G. Gibbs (ed.) *Improving Student Learning: Theory and Practice* (pp. 216–26). Oxford: Oxford Centre for Staff development.

Lea, M. and Street, B. (1998) 'Student writing in higher education: an academic literacies approach', *Studies in Higher Education*, 23, 157–72.

Lees, E. (1989) '"The exceptable way of the society": Stanley Fish's theory of reading and the task of the teacher of editing', in P. Donahue and E. Quandahl (eds) *Reclaiming Pedagogy: The Rhetoric of the Classroom* (pp. 144–63). Carbondale: Southern Illinois University Press.

Leung, C. (2005) 'Convivial communication: recontextualizing communicative competence', *International Journal of Applied Linguistics*, 15, 119–44.

Leung, C., Harris, R. and Rampton, B. (1997) 'The idealised native speaker, reified ethnicities, and classroom realities', *TESOL Quarterly*, 31, 543–75.

Lillis, T. (2001) *Student Writing: Access, Regulation, Desire.* London: Routledge.

Lisle, B. and Mano, S. (1997) 'Embracing a multicultural rhetoric', in C. Severino, J. C. Guerra and J. E. Butler (eds) *Writing in Multicultural Settings* (pp. 12–26). New York: Modern Language Association.

Lo Bianco, J. (2000) 'Multiliteracies and multilingualism', in B. Cope and M. Kalantzis (eds) *Multiliteracies: Literacy Learning and the Design of Social Futures* (pp. 92–105). London: Routledge.

Lovejoy, K. B. (2003) 'Practical pedagogy for composition', in G. Smitherman and V. Villanueva, Jr. (eds) *Language Diversity in the Classroom: From Intention to Practice* (pp. 89–108). Carbondale: Southern Illinois University Press.

Lu, M. (1999) 'Professing multiculturalism: the politics of style in the contact zone', in B. Horner and M. Lu *Representing the 'Other': Basic Writers and the Teaching of Basic Writing* (pp. 166–90). Urbana, IL: National Council of Teachers of English.

Lu, M. (2004) 'An essay on the work of composition: composing English against the order of fast capitalism', *College Composition and Communication*, 56, 16–50.

Lu, M. (2006) 'Living English work', *College English*, 68, 605–18.

Luke, A. (1998) 'Genres of power? Literacy education and the production of capital', in R. Hasan and G. Williams (eds) *Literacy in Society* (pp. 308–38). New York: Longman.

McKay, S. L. (2003) 'Toward an appropriate EIL pedagogy: re-examining common ELT assumptions', *International Journal of Applied Linguistics*, 13, 1–22.

Matsuda, P. (2002) 'Alternative discourses: a synthesis', in C. Schroeder, H. Fox and P. Bizzell (eds) *ALT/DIS: Alternative Discourses and the Academy* (pp. 191–6). Portsmouth, NH: Boynton/Cook.

Mejía, J. A. (2004) 'Arts of the US-Mexico contact zone', in A. A. Lunsford and L. Ouzgane (eds) *Crossing Borderlands: Composition and Postcolonial Studies* (pp. 171–98). Pittsburgh: University of Pittsburgh Press.

Milanés, C. R. (1997) 'Cross-talk: teachers, texts, readers, and writers', in C. Severino, J. C. Guerra and J. E. Butler (eds) *Writing in Multicultural Settings* (pp. 189–97). New York: Modern Language Association.

Mohan, B., Leung, C. and Davison, C. (eds) (2001) *English as a Second Language in the Mainstream: Teaching, Learning, and Identity*. London: Longman.

Nayar, P. B. (1997) 'ESL/EFL dichotomy today: language politics or pragmatics?', *TESOL Quarterly*, 31(1), 9–37.

Ohmann, R. (1996) 'Introduction to the 1995 edition', in *English in America: A Radical View of the Profession* (pp. xiii–lii). Hanover, NH: Wesleyan University Press.

Parakrama, A. (1995) *De-Hegemonizing Language Standards: Learning from (Post)Colonial Englishes about 'English'*. London: Macmillan.

Pennycook, A. (2003) 'Global Englishes, Rip Slyme, and performativity', *Journal of Sociolinguistics*, 7, 513–33.

Pennycook, A. (2004) 'Performativity and language studies', *Critical Inquiry in Language Studies*, 1(1), 1–19.

Petraglia, J. (ed.) (1995) *Reconceiving Writing, Rethinking Writing Instruction*. Mahwah, NJ: Erlbaum.

Pratt, M. L. (1987) 'Linguistic utopias', in N. Fabb, D. Attridge, A. Durant and C. MacCabe (eds) *The Linguistics of Writing: Arguments between Language and Literature* (pp. 48–66). New York: Methuen.

Rose, M. (1983) 'Remedial writing courses: a critique and a proposal', *College English*, 45, 109–28.

Singh, R. (ed.) (2000) *The Native Speaker: Multilingual Perspectives*. New Delhi: Sage.

Slaughter, S. and Rhoades, G. (2004) *Academic Capitalism and the New Economy: Markets, State, and Higher Education*. Baltimore, MD: Johns Hopkins University Press.

Smitherman, G. (2000) *Talkin that Talk: Language, Culture and Education in African America*. London: Routledge.

Street, B. (1995) 'Academic literacies', in D. Baker, C. Fox and J. Clay (eds) *Challenging Ways of Knowing in Maths, Science and English* (pp. 101–34). Lewes: Falmer Press.

Travis, P. W. (2005/6) 'The English department in the globalized university', *ADE Bulletin*, 138–9, 51–6.

Valdés, G. (1992) 'Bilingual minorities and language issues in writing', *Written Communication*, 9, 85–136.

Widdowson, H. G. (1994) 'The ownership of English', *TESOL Quarterly*, 28, 377–89.

Williams, J. (1981) 'The phenomenology of error', *College Composition and Communication*, 32, 152–68.

Williams, R. (1977) *Marxism and Literature*. New York: Oxford University Press.

References for Chapter 12

Arnberg, L. (1981) *Bilingual Education of Young Children in England and Wales*. University of Linkoping, Sweden: Department of Education.

Baker, C. (2003) *Foundations of Bilingual Education and Bilingualism*. Clevedon: Multilingual Matters.

Baker, P. and Eversley, J. (eds) (2000) *Multilingual Capital*. London: Battlebridge.

Brutt-Griffler, J. (2002) *World English: A Study of its Development*. Clevedon: Multilingual Matters.

Brutt-Griffler, J. (2005) '"Who do you think you are, where do you think you are?": language policy and the political economy of English in South Africa', in C. Gnutzmann and F. Intemann (eds) *The Globalisation of English and the English Language Classroom* (pp. 27–41). Tubingen: Gunter Narr Verlag.

Brutt-Griffler, J. (2006a) *Language and Globalisation: Myths and Realities*. Fremdsprachen Lehren und Lernen *(FluL)* 35.

Brutt-Griffler, J. (2006b) 'Race and ethnicity in the English-speaking world', in J. Brutt-Griffler and C. Davies (eds) *English and Ethnicity*. New York: Palgrave.

Brutt-Griffler, J. (2007) 'Bilingualism and Elearning', in R. Andrews and C. Haythornthwaite (eds) *Handbook of Elearning Research*. Thousand Oaks, CA: Sage.

Carrasquillo, A., Kucer, S. B., Abrams, R. (2004) *Beyond the Beginnings: Literacy Interventions for Upper Elementary English Language Learners*. Clevedon: Multilingual Matters.

Collins, J. L. (1998) *Strategies for Struggling Writers*. New York: Guilford.

Collins, J., Brutt-Griffler, J., Turner, S., Madigan, T. and Lee, J. (2006) 'Write to read and read to write: thinksheets and the development of reading and writing strategies'. Paper presented at the annual meeting of the American Educational Research Association, San Francisco, 11 April.

Cummins, J. (1977) 'Cognitive factors associated with the attainment of intermediate levels of bilingual skills', *Modern Language Journal*, 61, 3–12.

Elliot, A. (2003) 'Talking to me? No, the cabby's on his cell', *New York Times*, 17 July.

Fitzgerald, J. (2006) 'Multilingual writing in preschool through 12th grade: the last 15 years', in C. A. MacArthur, S. Graham and J. Fitzgerald *Handbook of Writing Research* (pp. 337–54). New York: Guilford.

Galambos, S. J. and Hakuta, K. (1988) 'Subject-specific and task-specific characteristics of metalinguistic awareness in bilingual children', *Applied Psycholinguistics*, 9, 141–62.

Gomez, R., Jr., Parker, R., Lara-Alecio, R. and Gomez, L. (1996) 'Process versus product writing with Limited English proficient students', *Bilingual Research Journal*, 20, 209–33.

Graddol, D. (2004) 'The Future of Language', *Science*, 303, 1329–31.

Guensburg, C. (2006) 'Why Johnny (still) can't read', *Edutopia*, February, 35–45.

Hull, G. and Schultz, K. (2002) *School's Out! Bridging Out-of school Literacies with Classroom Practice*. New York: Teachers College Press.

Mazrui, Alamin M. (2004) *English in Africa: After the Cold War*. Clevedon, England: Multilingual Matters.

Modern Language Association (2006) *MLA Language Map*; available at www.mla.org/census_map; accessed 27 April 2007.

Mufwene, S. S. (2004) 'Language birth and death', *The Annual Review of Anthropology*, 33, 201–22.

Nettle, D. and Romaine, S. (2000) *Vanishing Voices: The Extinction of the World's Languages*. Oxford: Oxford University Press.

Phillipson, R. (1992) *Linguistic Imperialism*. New York: Oxford University Press.

Purcell-Gates, V., Jacobson, E. and Degener, S. (2004) *Print Literacy Development: Uniting Cognitive and Social Practice Theories*. Cambridge, MA: Harvard University Press.

Skutnabb-Kangas, T. (2000) *Linguistic genocide in Education-or World Wide Diversity and Human Rights?* Mahwah, NJ: Lawrence Erlbaum.

Tunmer, W. E. and Herriman, M. L. (1984) 'The development of metalinguistic awareness: a conceptual overview', in W. E. Tunmer, C. Pratt and M. L. Herriman (eds) *Metalinguistic Awareness in Children.* Berlin: Springer-Verlag.

US Census Bureau (2006) *Language Spoken at Home, 2004 Community Survey.* Online document: factfinder. census.gov/; accessed 24 April 2006.

Valdes, G. (2004) 'Between support and marginalization: the development of academic language in linguistic minority children', in J. Brutt-Griffler and M. M. Varghese (eds) *Bilingualism and language pedagogy* (pp. 10–40). Clevedon: Multilingual Matters.

Vygotsky, L. S. (1934/1986) *Thought and Language* A. Kozulin (trans.). Cambridge, MA: MIT Press.

Vygotsky, L. S. (1978) *Mind in Society: The Development of Higher Psychological Processes.* Cambridge, MA: Harvard University Press.

Wertsch, J. (1991) *Voices of the Mind: A Sociocultural Approach to Mediated Action.* Cambridge, MA: Harvard University Press.

References for Chapter 13

Allington, R. L. (ed.) (2002) *Big Brother and the National Reading Curriculum: How Ideology Trumped Evidence.* Portsmouth, NH: Heinemann.

Alsup, J., Emig, J., Pradl, G., Tremmel, R. and Yagelski, R. P. with Alvine, L., DeBlase, G., Moore, M., Petrone, R. and Sawyer, M. (2006) 'The state of English education and a vision for its future: a call to arms', *English Education*, 278–94.

Boyd, F., Ariail, M., Williams, R., Jocson, K., Tinker Sachs, G. and McNeal, K. with Fecho, B., Fisher, M., Healy, M.K., Meyer, T. and Morrell, E. (2006) 'Real teaching for real diversity: Preparing English language arts teachers for 21st century classrooms', *English Education*, 329–50.

Collins, J. and Blot, R. K. (2003) *Literacy and Literacies: Texts, Power, and Identity.* Cambridge: Cambridge University Press.

Dyson, A. H. (2003) *The Brothers and Sisters Learn to Write: Popular Literacies in Childhood and School Cultures.* New York: Teachers College Press.

Fecho, B. (2004) *"Is this English?": Race, Language, and Culture in the Classroom*. New York: Teachers College Press.

Freire, P. (1970) *Pedagogy of the Oppressed*. New York: Continuum.

Freire, P. (1998) *Pedagogy of Freedom: Ethics, Democracy, and Civic Courage*. Lanham, MD: Rowman & Littlefield.

Gee, J. P. (1990) *Social Linguistics and Literacies: Ideology in Discourses*. London: Taylor & Francis.

Gee, J. P. (2000) 'The New Literacy Studies: from "socially situated to the work of the social"', in D. Barton, M. Hamilton and R. Ivanic (eds) *Situated Literacies: Reading and Writing in Context*. London: Routledge.

Gee, J. P. (2004) *Situated Language and Learning: A Critique of Traditional Schooling*. New York: Routledge.

Holland, D., Lachicotte, W., Skinner, D. and Cain, C. (1998) *Identity and Agency in Cultural Worlds*. Cambridge, MA: Harvard University Press.

Hull, G. and Schultz, K. (eds) (2002) *School's Out! Bridging Out of School Literacies with Classroom Practice*. New York: Teachers College Press.

International Reading Association (2001) *Integrating Literacy and Technology in the Curriculum: A Position Statement*. Retrieved 12 May 2006, from www.reading.org/resources/issues/positions_technology.html

Johnson, D. and Johnson, B. (2005) *High stakes: Poverty, Testing, and Failure in American Schools* (2nd edn). Lanham, MD: Rowman & Littlefield.

King, J. R. and O'Brien, D. G. (2002) 'Adolescents' multiliteracies and their teachers' needs to know: toward a digital détente', in D. E. Alvermann (ed.) *Adolescents and Literacies in a Digital World*. New York: Peter Lang.

Kress, G. (2000) 'Multimodality', in B. Cope and M. Kalantzis (eds) *Multiliteracies: Literacy Learning and the Design of Social Futures* (pp. 182–202). London: Routledge.

Luke, A. (2004) 'The trouble with English', *Research in the Teaching of English*, 39, 85–95.

Meier, D. and Wood, G. (2004) *Many Children Left Behind: How the No Child Left Behind Act is Damaging Our Children and Our Schools*. Boston: Beacon Press.

Miller, S. M. and Borowicz, S. (2005) 'City voices, city visions: digital video as literacy/learning supertool in urban classrooms', in L. Johnson, M. Finn and R. Lewis (eds) *Urban Education with an Attitude*. Albany, NY: State University of New York Press.

Miller, S. M. and Borowicz, S. (2006) *Why Multimodal Literacies? Designing Digital Bridges to 21st Century Teaching and Learning*. New York GSE Publications and SUNY Press.

Miller, S. M. and Fox, D. L. (2006) 'Reconstructing English education for the 21st century: a report on the CEE Summit' *English Education*, 38(4), 265–77.

Moll, L.C., Amanti, C., Neff, D. and Gonzalez, N. (1992) 'Funds of knowledge for teaching: using a qualitative approach to connect homes and classrooms', *Theory into Practice*, 31, 132–41.

Morrell, E. (2005) 'Critical English education', *English Education*, 37, 312–21.

National Council of Teachers of English (2003) *NCTE Position Statement: On Composing with Nonprint Media*. Retrieved 10 May 2006, from www.ncte.org/about/over/positions/category/media/114919.htm

New London Group (1996) 'A pedagogy of multiliteracies: designing social futures', *Harvard Educational Review*, 66, 60–92.

Street, B. (1984) *Literacy in Theory and Practice*. Cambridge: Cambridge University Press.

Street, B. V. (1995) *Social literacies: Critical Approaches to Literacy in Development, Ethnography and Education*. London: Longman.

Vygotsky, L. S. (1978) *Mind in Society*. Cambridge, MA: Harvard University Press.

References for Chapter 14

Alsup, J., Emig, J., Pradl, G., Tremmel, R. and Yagelski, R. P. with Alvine, L., DeBlase, G., Moore, M., Petrone, R. and Sawyer, M. (2006) 'The state of English education and a vision for its future: a call to arms', *English Education*, 38(4), 279–94.

Assessment and Qualifications Alliance (AQA) (2007) *GCSE English/English Literature (Specification A) (3702/3712) Anthology*. Manchester: AQA.

Attlee, J. (2007) *Isolarion. A Different Oxford Journey*. Chicago, IL: University of Chicago Press.

Beaumont, R. (2007) 'Developing critical and independent readers of extended whole texts at Key Stage 3'. Unpublished PGCE assignment, Oxford: University of Oxford.

Benton, P. (ed.) (1990) *The Oxford Internship Scheme*. London: Calouste Gulbenkian Foundation.

Britzman, D. P. (1992) 'Structures of feeling in curriculum and teaching', *Theory into Practice*, 31(3), 252–8.

Browning, R. (1849/2007) 'My Last Duchess', in AQA (2007) *GCSE English/English Literature (Specification A) (3702/3712) Anthology*, Manchester: AQA. Also available at the University of Toronto poetry library online rpo.library.utoronto.ca/poem/288.html; accessed 27 April 2007.

Bullough, R. V. (1989) *First Year Teacher: A Case Study*. New York: Teachers College Press.

Cole, M. (1996) *Cultural Psychology*. Cambridge, MA: Harvard University Press.

Daniels, H. (1994) *Literature Circles: Voice and Choice in the Student-Centred Classroom*. Portland, ME: Stenhouse Publishers.

Department for Education (DfE) (1992) *Circular No 9/92 Initial Teacher Training (Secondary Phase)*. London: DfE.

Dickson, R. and Smagorinsky, P. with Bush, J., Christenbury, L., Cummings, B., George, M., Graham, P., Hartman, P., Kynard, C., Roskelly, H., Steffel, S., Vinz, R. and Weinstein, S. (2006) 'Are methods enough? Situating English education programs within the multiple settings of learning to teach', *English Education*, 38(4), 231–36.

Ellis, V. (2005) *Voices: making the Phoenix*. Oxford: Pegasus Theatre/University of Oxford.

Ellis, V. (2007) *Subject Knowledge and Teacher Education: The Development of Beginning Teachers' Thinking*. London: Continuum.

Engeström, Y. (1991) 'Developmental work research: reconstructing expertise through expansive learning', in M. I. Nurminen and G. R. S. Weir (eds) *Human Jobs and Computer Interfaces*, Amsterdam: Elsevier.

Engeström, Y. (1999) 'Innovative learning in work teams: analysing cycles of knowledge creation in practice', in Y. Engeström, R. Miettinen and R. Punamäki (eds) *Perspectives on Activity Theory*. Cambridge, MA: Cambridge University Press.

Engeström, Y. and Miettinen, R. (1999) 'Introduction', in Y. Engeström, R. Miettinen and R. Punamäki (eds) *Perspectives on Activity Theory*, Cambridge: Cambridge University Press.

Furlong, J., Barton, L., Miles, S., Whiting, C. and Whitty, G. (2000) *Teacher Education in Transition: Re-forming Professionalism?* Buckingham: Open University Press.

Greeno, J. G., Collins, A. M. and Resnick, L. (1996) 'Cognition and learning', in D. Berliner and R. Calfee (eds) *Handbook of Educational Psychology* (pp. 15–46), New York: Macmillan.

Grossman, P., Thompson, C. and Valencia, S. (2001) *District Policy and Beginning Teachers: Where the Twain Shall Meet*. Seattle, WA: Center for the Study of Teaching and Policy, University of Washington.

Hoyle, E. and John, P. (1998) 'Teacher education: the prime suspect', *Oxford Review of Education*, 24(1), 69–82.

Koertge, R. (2001) *The Brimstone Journals*. Cambridge, MA: Candlewick Press.

Lave, J. (1988) *Cognition in Practice*. Cambridge: Cambridge University Press.

Lu, M.-Z. (2006) 'Living-English work', *College English*, 68(6), 605–18.

Moll, L. C., Amanti, C., Neff, D. and Gonzalez, N. (1992) 'Funds of knowledge for teaching: using a qualitative approach to connect homes and classrooms', *Theory into Practice*, 31, 132–41.

Smagorinsky, P. (2007) 'Foreword', in V. Ellis *Subject Knowledge and Teacher Education: The Development of Beginning Teachers' Thinking*. London: Continuum.

Stewart, S. (2006) 'Performance, personality and pedagogy: engaging children's cultural worlds in the classroom'. Unpublished PGCE assignment, Oxford: University of Oxford.

Street, H. and Temperley, J. (eds) (2005) *Improving Schools Through Collaborative Professional Enquiry*. London: Continuum.

Sumara, D. (1996) *Private Readings in Public: Schooling the Literary Imagination*. New York: Peter Lang.

Teitel, L. (2003) *The Professional Development Schools Handbook, Starting Sustaining, and Assessing Partnerships That Improve Student Learning*. Cambridge, MA: Corwin Press.

Vygotsky, L. S. (1986) *Thought and Language*. Cambridge, MA: MIT Press.

Williams, R. (1958/1989) 'Culture is Ordinary', in *Resources of Hope*. London: Verso.

Williams, R. (1965) *The Long Revolution*. Harmondsworth: Pelican Books.

References for Afterword

Cognard-Black, J. and Cognard, A. (2005) *Advancing rhetoric*. New York: Kendall Hunt.

Flood, J., Heath, S. B. and Lapp, D. (1997). *Handbook for literacy educators: Research in the visual and communicative arts*. New York: Macmillan.

Flood, J., Heath, S. B. and Lapp, D. (2007). *Handbook for literacy educators: Research in the visual and communicative arts. Vol. 2.* New York: Routledge.

Heath, S. B. (1996) 'Ruling places: Adaptation in development by inner-city youth'. In R. Shweder, R. Jessor, and A. Colby, (eds) *Ethnographic approaches to the study of human development* (pp. 225–51) Chicago: Chicago University Press.

Heath, S. B. (2002) 'Working with community'. In G. Dees, J. Emerson and P. Economy (eds) *Strategic tolls for social entrepreneurs* (pp. 204–243) New York: John Wiley.

Heath, S. B. (2004) 'Risks, rules, and roles: Youth perspectives on the work of learning for community development'. In A. N. Perret-Clermont et al (eds) *Joining society: Social interaction and learning in adolescence and youth.* (pp. 41–70) New York: Cambridge University Press.

Heath, S. B. (2006) 'Dynamic of completion: Gaps, blanks, and improvisation'. In M. Turner (ed) *The artful mind.* (pp.133–152). New York: Oxford University Press..

Heath, S. B. and Robinson, K. (2004) 'Making a way:Youth arts and learning in international perspective'. In N. Rabkin and R. Redmond (eds) *Putting the arts in the picture: Reframing education in the 21st century* (pp. 107–126) Chicago: Center for Arts Policy, Columbia College.

Heath, S. B. and Smyth, L. (1999) *Art*Show: *Youth and community development.* Washington, D.C.: Partners for Livable Communities.

Laddaga, R. (2007) 'From work to conversation: Writing and citizenship in a global age'. *PMLA* 122.2:449–463.

Liestol, G. Morrison, A. and Rasmussen, T. (eds.) (2003) *Digital media revisited.* Cambridge, MA: MIT Press.

Lunsford, A. (2005) 'Performing writing, performing literacy'. *College Conference on Communication and Writing* 57.2:224–252.

Spivak, G. C. (2003) *Death of a discipline.* New York: Columbia University Press.

Viechnicki, G. B. and Kuipers, J. (2006) "It's all human error!': When a school science experiment fails'. *Linguistics and Education* 17:107–130.

Wardrip-Fruin, N. & Harrigan, P. (Eds.) (2004) *First person: New media as story, performance, and game.* Cambridge, MA: MIT Press.

Index